Adlai Stevenson's Lasting Legacy

Adlai Stevenson's Lasting Legacy

Edited by Judge Alvin Liebling

ADLAI STEVENSON'S LASTING LEGACY
Copyright © Judge Alvin Liebling, ed., 2007.

First published in 2007 by
PALGRAVE MACMILLAN™
175 Fifth Avenue, New York, N.Y. 10010 and
Houndmills, Basingstoke, Hampshire, England RG21 6XS.
Companies and representatives throughout the world.

PALGRAVE MACMILLAN is the global academic imprint of the Palgrave Macmillan division of St. Martin's Press, LLC and of Palgrave Macmillan Ltd. Macmillan® is a registered trademark in the United States, United Kingdom and other countries. Palgrave is a registered trademark in the European Union and other countries.

ISBN-13: 978-1-4039-8195-0
ISBN-10: 1-4039-8195-7

Library of Congress Cataloging-in-Publication Data
Adlai Stevenson's lasting legacy / edited by Alvin Liebling.
      p. cm.
Includes bibliographical references and index.
ISBN 1-4039-8195-7 (alk. paper)
1. Stevenson, Adlai E. (Adlai Ewing), 1900–1965—Influence. 2. Statesmen—United States—Biography. 3. Legislators—United States—Biography. 4. Governors—Illinois—Biography. 5. United States—Foreign relations—1945–1989. 6. United States—Politics and government—1945–1989. 7. Nuclear arms control—History—20th century. 8. United Nations—History—20th century. I. Liebling, Alvin.
    E748.S84A64 2007
    973.921092—dc22   2006053295

A catalogue record of the book is available from the British Library.

Design by Scribe Inc.

First edition: October 2007

10 9 8 7 6 5 4 3 2 1

Printed in the United States of America.

Appreciation is extended to those who have materially assisted in the editorial process, including the Princeton University and Abraham Lincoln and Franklin Roosevelt Presidential Libraries, and the Chicago-based eProduction Group—document management and electronic discovery and Gamma Photo Labs; also Christopher Cecot of San Diego for his index assistance.

CONTENTS

List of Illustrations

RECOLLECTIONS OF ELEANOR ROOSEVELT

Eleanor Roosevelt and Adlai Stevenson
Source: Abraham Lincoln Presidential Library

ON MY OWN (New York: Harper and Brothers Publishers, 1958), 158–60—In 1952, it was my opinion that Governor Stevenson would probably make one of the best Presidents we ever had had, but I also believed that it was practically impossible for the Democrats to win the election because of the hero worship surrounding General Eisenhower. I did make a speech on the United Nations at the Democratic National Convention that year at the request of President Truman, and I came out for Governor Stevenson, but I did not intend to be active in that campaign, and I was not.

Why then did I re-enter politics in 1956? For one thing, I was out of the United Nations delegation by that time and, as a private citizen, I had no feeling that I was barred from taking part in a political campaign. In addition, I believed as strongly as before that Adlai Stevenson would make a good President. . . . President Eisenhower had seen much of the international scene and was keenly aware of the vital importance of our role in world affairs, but the net result of his administration had not been impressive, because there were enough old-line Republicans in powerful positions to keep the party, on the whole, a conservative, businessmen's party.

Of course, the Democratic Party had many conservatives in powerful positions, too, but in general it was more progressive. . . . Still another thing that influenced me in getting back into politics as the 1956 campaign approached was Governor Stevenson's high standing among statesmen of other countries which are our allies or which we want to have on our side in the world struggle against Communism. After his defeat in 1952, Governor Stevenson had taken a trip around the world to study conditions in other countries and, during my own world travels, I had been greatly interested in the impression he had made on foreign statesmen. Again and again, they told me that Mr. Stevenson was the kind of man who listened, who wanted to learn all the facts. I came to the conclusion that it might be a good thing if more of us did more listening and did not try to ram our own ideas down other people's throats.

⟶☰◎☰⟵

MY DAY (New York: United Features Syndicate, May 19, 1960)— The suggestion made the other day by Adlai Stevenson would, I think, go a long way toward bringing real knowledge to the people about Presidential candidates and their policies. . . . [His] suggestion to have a "great debate" on television would be a real step forward in having a rational campaign conducted. . . . [People] would get a far clearer concept of what was at stake and of which was the candidate best equipped by character and knowledge as well as experience to meet the issues of the future.

⟶☰◎☰⟵

ON MY OWN, ibid., 167–68—One of the important duties of the President—and one that the Republican administration neglects—is to be the educator of the public on national problems. Most people do not have the time or inclination to inform themselves fully on the complex and perhaps seemingly remote problems that must be settled by government. But, if he knows the issues and explains them clearly, the President is in a position to make the people aware of what must be decided and to make them feel their responsibility as citizens in reaching a decision. Without such "education" of the public, democracy can become a dangerous kind of government because voters are called upon to make decisions or to support decisions without having sufficient knowledge of the factors involved.

Ibid., 165–66—I am not an Egghead, but I am in favor of Eggheads if that means the application of our best intellects to the problems of government. I believe most voters feel the same way and I do not think that the description of Governor Stevenson's advisers—or some of them—as Eggheads was detrimental to his campaign. I don't believe the voters want their candidates to be dumb.

Let me cite a couple of Egghead ideas that were bitterly attacked by the Republicans during the [1956] campaign. First, there was the question of abolishing the draft. Since [then] it has become more and more obvious that drafting young men for a big standing army is unwise and unfair. . . . Another Democratic issue in the campaign was the continued test explosion of atomic bombs. This was derided by the Republican leaders as just an Egghead idea, but, as everybody knows, it has since become a problem of great concern to people everywhere.

-⊶≡◐⊂≡⊷-

AUTOBIOGRAPHY OF ELEANOR ROOSEVELT (New York: Harper and Brothers Publishers, 1961), 422–23—Now, while I was determined to take no further part in presidential campaigns, I was stirred by reading a statement . . . that, while Adlai Stevenson was undoubtedly the best candidate for the Presidency, they did not think he could be nominated [a third time] and consequently they were going to support John Kennedy. It seemed absurd to accept anyone as second best until you had done all you could to get the best. For my part, I believed the best ticket would be Stevenson and Kennedy, with the strong chance that the latter would become president at a later time. . . . I was finally persuaded to go to the convention, when I was distressed to find that once again [as 1956] I was in opposition to Mr. Truman's political stand, and I made a seconding speech for Mr. Stevenson's nomination.

MY DAY, ibid., July 5, 1960—Mr. Stevenson will remain a great figure in the country, whether he is nominated or not. Without any office, he is still the only one of all the candidates who forces the knowledge upon you that he has entered a room even before he speaks.

INTRODUCTION

Alvin Liebling

Alvin Liebling, Sr. U.S. Administrative Law Judge and editor of this volume, met Adlai E. Stevenson II in 1947 as an undergraduate at Northwestern University in Evanston, Illinois. He headed an Illinois college student campaign for Stevenson for Governor in 1948. During Adlai Stevenson's governorship, he attended Northwestern's Law School in Chicago where Stevenson had graduated. A number of the Governor's associates were from that school, and as a student, he came to know many of them. Like them, his career was greatly influenced by the Governor. Starting with military service after graduation, he spent two years in the army and in the air force as an Assistant Staff Judge Advocate and advisor to its rehabilitation program. On his return to Rockford, Illinois in 1954, he became an Assistant State's Attorney, and in 1956–58 in Washington, DC, a Special Attorney (contracts) with the U.S. Department of Justice and in Chicago, an Assistant U.S. Attorney.

During 1958–70, Attorney Liebling practiced law in Rockford and was Chairman of its Planning Commission. In 1971, he moved to Springfield and Chicago, as an Assistant Attorney General of Illinois in condemnation and environmental law. He then became Assistant Regional Counsel in Chicago of the newly formed U.S. Environmental Protection Agency, and for a long period, he was its acting Regional Counsel. In 1978, he became GATX Corporation's Environmental Counsel, and in 1980, taught environmental law at Northwestern. In 1983, he returned to the EPA as a senior attorney. In 1991, he became a U.S. Administrative Law Judge, assigned to the Social

Security Office of Hearings and Appeals in the Chicago area. He retired from that position in February 2000 with some twenty-seven years of U.S. Government service. He is currently engaged in governmental regulatory matters in Illinois and Chicago, where he resides with his wife, Jacquelyn. Fax: 312-609-0626.

-⊷⇒⇐⊷-

Your days are short here;
This is the last of your springs.
And now in the serenity and
Quiet of this lovely place,
Touch the depths of truth,
Feel the hem of Heaven.
You will go away
With old, good friends. And
Don't forget when you leave,
Why you came.

—Adlai Stevenson, 1954

Adlai E. Stevenson II became Illinois' thirty-third Governor, twice Democratic candidate for the presidency, and a revered founder of and diplomat to the United Nations. He was a patient man with an impatient mission, and the courage to pursue it. As United States Ambassador to the United Nations in an emotional exchange, he told Soviet Ambassador Valerian Zorin that he was willing, if necessary, to wait "until hell freezes over" for a response. That was 1962, and his challenge to the Soviets to admit that atomic-tipped missiles of imminent, substantial threat to the United States and the Western Hemisphere had been placed in nearby Cuba. His demand was based on convincing U-2 photographic evidence he then presented to the Security Council. This was in character for Stevenson, whose entire career had addressed the pressing needs of his state and the nation.

Above all, Adlai Stevenson's mission had been one of peace. As he said of that fateful day, "Let it be remembered not as the day when the world came to the edge of nuclear war but the day when men resolved to let nothing thereafter stop them in their quest for peace." Before the advent of the United Nations, he had said the United States and its allies this time must not be unprepared to "insure" the peace of the world. And he undertook a long series of assignments during and following World War II on behalf of the United States in connection with the organization and initial functioning of the UN. It was a driving force of his mentors, Woodrow Wilson and Abraham Lincoln. On his return to the UN in the 1960s, as he had advised others, he had not forgotten why he first had come. His awesome revelation was intended to help keep the peace, and it did.

Adlai Stevenson's legacy in this nuclear age was a demonstration of the absolute value of patient international collaboration in resolving the myriad of perplexing challenges to world peace that he faced. And with that, providing America, in a position of strength, the opportunity to foster freedom among others by our example and assistance, not an impatient arrogance productive of resentment and resistance. It was a matter of consistently seeking a necessary multilateral consensus and effectively carrying it out.

This was his guide for the nation for the two score years following his unexpected demise in 1965. Now, it is a lesson that remains for Iraq, Iran, Korea, and elsewhere, combating terrorism, assisting basic human needs, and protecting the world's environment—as well as for achieving nuclear nonproliferation, retrieval of fissionable materials, disarmament, and a continued ban on nuclear testing. Yet, since 2001, the Bush Administration is seen to have turned away from this course toward a policy of unilateralism at critical junctures in our national security and foreign relations, with considerable loss to our country and others. Unless consistently changed, many fear it will be difficult in the future to maintain our traditional position of world leadership in many spheres of vital security and economic interest.

So, it was fitting for the friends of Adlai Stevenson to have celebrated his one-hundredth birthday, February 5, 1900, with personal reminiscences about him, at Princeton University where he had graduated in 1922. Significantly, this and today's events have sparked a renewed assessment of the societal impact of this extraordinary man. This book is about that impact as related in the following incisive chapters by those familiar with his life and what he stood for.

It begins with a sketch by his eldest son, Adlai Stevenson III, former U.S. Senator from Illinois. I remember the unusual tonal quality in the Governor's voice, which attracted audiences to the special messages in his statements. Presented over an extended period, they are at the core of his public legacy. They have survived through this date, some forty years after his too early passing on July 14, 1965, at age 65.

Adlai Stevenson, indeed, is thought to have been among our great American political speakers, Presidents Franklin D. Roosevelt, John F. Kennedy, and Ronald W. Reagan included. And his utterances are perceived to have had a positive, continuing influence on the public. As the ancients have said, words of that impact are considered to be actions of the greatest character. U.S. Senator Eugene J. McCarthy expressed this in his 1960 nominating speech of Stevenson for yet a third try at the U.S. presidency. And even now, those remembering his words and his record continue to admire his impressive role at the United Nations, as elsewhere. As John D. Philipsborn of his UN staff wrote, "I maintain my memory of him as a fine, exemplary man—a friend at times; always the boss," attentive and in charge.

Our grasping of the moment to assess the scope of Stevenson's legacy is central to understanding its public relevance today. Clearly, one direction that could take would be to reinforce the authority of the United Nations, which he had played a key role in organizing and later nourishing. That could translate into providing the Security Council with continuing, limited instruments of peacekeeping and enforcement available for use against acts of external violence and violation of international human rights, though emanating from within sovereign national borders. They thus could be more timely and effectively employed and viewed as acts of the world community, not a single nation.

I first met Adlai Stevenson when he was 47 in the fall of 1947 in his offices at the Chicago Sidley, Austin law firm. He had just returned from New York as an Alternate UN General Assembly Delegate to former First Lady Eleanor Roosevelt. He was being prominently mentioned as a possible Democratic candidate for the U.S. Senate from Illinois. My friend Newton Minow was head of the UN Club at Northwestern University in Evanston and I, its program chairman. We decided to invite Mr. Stevenson to speak before our group, particularly because he had been one of the UN's organizers.

I waited some length and finally talked to Mr. Stevenson. Our very pleasant conversation, like what must have delayed it, was frequently interrupted by inquiries and well-wisher telephone calls. I presented our invitation, and in explaining why he could not presently commit to coming, he turned to the U.S. Senate race he was considering. He also talked about running concurrently with University of Chicago economics professor and Marine Corps hero Paul Douglas, as the candidate for Governor. Later, their political roles were switched, with Stevenson running for Governor and Douglas for the U.S. Senate. I was thus introduced to Stevenson's first personal foray into politics.

Those of us involved early in that campaign—Lou Kohn, an attorney with Mayer, Brown; Steve Mitchell of his own law firm; Herrnon Dunlap (Dutch) Smith of Chicago insurance fame; Mrs. Edison (Jane) Dick, a longtime family friend from Lake Forest; also, myself, to head a state college campaign—were initially thinking of a possible joint campaign with Professor Douglas. Not long after this, however, a decision was made to have separate campaign organizations, and we set up our offices at 7 South Dearborn Street in downtown Chicago. Many contacts continued with the Douglas campaign and my counterpart Jack M. Siegel, who remains a friend and later became Evanston's longtime Corporation Counsel.

Of collateral interest, our headquarters site in 1999 was mentioned in a developer's plan to recapture for Chicago the title, "World's Tallest Building." I thought, if the plan had matured, naming it after Stevenson would have been an even more fitting physical memorial to him than the southwest industrial expressway in Chicago that bore his name. Like such a building, the scope of Stevenson's ideas had stretched skyward.

Adlai Stevenson has surely been viewed as a far-thinking man, some have said consummately. In a later election, he was pictured with a hole in the sole of his shoe, distracted by his thoughts. So many people over the years I have spoken to—on both sides of the political spectrum—have said they have known, voted for, or admired him. He won the Illinois governorship over Governor Dwight Green with over a 570,000 vote plurality, with a like result for Professor Paul Douglas. They both very much helped to carry the state for President Harry S. Truman and Stevenson's cousin Alben Barkley, who everybody thought to be in a very close race. Indeed, that was the election the *Chicago Tribune* in an early edition mistakenly headlined, "Dewey Defeats Truman."

For me at 21 in 1948, as Adlai Stevenson ran for his first political office, he was an inspiring role model. I looked upon him as a good friend and treasured his calling me a colleague. He was at once, industrious, thoughtful, and eloquent. On the campaign trail for Governor—exhibiting a trait I have come to emulate—I witnessed him constantly editing his speeches down to the very moment before delivery. I remember him at his desk before presentation with his hand on his forehead, pondering and preparing his thoughts.

He generally preceded his well-crafted formal texts with *impromptu* pieces of personal wit, and followed with a favorite story or two of Lincoln. He was not only very thoughtful but also possessed a wonderful sense of humor—humbly able to see it, especially when it applied to himself. He later accepted his first national nomination in 1952, after President Truman had decided not to run, saying: "I did not seek it, I did not want it, . . . but to refuse it would be to meet honor with dishonor." In his election night concession, quoting Lincoln, he noted "he was too old to cry, but that it hurt too much to laugh." Now, it is we who cry for politicians of his substance and grace, and we remember the eloquence of his eulogy of our country's slain President John F. Kennedy.

Adlai E. Stevenson II, by intellect and heritage, perhaps destiny—from his maternal great grandfather Jesse Fell, an early key supporter of Abraham Lincoln, and his paternal grandfather Adlai E. Stevenson I, Vice President under Grover Cleveland, to his father Lewis G. Stevenson, an Illinois Secretary of State—had from the start been a most dedicated public person and a courageous civil libertarian. In his early years of the 1930s, he toiled as a lawyer with the Federal Government in Washington.

Later, in Chicago, he was part of our area's leadership that sought to arouse America and the free world against the aggressions of the Nazi regime. During World War II, his brave but humble exploits for the country as Secretary of the Navy Frank Knox's assistant and later, in Europe, were further testimony of his preparation for greatness. At the end of the war, being in the forefront of the U.S. participation in the organization of the United Nations, he helped fulfill the dream of Woodrow Wilson and Franklin Roosevelt and Winston Churchill under the Atlantic Charter.

He later gave the UN dramatic, further life. And toward the end of 1964, he began private talks with UN Secretary General U Thant about initiating efforts to end the war in Vietnam, in his mode long before its conclusion in 1974. It is noteworthy that two years after Stevenson's death, Secretary of Defense Robert

McNamara resigned, also opposing continuation of that struggle. Previous to this period, in repeated tries at the presidency, Stevenson had striven, with marked determination, to render the highest level of elective leadership.

In 1948, when Adlai Stevenson ran for Governor, he similarly sought to turn around Illinois' low rank in providing for the public education of its youth. Like Thomas Jefferson, he saw the state's role as a primary governmental responsibility, not exceeded by any other. During his term, he worried that the loyalty oaths required under the Broyles Bill would needlessly inquire concerning the state's civil servants contrary to federal interests, and he vetoed it.

When he ran a second time for the presidency in 1956, with an enlightened conscience and against the advice of some of his political strategists, he warned the country against the continued release of strontium-90 into the atmosphere from unbridled, advanced nuclear testing. On the side of scientists and in the spirit of America's elder statesman Bernard Baruch, he saw this as the right thing to seek of the American public, though well ahead of its opinion. It amounted, he was convinced, to an unsupportable, serious risk to citizens not only within but also widely across the borders of testing nations, including our own. It was, as he had said, "time to talk sense to the American people" before the election, which he viewed as an institutionalized learning process. Because of his stand, he contributed substantially to the later test ban treaty with the Soviets.

In the early 1960s, the nation watched and admired Ambassador Stevenson's skill and courage in presenting this country's case before the United Nations during the Cuba missile crisis. Now, several have pointed to his actions as the model for proving-up the presence of an imminent, substantial threat to the peace—as the prerequisite to military action. However, as former U.S. Senator Adlai Stevenson III pointed out in a *New York Times* op-ed piece early in 2003, his father's actions were not the predicate for that end, particularly against a Great Power. Rather, as he explained, they were undertaken for the purpose of maintaining the peace. What was sought was the peacekeeping effect of the international opprobrium and fear of retribution that could be expected from such an awesome disclosure. Coupled with other diplomatic efforts, the point is, that it worked.

It also has been said that Adlai Stevenson, though not elected to the presidency, laid down the foundations in substance and style for the New Frontier and Great Society programs that followed his national candidacies. Many of his associates fueled those successor administrations in key positions. Indeed, he humorously said that he "regretted he only had one law firm to give to his country."

Like his mentor from Springfield a century before, Adlai Stevenson viewed the role of government as that required reasonably and effectively to respond to the otherwise unsatisfiable needs of the public in education, physical and mental health, development, employment, and the protection of individual rights and the public's peace. His courage was to support what he perceived to be significantly required of the public, whatever the personal cost. With that, his legacy now has an even wider, more profound impact. The main reason, I would submit, is today's challenge to the UN and the desperate need the world has for renewed and lasting international collaboration.

In his sketch, Senator Stevenson laments the change in our national security policy of recent years, from the days of his father through the years that followed. It was different then, he notes, a time when America "was strong and secure in the world" and the Governor and his compatriots were "waging peace, not war, seeking cooperation, not preemption."

They were the architects of "a post world war international order built around containment" and multinational collaboration, "the Marshall Plan, Point Four and the U.N." And "the Guv would . . . say, peace was a condition of human survival in the nuclear age." Others have continued that course. Now, "[t]he reaction waits," he notes, "as the new America of George Bush demonstrates the limits of its military and economic power, rendering it dependent on China and Japan to shore up a newly unsound dollar." A policy of unsupported, essentially unilateral preemption in Iraq is seen to have failed; a permanent return to the multilateral collaboration it replaced, as necessary.

Adlai Stevenson's goddaughter, Dr. Adele Simmons, former President of Hampshire College and of the MacArthur Foundation in Chicago, quotes him concerning the proper conduct of our foreign relations: "There is no room for the 'Big Stick' or the ultimatum. . . . Ours must be the role of the good neighbor. The good partner, the good friend. Never, the big bully." She admired his perception and courage and reminds, in his words, that we "should look at the UN, as we do other political instruments, see what it is not, disabuse ourselves of any illusions, and appreciate how useful it still can be." And she adds, "there is no other forum of its kind. In our arrogance, we cast it aside to go our own way in Iraq."

Barbara Ward, distinguished British author, economist, and wife of Sir Robert Jackson, a consultant to the UN, also wrote that Stevenson "found any form of . . . national arrogance or bullyboy pretensions profoundly antipathetic." Also, that his "presence at the United Nations and his participation in the American Cabinet's decision-making were taken by vast numbers of people abroad as a guarantee that the overwhelming, irresistible power of the United States would not be used arrogantly or unthinkingly to override the interests and susceptibilities of other, smaller communities." She said, "his last years" were "entirely dedicated to the task of convincing the world that America . . . would . . . be ready for some mediation of its power through the institutions of the United Nations." At the root of his actions, she continued, was his "known conviction, expressed in a hundred different speeches, that the world has to find its way to a rule of law and neighborly responsibility or perish" (*As We Knew Adlai* [New York: Harper and Row, 1966], 225–26).

That conviction is seen as the critical difference between "Adlai's Legacy" and America's current often unilaterally based national security actions and what the debate outside and within the Bush Administration these immediate past years has been all about.

While the national security threat surrounding Stevenson's time appears to have taken a turn away from the Big Powers, it still remains awesome in a nuclear age, and even more real and direct to many Americans. It comes now from smaller nations and groups of terrorists and individuals from a variety of places, seemingly not as affected by the concerns nations have had in the past. But the challenge remains serious and reflects the conviction of Stevenson that somehow, with others, we need to figure out a lawful way to achieve protection against these threats without sacrificing our treasured way of life in America. "[E]ven when . . . under heavy and ruthless fire," he asserted, "the challenge to all of us is to prove that a free society can remain free, humane, and creative," and "while resisting a monstrous foreign despotism," we can still attend to our basic precepts.

So, the debate has raged on and may be expected to continue at least into the short term—its outcome as to Iraq already determined. And it could be extended, if, among other reasons, scientific forebodings of a move to modify the long-standing ban on nuclear weapon testing in the second segment of the current Bush Administration were to occur.

As a politician, in the highest sense, Adlai Stevenson gave both definition and example to modern, civilized human behavior abroad, as at home. For voters in this country who looked in on his actions, it was a need to know the truth on the issues, which in a democracy each had the right to help decide. For those, wherever engaged in politics, it was an elevation of the representative status of each.

For a younger compatriot, the late U.S. Senator Paul Simon— initially, as Stevenson was, a downstate Illinois journalist—the career of the Governor had a profound meaning. On the Governor's passing, the Senator wrote that Stevenson "was a politician who dared to think, who like the ancient god Janus looked both at yesterday and tomorrow, who matched compassion with wisdom." And that "[b]y being all this and more, he gave each of us a spark of hope which I trust never will be dimmed, even though we may often reflect that hope most inadequately" (ibid., p. 137). Thirty years later, Senator Simon made his own bid for the White House, doing well in the Iowa caucuses but abbreviating his efforts afterward. His unexpected death intervened in his plan to contribute a chapter to this book, which, beyond enriching readers now, he thought could be "valuable to historians in the years to come."

For his election research directors in 1955–56, Dr. John Brademas and Ken Hechler, also Dr. Adele Simmons, Ambassadors Harlan Cleveland, Charles Yost, William vanden Heuvel, George Bunn and James Goodby, Dr. Arthur Schlesinger Jr., and Dr. Sidney Drell, Adlai Stevenson helped to stimulate a set of indefatigable public and education-based careers. And there were many others. Like him, they have often traveled abroad in pursuit of knowledge and improving world understanding. As Dr. Brademas, now President Emeritus of New York University, has said, "Ignorance of the histories, languages and religions of those societies," has been "among the reasons . . . the United States has experienced calamities in Vietnam, Central America and now Iraq."

For all of us, Adlai Stevenson's far-thinking and dedicated service to the public has been and remains a lasting inspiration.

After the 1948 election, I went back more fully to my senior year at Northwestern, periodically visiting the Governor in Springfield and some of my good friends there. Once, I recall driving Mrs. Stevenson down to Springfield with some items for decorating the mansion. I remember the next morning's breakfast with the Governor, the head of the Democratic State Central Committee, and the Governor's Revenue Director, Richard J. Daley, the later famed Mayor of Chicago and father of our current outstanding Mayor. I still recall that heaping platter of scrambled eggs we all enjoyably shared.

In the fall of 1949, I entered law school at Northwestern in Chicago. Lou Kohn suggested we not feel badly for ourselves who needed to stay behind. I was later appointed an Illinois representative to the 1950 White House Conference on Children and Youth, which didn't take much time away from my law school study. Upon graduation, I entered the armed services in 1952. Other classmates not then so occupied, Newt Minow, Dan Walker, and Dawn Clark Netsch, were able to become involved on the Governor's staff.

Newt Minow later became Chairman of the Federal Communications Commission under President Kennedy. Dawn went on to teach at Northwestern Law School and became a State Senator and, a few years ago, the first female candidate for Governor of Illinois. Dan later became governor. Others, law school professors Carl McGowan, Willard Wirtz, and Walter Schaefer, also joined the Stevenson Administration. The first two later were, respectively, appointed as a U.S. DC Court of Appeals Judge and Secretary of Labor under Kennedy. The third eventually became Chief Justice of the Illinois Supreme Court.

I had thought of pursuing the collection and presentation of the following chapters about the Governor for some time since his untimely and sad passing. It seemed he had been with us longer because of his repetitive impact on history and our pride in his actions. I attempted to rationalize it by a reminder of the early passing of his father and other family members from heart ailments. Yet, it seemed incongruous, given that as Ambassador to the UN he had only a short while back survived his own alarming experience with Dallas's unrest and how alive he had been before being struck down in London by a heart attack.

Personal career demands had postponed putting this book together in the past, but the Governor's one-hundredth anniversary and the nature of the times have now made it a compelling task. Senator Stevenson felt that as "a friend from the earliest days and knowing the history and the survivors," I should be in a good position to undertake this project. Although time has thinned the ranks of those remaining, recollections are still clear, even stronger considering the importance today of what the Governor left behind for all of us to use.

The initial part of the prologue hereafter sets the stage for the chapters that follow, of the Governor's son and others, also of the Governor himself on his 1956 proposal for a ban on further H-bomb testing—first, about his preparation for a life in the public service, the years during World War II and his work for the United Nations, and then his entry into politics. It was written by a longtime friend of mine, Don Campbell, a former public relations manager at General Electric, who actively participated in our college campaign for the Governor before graduating from Northwestern University in 1948.

PROLOGUE

THE ROAD TO SPRINGFIELD

Donald C. Campbell

Donald C. Campbell was employed by the General Electric Co. as an employee and public and government relations manager after graduation from Northwestern University and working on the Stevenson campaign in 1948, service in the Army as head of the central news agency, and a period with the International News Service. He had many special assignments at GE, during which he came to know future and past Presidents Ronald Reagan and Herbert Hoover. He retired from the company in 1987 and since has been a consultant to a number of major firms, board chairman of a Portsmouth Veterans Affairs hospital and member of several foundation boards. The pages that follow about the Stevenson years after 1935, with his permission, are taken from columns he wrote in the Ohio *Ashland Times-Gazette* (1952).

⤞══◯══⤝

I have stood in awe and been moved down deep in my soul by the music of great symphonies, by Carl Sandburg reciting some of his beautiful poetry with deep-voice inflections, before some of Michelangelo's great masterpieces in Italy, by the sheer beauty of Yosemite Park in California, and the breathtaking majesty of the world's great cathedrals; yet, I have heard no one who could use the English language to such perfection as Adlai Stevenson (only Franklin Roosevelt and Winston Churchill, in the recent past, were comparable).

I had worked with my friend Al Liebling on the Stevenson gubernatorial campaign during the first half of the year, before my graduation from Northwestern University in Evanston, Illinois in 1948.
Afterward, he kept me informed of Stevenson's successful campaign
and election. He had organized a large contingent of Northwestern
and other college students who spent weekends traveling the state in
buses. They entertained crowds on street corners, at political rallies,
and handed out literature and "Adlai" balloons wherever they went.

Stevenson was a very likeable person, and he thoroughly enjoyed
having a group of young people around him. I really believe he
missed his three young sons and spending time with them on his
farm near Libertyville. He had given much of his time to his country
and to the world and strongly desired some time now for himself and
his family, but he was to find very rare moments for this. And it was
my impression that it was hard even for him to relax there on the
farm, for his idea of relaxation was to work hard on the farm, riding
the tractor or whatever else involving manual labor—so long as it
also involved his sons. Whenever he had the opportunity, he played
an intense and vigorous game of tennis—a great love, next to his
young sons.

So, I sensed that Stevenson felt he could relax around us young
college men and women. He especially enjoyed Al, because Al could
be serious but also has a hearty, lusty laugh and Stevenson would
simply beam whenever he could cause Al to laugh. Or, if he heard us
laughing, he often would stop whatever he was doing to find out
what had amused us, so he could join in. Otherwise, he was a very
intense person. When you spoke to him, he always listened very
intently and seriously. Yet, he had a wonderful, dry sense of humor
and never took himself as seriously as you viewed him as being.

AROUND THE WAR

The years 1935 to 1941 found Adlai E. Stevenson in Chicago, prac-
ticing law as a partner in the firm of Sidley, Austin, Burgess, and
Harper. Stevenson's civic interest was reflected in his work as direc-
tor of organizations like Hull House, International House, Immigrants
Protective League, and the Illinois Children's Home and Aid Society.
But his real interest was in international affairs.

During 1939 and 1940, when political thinking in this country was divided over our relationship with the rest of the world, Stevenson was working actively to arouse Midwesterners to the menace of Hitler and the Nazis. As a director of the Chicago Council on Foreign Relations, he organized a number of mass meetings and persuaded Wendell Wilkie and Carl Sandburg to come to Illinois to address them.

When asked by a Chicago newspaper how he intended to vote in the 1940 election, Stevenson said he had nothing against Wilkie but was going to vote for a third term for Roosevelt. In explaining his stand, he said he saw the world "in a death struggle of ideals, of which armed conflict is only one manifestation."

In mid-1941, Stevenson was called to Washington by Secretary of the Navy Frank Knox to act as his special assistant. He filled this post during the period of the nation's expansion to wartime strength but was as yet an unknown in diplomatic circles. An example of this was a story told by Joseph Driscoll of the *St. Louis Post-Dispatch*. Secretary Knox had gone to the Pacific on an inspection tour, during which he and his staff members were bombed at Guadalcanal and at Espiritu Santo. It was rumored that their presence had been tipped off to the Japanese, and everyone was very tense.

At Pearl Harbor, Admiral Nimitz arranged a press conference for Secretary Knox in his cement-and-steel bomb shelter. When the correspondents were summoned from their billets, they came complete with gas masks. Nimitz invited Secretary Knox to occupy the chair behind the admiral's desk, and he sat on the left. Selecting at random, he invited one of the newspapermen to occupy a third chair, on the right. The rest of the correspondents sat in front of the desk.

Presently, the correspondent behind the desk was tapped on the shoulder by a mild-mannered man who asked: "Pardon me, but do you mind if I occupied your chair?" "I certainly do," the correspondent blustered. "After all, Admiral Nimitz invited me to sit here." "Oh," said the man, as he retired to the background. The mild-mannered man was Adlai Stevenson.

Although reserved on this occasion, Stevenson was never timid in expressing his views on international affairs. He often preached in public appearances his belief that the United States, Great Britain, and the Soviet Union "can and must insure peace of the world" after the war. At a formal dinner of the Chicago Real Estate Board in 1943, he reaffirmed this belief and further stated that the United States must not be unprepared "when peace breaks out," as she was when war descended. In December of that year, he was assigned to the newly established Foreign Economic Administration.

At President Roosevelt's direction, Stevenson headed a mission that followed in the wake of the Allied armies in Italy. The mission surveyed the economic condition of that country and developed the first U.S. program for coordinated relief and reconstruction in a major liberated area. While on this six-week trip, Stevenson made a practice of slipping away from the official party to talk unofficially with Italians. Italian-speaking GI's often served as his interpreters during these "secret missions."

Stevenson returned to Europe in 1944 as a member of a War Department mission for the Air Force to study the effects of American bombing of German cities. In 1945, the Chicago lawyer became a special assistant to Secretary of State Edward Stettinius and then, James Byrnes. At the United Nations Conference on International Organization, which opened in San Francisco in April 1945, Stevenson was press spokesman for the United States delegation. He is said to have persuaded the State Department to relax the censorship of its reports and to issue statements instead of "no comment."

AFTER THE WAR

Later in 1945, he was appointed U.S. Minister and Representative to the Preparatory Commission for the United Nations, which met in London from August to December. The chief American delegate in the absence of Stettinius, Stevenson was described by columnist Edgar Ansel Mowrer as having done "what most representatives of foreign countries here consider a magnificent job," and as having "won himself immense popularity . . . by his tact and his ability to understand the other fellow's viewpoint."

When the first UN General Assembly opened in London in January 1946, Adlai Stevenson was senior advisor to the American delegation. The delegates included Byrnes, Stettinius, Eleanor Roosevelt, Sol Bloom, and Senators Tom Connally and Arthur Vandenberg. Stevenson was mentioned in press accounts as representing his country in private negotiations with the other Big Five nations. He resigned after the session ended in March, but in July, President Harry S. Truman appointed him alternate delegate to the second meeting of the assembly. During this session, he and Representative Helen Gahagan Douglas served on the economic and financial committee. In November 1946, Stevenson presented his government's view that a new organization need not be created to succeed the United Nations Relief and Rehabilitation Administration (UNRRA). Reappointed for the 1947 sessions at Lake Success, the Chicagoan worked with Warren Austin on the administrative and budgetary committee.

RUNNING FOR GOVERNOR

Stevenson opened his campaign for the Democratic nomination for the governorship of Illinois in February 1948. He credited his decision to enter politics in large part to an item he read during the war in the Army newspaper, *Stars and Stripes.* The story reported a public opinion poll that showed that seven out of ten parents in America didn't want their boys to enter public life.

"Think of it!" Stevenson said later: "Boys could suffer and die in their cold, muddy, bloody campaign for the things we believe in, but parents didn't want their children to work for these same things. I decided then that if I ever had a chance, I'd go into public life." There was one serious drawback. The politicians had never heard of Stevenson.

Col. Jacob M. Arvey, Chairman of the Cook County Democratic Committee, was the one politician chiefly responsible for Stevenson's emergence into the Illinois political spotlight. A product and heir of the Kelly-Nash machine in Chicago, Arvey grew up in the downtown Loop district and worked as an errand boy. He studied for his law degree in night school and spent the remainder of his time rounding up votes for precinct leaders. Arvey was elected to the city council in 1923, and thereafter followed his rapid rise to power.

Arvey first learned about Stevenson at a luncheon given by Lester Biffle, the Senate secretary, in July 1947. The meeting was attended by Senators Scott Lucas and Tom Connally, and Secretary of State James Byrnes, as well as Arvey and a group of his associates. During a discussion dealing with an appointment Arvey was seeking to be filled, Byrnes interrupted to inquire: "Don't you people in Illinois know you've got a gold nugget out there?" "Who do you mean?" Arvey asked. "I mean Adlai Stevenson," replied Byrnes. Byrnes and Connally proceeded to enlighten him.

When Arvey returned to Chicago, he telephoned his good friend Judge Harry M. Fisher, who he found was already a Stevenson admirer. It was from Fisher that Arvey learned about a group of Chicago lawyers who were already banding together in a Stevenson-for-Senator committee. This was enough for Arvey; now he wanted to meet this "nugget" he had somehow missed in the Chicago political scramble. So Fisher arranged a luncheon for the two men. Arvey spent most of the meal asking Stevenson for his views on labor, civil rights, the economy, and other controversial state and national issues. Stevenson's replies impressed him. After further meetings with Stevenson, which included a weekend at Lake Forest, Arvey became convinced. Recommendation by Arvey was tantamount to nomination.

The group of Chicagoans who had met and discussed Stevenson as a candidate for U.S. Senator from Illinois included Stephen A. Mitchell, a lawyer and the man Stevenson later named as national chairman of the Democratic Party; Louis Kohn, another Chicago attorney and later an advisor and special assistant to Stevenson; and Hermon Dunlap Smith, an insurance broker and later national chairman of the Volunteers-for-Stevenson committee. These men enlisted the support of fifty prominent Chicago persons, who granted permission for the use of their names on Stevenson stationery.

They approached Arvey and were granted permission to use the offices formally inherited by Martin Kennelly in his successful campaign for election as Mayor of Chicago. Located at 7 South Dearborn Street, the offices were the central headquarters for the Volunteers-for-Stevenson organization and were considered a political omen of victory. Stevenson changed his office to his campaign headquarters.

In January 1948, when the party's State Central Committee met, most of the Democrats were at an emotionally low state and were even looking for a national candidate to replace President Truman. It was at this time that Stevenson's supporters had approached Arvey, who was already receptive to Stevenson as a candidate for one of the state offices.

Arvey had the native instinct to see that in a bad year it might be well to put some new and fresh faces on the Democratic ticket in Illinois.

Arvey ultimately prevailed upon Stevenson to switch his campaign plans and become the candidate for governor rather than senator, in favor of another reform candidate Paul Douglas. Douglas was an economics professor at the University of Chicago and had served as a Marine in the Pacific during World War II and had been wounded in action. He would oppose World War I veteran incumbent Senator C. Wayland Brooks. Lacking a combat record, after some misgivings Stevenson accepted the change.

Adlai E. Stevenson defeated Dwight Green by 572,000 votes to capture the governorship of Illinois in 1948, while President Truman nosed out Governor Thomas E. Dewey in that state by a 34,000 vote plurality. Douglas handily won his race, as well. Never having been in politics before, Stevenson was unencumbered by the political obligations normally incurred before reaching such eminence. He brought to politics only honesty of the lay variety and acted as though that were the only kind. As the conclusion of his first term neared, Stevenson felt his work as Governor was unfinished. He was nominated again for that office, before the Democratic National Convention selected him as its presidential nominee.

QUEST FOR THE PRESIDENCY

Eugene J. McCarthy

Eugene J. McCarthy was a U.S. Senator from Minnesota. This section of the Prologue was originally a part of his third Presidential nominating speech of Adlai E. Stevenson, presented on July 13, 1960, in Los Angeles—also, a eulogy. With his permission, this portion of his speech and eulogy are from pages 196–98 of the *Hard Years* by Eugene J. McCarthy (Lone Oak Press, 2000).

-->≡○⊂≡<--

[T]here was one man who did not prophesy falsely, let me remind you. There was one man who said, "Let's talk sense to the American people."

What did the scoffers say? The scoffers said, "Nonsense." They said, "Catastrophic nonsense." But we know it was the essential and the basic and the fundamental truth that he spoke to us. This was the man who talked sense to the American people.

There was one man who said: This is a time for self-examination. This is a time for us to take stock, he said. This is a time to decide where we are going.

This, he said, is a time for virtue. But what virtues did he say we needed? Oh, yes, he said, we need the heroic virtues—we always do. We need fortitude; we need courage; we need justice. Everyone cheers when you speak out for those virtues.

But what did he say in addition to that? He said we need the unheroic virtues in America. We need the virtue, he said, of patience. There were those who said we have had too much of patience.

We need, he said, the virtue of tolerance. We need the virtue of forbearance. We need the virtue of patient understanding.

This is what the prophet said. This is what he said to the American people. I ask you, did he prophesy falsely? Did he prophesy falsely?

He said this is a time for greatness. This is a time for greatness for America. He did not say he possessed it. He did not even say he was destined for it. He did say that the heritage of America is one of greatness.

And he described that heritage to us. And he said the promise of America is a promise of greatness. And he said this promise we must fulfill.

This was his call to greatness. This was the call to greatness that was . . . issued in 1952.

He did not seek power for himself in 1952. He did not seek power in 1956.

He does not seek it for himself today.

This man knows, as all of us do from history, that power often comes to those who seek it. But history does not prove that power is always well used by those who seek it.

On the contrary, the whole history of democratic politics is to this end: that power is best exercised by those who are sought out by the people, by those to whom power is given by a free people.

And so I say to you Democrats here assembled: Do not turn away from this man. Do not reject this man. He has fought gallantly. He has fought courageously. He has fought honorably. In 1952 in the great battle. In 1956 he fought bravely. And between those years and since, he has stood off the guerrilla attacks of his enemies and the sniping attacks of those who should have been his friends.

Do not reject this man who made us all proud to be called Democrats. Do not reject this man who, his enemies said, spoke above the heads of the people, but they said it only because they did not want the people to listen. He spoke to the people. He moved their minds and stirred their hearts, and this was what was objected to. Do not leave this prophet without honor in his own party. Do not reject this man.

I submit to you a man who is not the favorite son of any one state. I submit to you the man who is the favorite son of fifty states.

And not only of fifty states, but the favorite son of every country in the world in which he is known—the favorite son in every country in which he is unknown but in which some spark, even though unexpressed, of desire for liberty and freedom still lives.

This favorite son I submit to you: Adlai Stevenson of Illinois.

When Adlai Stevenson died, we lost the purest politician of our time.

Stevenson's approach to politics was marked by three principal characteristics:

First, a decent respect [for] the opinions of mankind in world affairs.

Second, a willingness to accept the judgment of the majority in domestic politics and in general elections.

Third, the unselfish surrender of his own personal reputation and image for the good of the common effort if, in his judgment, that surrender would advance the cause of justice and order and civility. Adlai Stevenson did not grow in honor and in reputation through the organizations which he served, but rather they grew by virtue of his service.

He demonstrated early in his career and throughout his public life the highest degree of political humility in his indifference to what historians and biographers might say about him.

Stevenson was not ahead of his times or outside of his times, as some of his critics said. He was a true contemporary, passing judgment on his own day, expressing that judgment in words that proved his deep concern for the integrity of the language, and finally committing himself to the consequences of his judgment.

In the words of Chaucer, he was a worthy knight who from the time he first rode forth "loved chivalry, truth and honor, generosity and courtesy."

Part I

His Concern for Humanity and Its Survival

Adlai Stevenson congratulating son Adlai Stevenson III on birth of his son Adlai Stevenson IV at hospital in Boston, Nov. 6, 1956
Source: Abraham Lincoln Memorial Library

CHAPTER 1

ANOTHER TIME, ANOTHER POLITICS

Adlai E. Stevenson III

Adlai E. Stevenson III is the eldest son of former Governor
Stevenson. A former U.S. Senator from Illinois, he is now Board
Chairman of SC&M Investment Management Co., an investment
banking firm in Chicago. After he graduated from Harvard College in
1952, he served as a Marine Corps tank platoon commander in
Korea. He graduated from Harvard Law School in 1957. In 1958, he
joined the Chicago-based law firm of Mayer, Brown, and Platt,
becoming a partner in 1966. With record-breaking margins, he was
elected to the Illinois House of Representatives in 1965–67 and as
Illinois State Treasurer in 1967–70 and U.S. Senator from Illinois
from 1970 to 1981. In the Senate, Stevenson was the first Chairman
of the Ethics Committee and the Chairman of the Special Committee
for Senate reorganization in 1976–77. Membership on the Senate
Commerce and Banking Committees led to special responsibilities for
energy, science, technology, space, international trade, the monetary
system, and international finance. He also was a member of the
Majority's Policy Committee and principal author of the International
Banking Act, the Stevenson-Wydler Technology Innovation Act, the
Bayh-Dole Act, Export Administration Act amendments and the
Export Trading Company Act. As a member of the Senate
Intelligence Committee and Chairman of the Subcommittee on the
Collection and Production of Intelligence, he conducted numerous
investigations and the first in-depth congressional study of terrorism
and introduced the Comprehensive Anti-Terrorism Act of 1979.

After retiring from the Senate, Stevenson engaged in close races for the Illinois governorship in 1982 and 1986. He has visited more than eighty foreign countries. His private career as lawyer, investment banker, and public policy expert has focused on international matters, especially in finance and East Asia. He is a director and past President of the U.S. Committee of the Pacific Economic Cooperation Council and has been a leader in the Japan America Society of Chicago, U.S. Midwest Japan Association, U.S.-Korea Wisemen Council, Pacific Basin Council, Advisory Board of the Korea Economic Institute, U.S. Committee of the Council for Security Cooperation in the Asia Pacific and the Council on Foreign Relations, also other civic and business organizations. He manages a farm and continues to travel overseas and do research, lecturing widely, authoring numerous articles and receiving several honorary degrees and awards, including Japan's Order of the Sacred Treasure with gold and silver star. He is an Honorary Pprofessor of Renmin University, Beijing, PRC. Stevenson and his wife, Nancy, have two sons, two daughters, and five grand-children. Their home is in Hanover, Illinois, and they maintain a res-idence in Chicago.

⋅⊱═⊙⊜═⊰⋅

He was known to friends as the Guv. A child of the American heartland and center of isolationism, he was from the beginning a student and citizen of the world. He had lived through the horrors of World War I, precipitated by the Austro-Hungarian Empire's reaction to a Serb nationalist's act of terrorism. A boy correspondent for the *Bloomington Pantagraph*, the family owned central Illinois newspaper, he had seen starving street children in Russia, innocent victims of civil war. He had pondered the military cemeteries in Europe, and, a Princetonian, he was influenced by Woodrow Wilson's internationalism, which postulated self-determination and a League of Nations to resolve disputes peacefully and end war for all time.

Wilson accounts in some measure for the enlightened interna-tionalism, Lincoln for the politics, of the Guv. Lincoln was a con-stant presence in our family, revered above all others. Another product of the prairies, Lincoln had been a presence in the family for generations. He gave his sublime autobiography to great, great grandfather Jesse Fell, his friend and confidante, founder of the *Pantagraph*. Fell, a Quaker immigrant to Illinois from Pennsylvania, had proposed the Lincoln-Douglas debates and then used the auto-biography to promote Lincoln's candidacy for the presidency.

As a young lawyer, the Guv led the Chicago Council on Foreign Relations and the William Allen White Committee to Defend America by Aiding the Allies. When war broke out, we were living in Washington where he served as an assistant to Frank Knox, Secretary of the Navy and a Republican from Chicago. That assignment included trips to the Pacific from whence he would return with tales of meetings with General Douglas MacArthur and Admiral Chester Nimitz and near mishaps at the edge of combat. Before the war was over he served on missions to Europe, including the Strategic Bombing Survey, and then with Archibald MacLeish at the State Department to help articulate America's post war policies to the world. He was present at the birth of the United Nations in San Francisco and represented the United States at its Preparatory Commission in London starting late in 1945. Our little home on a mews off Grosvenor Square became a nightly watering hole for great men excitedly planning the new world order and rebirth of Europe. Jan Masaryk of Czechoslovakia was there. He, by then Foreign Minister, would later die a mysterious death in Prague. Gladwyn Jebb of Great Britain was there, Paul Henri Spaak of Belgium and Andrei Gromyko of the Soviet Union with whom we both would clash in later years.

He was one of the architects of the post world war international order built around containment, the Marshall Plan, Point Four, and the UN family of international institutions. Peace, the Guv would later say, was a condition of human survival in the nuclear age. He started the strategic arms control process with his proposal for cessation of nuclear testing. He warned that the planet Earth was a fragile spaceship dependent on its vulnerable reserves of air, water, and soil. To the day he died while serving as U.S. Ambassador to the UN, he warned that a world divided against itself, "haves and have nots," would not stand.

The Guv was a student of the world all his life, on the ground, rummaging in markets and *favelas* to learn how people lived, in their ruins and monuments to discover their past, everywhere in the last years courted by the wise and the mighty, cheered by the humble. Virtually everywhere he received a hero's welcome, the embodiment of principles that made America secure and leader of the "free world," its embassies everywhere outposts of hope, even inspiration. Now, they lie behind barriers, and U.S. ambassadors dare not fly the flag on their armor-plated limousines.

Adlai Stevenson profiled with sons Adlai Stevenson III and John Fell
Source: Archie Lieberman

Our home in Libertyville, northwest of Chicago, was something of a museum, reflecting the Guv's itinerant life and his political antecedents. Mementos from his travels littered the house. The floor of a large room in the basement was covered by a magnificent Arab rug. It seems the Guv was warned by U.S. officials in Riyadh, Saudi Arabia, not to admire objects in the palace, for the King, Ibn Saud, would then be obliged by Arab custom to give them to him. The Guv was a tight man with the dollar—Scotch-Irish, the Scotch predominated. He may have admired the King's rugs selectively, thus furnishing some of his home's bare floors. Over the fireplace in this basement room was a framed Democratic poster from the 1900 campaign, which bore the slogan, "The Republic, not the Empire." Empire won, as it often does—for a time. The Philippines was colonized. William Jennings Bryan and his running mate, Adlai I, Vice President under Grover Cleveland, lost the election. But reaction to the excesses of the Gilded Age followed the assassination of President McKinley. President Theodore Roosevelt, Adlai I's opponent in 1900, railed against "malefactors of great wealth." He fought the trusts and preserved the country's natural wonders. Wilson carried on.

There was a rhythm to our politics, occasional bursts of energy and innovation, occasional statesmen. Democrats ran under the banners of a New Deal, Fair Deal, New Frontier, Great Society—and the New America of Adlai Stevenson. The Gilded Age, the malefactors have returned. The reaction waits. The "haves and have nots" divide even more at home and in an interdependent world. A popularly unelected president trailed in the failed footsteps of Leninists, seeking Empire in the guise of ideology, little recognizing that America was strong and secure in the world when the Guv and his compatriots of another generation were waging peace, not war, seeking cooperation, not preemption. As ideologies in China lost power, they began to win power in a new America. The reaction waits as the new America of George Bush demonstrates the limits of its military and economic power, rendering it dependent on China and Japan to shore up a newly unsound dollar.

The Guv's was a different politics—and time. I was a sergeant at arms at the 1948 Democratic Convention in Philadelphia. That was a convention of politicians assembled for serious business. The air was heavy with sweat and tobacco smoke. A young, unknown Mayor of Minneapolis and candidate for the U.S. Senate made an impassioned speech challenging those politicians to approve a strong civil rights plank. That convention rose to his challenge. The South stormed out. Harry Truman, a product of the St. Louis Prendergast machine, went on to barnstorm across the country, campaigning against the "Do Nothing" Republican Congress.

The Guv, bureaucrat, diplomat, and partner in a blue ribbon Chicago law firm and Paul Douglas, Professor of Economics at the University of Chicago, were the candidates for Governor and U.S. Senator, respectively, of the regular Democratic organization of Illinois and the Cook County machine. Like Truman, they were given little chance of winning. They each headed a caravan of candidates who traversed the state day in and day out, occasionally converging for large rallies. They took no polls. They had little money and no consultants. My cousin, Tim Ives, and I were the drivers. From one end of the state to the other, at county fairs and county courthouses, at factory gates and Chicago ward meetings, the candidates pressed the flesh and railed against a corrupt Republican administration in Illinois, the "Do Nothing" Congress in Washington—"the flesh, the devil and all the other enemies of the Democratic Party." People responded; they were engaged in their politics and their parties. Political organizations and volunteers got out the vote. The Guv won by the largest plurality in Illinois history to that time and with Douglas, helped Harry Truman carry Illinois and win the presidency.

Illinois' governor-elect recruited professionals and academics from outside politics. Citizens doing their duty poured into state government, as they had the New Deal and would, the New Frontier of John F. Kennedy. Few bore the endorsements of campaign contributors and political leaders. State Senator Richard J. Daley, Director of the Department of Revenue, was something of an exception. A constitutional convention was organized which would later reform state government. Departments were overhauled, the State Police put under civil service. Gambling was shut down. Fair employment and housing practices were enforced. At night, the Guv would walk alone from the Governor's Mansion to Lincoln's home and commune in the darkness, seeking some wisdom from the martyred president.

Many of those good citizens who heeded his call went from the Stevenson Administration to the Kennedy and Johnson Administrations. At his Senate confirmation hearing for Ambassador to the UN, he would remark that he regretted he had but one law firm to give to his country. Willard Wirtz, Professor of Law at Northwestern University and chairman of the Illinois Liquor Control Commission, would become Secretary of Labor. George Mitchell, Illinois Director of Finance, would become Vice Chairman of the Federal Reserve Board. Newton Minow became Chairman of the Federal Communications Commission. William McCormick Blair became Ambassador to Denmark, Carl McGowan a U.S. Appellate Judge, and so it went. Richard J. Daley would become the legendary Mayor of Chicago and "Boss," supported by the Guv in a primary contest with the incumbent Mayor Kennelley.

The Guv wanted to finish the job in Springfield, but after an eloquent welcoming address, he was drafted by the 1952 Democratic National Convention in Chicago. His campaign started at that convention with no staff, no program, and no money, only a band of sturdy, talented volunteers who congregated at the Elks Club in Springfield. He went on to lose the election to the returning war hero, General Dwight Eisenhower, and win the hearts and minds of people the world over. Before veterans, he did not beat the drums or wave the bloody flag though that was expedient in Joe McCarthy's time.

Patriotism was the "quiet steady dedication of a lifetime." He refused, unlike Eisenhower, to say he would go to Korea where the war raged, knowing his negotiating hand as President would be weakened. (I went as a Marine Corps platoon commander.) He refused to trade the national patrimony, the tidelands, to the oil industry for money or votes and forfeited the support of the Democratic Governor of Texas. And he lost. It was "time for a change."

The Guv would not have been possible in today's money drenched, mass media driven politics. He was a rarity even for his time. A campaign was a device for informing the people, so they could make an informed judgment. Trust the people with the truth, he said, all the truth. What won was more important than who won.

After the 1952 campaign, he organized the Democratic Advisory Council to develop public policy for the party. He was its titular leader and took the responsibility seriously—which meant more than raising money. Today, there is no such advisory council or titular leader to speak for the party. The national committees are machines for raising and distributing money.

In 1956, he contested in three primaries, locking up the nomination in California. By then, television had intruded and was beginning to trivialize American politics, but he took half-hour blocks of time on national television for eloquent speeches to cheering partisans, always mindful that the world was listening. He lost the election after the invasions of Hungary and Suez rallied the people to their president, but in losing, he laid the programmatic foundation for the New Frontier and the Great Society. Federal aid to education and Medicare have roots in the New America of the Guv.

The Guv's partisans converged from across the country to literally storm the 1960 Democratic National Convention in Los Angeles, demanding another nomination. He had entered no primaries and encouraged his followers to support others. Many refused, including Eleanor Roosevelt who supported him to the end. The outcome was foreordained. John F. Kennedy won the nomination and went on to win the presidency with the Guv's active support. The country experienced one of those bursts of energy and innovation—the New Frontier and Great Society. And the Guv returned to his beginnings, the United Nations, as America's Ambassador to the World. It was not the office he sought. He wanted to be an architect of policy, Secretary of State, not an advocate. He had no illusions. A cabinet position and promises notwithstanding, he would be an advocate of policies decided by others. He could have supported Kennedy's quest for the nomination and been Secretary of State but thought it right for the titular leader to be neutral.

At the UN, the Guv is remembered best for his indictment of the Soviet Union before the Security Council during the Cuba missile crisis. Little remembered is his presentation to the Security Council during the Bay of Pigs crisis. He was fed erroneous information, which he innocently presented to the Council. When the truth was found out, that the U.S. had orchestrated the invasion, he feared his reputation and effectiveness would be compromised. But UN members rallied behind him. None were deceived. The Kennedy Administration was compromised, not the Guv. Toward the end, he was called upon to support a policy in Southeast Asia, which had lost his support. He decided to resign at the end of 1965 but died on July 14, in London, a few blocks from the site of our old home where this tale, as I remember it, began.

CHAPTER 2

WOULD THAT THE GUV WERE HERE

Adele Simmons

Dr. Adele Simmons is Vice Chair of Chicago Metropolis, a public interest group dedicated to the development of a Greater Chicago. She is the daughter of famed Chicago insurance executive, Hermon Dunlap Smith and the goddaughter of Adlai E. Stevenson II. She attended Radcliffe and Oxford, taught and served in the administrations at Tufts and Princeton Universities, was President of Hampshire College in Amherst, Massachusetts, and of the MacArthur Foundation in Chicago. In each position, she was strongly committed to Stevenson's goals and values.

Adlai Stevenson was in our house, on our minds, and in our hearts as I grew up, went to college, and moved into the professional world. My father met Adlai when they were ten, and they were close friends thereafter. My parents were not particularly political— though my father later became head of the Volunteers for Stevenson. My parents were friends in the best sense of the word. They relaxed together, often discussing Illinois politics or world affairs, but my parents wanted nothing from the Guv and provided him with a safe space to laugh, think out loud about his political career and his personal life, and relax.

As friends, my parents were a part of a small group of people who were with the Guv to celebrate successes and regroup after disappointments. My parents and Adlai were together in Washington when the Japanese bombed Pearl Harbor in 1941. My father participated in key conversations leading to the decision that Stevenson would run for governor in 1948. My mother contributed the parody of "I'm in Love with a Wonderful Guv" that was sung on the convention floor when her friend's name was placed in presidential nomination in 1952. Originally penned for Adlai's fiftieth birthday, it had several verses, among them the following:

> He's as honest as Abraham Lincoln,
> He's the man no money can buy,
> He's the best guy on earth,
> So let's sing to his worth,
> He's our guv, he's a wonderful guy.

It was not long after and on Adlai's account that I felt like a pariah among my peers. In my sixth-grade class in Lake Forest, Illinois, in 1952, I was the only Stevenson supporter, Eisenhower being that Chicago suburb's candidate. I could live with the ostracism that was the result because I knew that my ascendancy was mere months away, when I would be a guest in the Stevenson White House. That this did not come to pass proved to be a formative experience. I could stand alone, and I could see there was a certain reward in the stand itself.

Thus, I was well girded for the 1956 campaign. That September, I went off to a boarding school near Baltimore. An optimist might say that I found Stevenson's support had doubled: in the entire school, there were now two students who supported him—the president of the student government and I. We were absolutely surrounded. Everywhere we looked was a lapel adorned by an "I like Ike" button.

I thought it important that the candidate know of my predicament, and, unaware of the hubris in the act, I put pen to paper. It was characteristic of my older friend that I received a reply by return mail. The envelope contained a button that proclaimed, "Adlai likes Me."

The following summer, the soundly defeated candidate arrived at my family's summerhouse in Desbarats, Ontario. It was a trip he made often in the years between 1930 and 1964. In 1957, the assembled children thought he deserved a particular welcome, fearing perhaps that his spirits might have declined in the wake of his second colossal defeat. Lacking 21 cannon, they assembled on the pier with 21 rocks, which they systematically propelled into the water as Adlai arrived by motorboat. Adlai understood this honor instantly. He stood up in the boat and saluted, causing significant anxiety in one of my nieces, who had been drilled in the maxim that one must never stand in a moving boat.

As I re-read biographies of Stevenson, his speeches, and personal letters from him, to him, and about him, the Guv rests in my memory as that man standing in the boat. He stood for principles when others sat. He saw things from a higher perch. He was a complex man in a simpler time, a visionary when Americans wanted concrete, when they truly believed that what was "good for General Motors [was] good for the country." He listened to and saluted the young. When many men shared the view of Lord Chesterfield that those of the opposite sex were "only children of a larger growth," Adlai valued and sought out the opinions of women.

In 1961, when I was a sophomore in college, I spent a summer in a YMCA work camp in Nairobi and came home through New York, stopping to visit Adlai at the Waldorf Astoria. I walked in, covered with dust and dirt, carrying a duffel bag and a Masai spear and shield. I doubt the Waldorf would let anyone in such attire in the discreet Towers entrance today, but on that occasion, the doorman looked askance, but let me by.

The Guv was not deterred by either my spear or my shabby look, and knowing Kenya from a 1953 visit, he asked me questions about it for what seemed like hours. What did I think of Kenyatta? What were the people around him like? What would happen to the British farmers who had been in Kenya for decades? Was the Mau Mau rebellion really over? How deep were the tribal divisions? Was a union among Kenya, Uganda, and Tanzania possible? He was intrigued that the leading business group in Nairobi had asked me, a 21-year-old American working in a multiracial work camp, to be a luncheon speaker. And we discussed at some length the offer I was to convey to my father from one Kenyan dignitary: 22 cows in exchange for his daughter.

I doubt that my answers shaped U.S. policy toward East Africa. But the questions had a profound effect on me. He took me very seriously. He seemed to care about my answers, which I, of course, believed to be far more authentic than any information he would be getting from the U.S. Embassy. On this and other occasions, he valued me and my ideas, and with a twist of phrase, he had me believing that what I was trying to say was worthwhile. As a young woman in that era, when feminism was far from a household word, his belief in me was the foundation of a self-confidence that I carried into various theatres—Radcliffe, South Africa, Mauritius, Alabama.

On July 14, 1965, I was working in the civil rights movement in Birmingham, Alabama, when I heard of his sudden death in London. I was moved to write my parents, who had lost their good friend of so many decades. I recalled his effect on me, but his effect on the world was also on my mind. Stevenson had opposed military action in Vietnam until all peaceful remedies through the UN had been exhausted, and in March 1965, he had noted to himself, "Military track runs into dead end." I wrote home saying, "Without this voice of moderation and reason, bombs may end up falling indiscriminately in Vietnam and who knows where else." And not too long thereafter, bombs did start falling indiscriminately in Southeast Asia.

John Bartlow Martin points out that when the Guv died, he was mourned by high and low alike around the globe. I could understand this. I had traveled with him and other family friends on a boat in the Western Mediterranean in 1959. Wherever we docked, Stevenson was a celebrity. Local mayors received him. He was invigorated by people in the local markets. I was initially skeptical of the value of visits that seemed to me scripted and too brief, but I was won over by Adlai's ability to see and hear between the lines. When he returned to the boat, I was invariably struck by his quickly gathered impressions of the nature of the government, the contentment or discontent of the people, the future of the local economy and how it fit with the direction of the nation, the continent, and world markets. This should not have surprised me. I knew that in earlier world tours, he had visited slums as well as palaces and chatted with street vendors as well as prime ministers—and it was all of a piece for him.

I learned from it. When I later lived in Tunisia, I recoiled from the Americans there who never strayed beyond the embassy parties and who made sweeping judgments about what was happening in the country, without breaking out of a very narrow circle of English-speaking Tunisians. With the support of U.S. Ambassador Francis

Russell, and with the help of Joanna Macy, then wife of the Director of the Peace Corps, I started a newsletter about Tunisian politics, culture, and economic development that was circulated to the English-speaking community. Unless Americans in particular understood the country they lived in, they could not engage it. But by the time I ended up living in Tunis, I had had the advantage of years of tutoring by the Guv. I never became as good as he was at eyeballing villages, but throughout Africa, I saw things that I never would have without his tutoring. And it was this perspective—that street markets, slums, offices, and palaces were all libraries of information on the public welfare—that shaped a foreign policy that earned the United States respect in the world.

The Governor did not talk at people, he talked with them. My father was in the car with him when he rode to the Amphitheater in Chicago in 1952 to accept the party's nomination for president. As a result of the crowds of spectators in the street, the car was repeatedly mired in traffic. At one such stop, a woman asked the Guv who he would choose for vice president. I can hear a modern-day candidate saying, "Well, we have many fine people in the party," and droning on from there. Stevenson's response was, "Who do you suggest?" As it turned out, the woman wasn't too particular. "Anybody but Kefauver," she said.

A few days later, the press descended *en masse* on the Governor's Mansion in Springfield for his first press conference as a candidate. He came out dressed in a suit, which he told reporters was "not more than four inches too long in the trousers." When pressed about its origins, he said it had been sent from Spain. A correspondent commented that he did not know that Sears Roebuck had stores in Spain. The Governor said the suit was not from Sears, that it had been sent to him by the artist Joseph Allsworthy.

"Friend of yours?" asked a reporter.
"Enemy?" asked another.
"He's a friend," Adlai said. "Or was."

He had that endearing sense of humor, that ability to laugh at himself. I haven't seen anything to match it since in a presidential candidate from either party. I recall him coming down to the lake in Desbarats one afternoon. We were playing nearby, and he was intent upon filling a bucket. As he stepped onto the mossy rock at water's edge he slipped. Over the years, I witnessed several of these unintentional dunkings by fully clad adults, and I can assure you that the other entries into the lake were invariably accompanied by a vocabulary unsanctioned for the ears of children. The Guv's entry, however, was done with characteristic charm. He ended up, neck deep, the water bucket held over his head, the only item kept dry. And he laughed the whole time.

Now, at first glance, there is a certain absurdity to keeping a water bucket dry, but I like to look at this another way. If you are about to enter the water unwillingly, even if the cost is only to your vanity, it nonetheless takes a certain presence of mind to realize that you will have a much harder time getting out if you are carrying a full bucket of water. Stevenson had an exit strategy, realistic and achievable. At this point in our history, I need say no more.

When I reflect now on Stevenson's life and times, I am at times impressed by how far we have come. As assistant to the Secretary of the Navy during World War II, when that office was daily engaged with huge logistical problems in the Atlantic and Pacific, Stevenson later said that the hardest part of the job had been desegregating the Navy. Today, the American military actually looks more like America. Not so long ago, it didn't. I like to think, however, that the Guv would have worked hard to keep the draft, so that the Army would not only reflect the racial diversity in the country but also the class diversity. He would, I think, argue that the children of the rich and powerful should be on the front lines too.

A few years later, while the Guv saw the dire need for the United Nations, many in the United States thought we could go back to simpler times, when the rest of the world did not interfere with us or even enter most people's thoughts. Today, everyone recognizes that the rest of the world has a daily impact on our lives.

When Stevenson ran for Governor of Illinois in 1948, good government was a somewhat foreign notion in the Land of Lincoln. Part way through his administration, he noted, "We [Democrats] have just been trying to give the people the right change, which seems to be a novel and appealing idea." Today, we don't always get good government, but we expect each new governor to deliver it.

In other ways, however, reading and reflecting on Stevenson's life and time, I am simultaneously impressed and depressed by the relevance of his thoughts and words. In 1949, in his "The Kind of Democrat I Am" speech, he defined himself as a man who had no fixed standards by which every issue was to be automatically resolved.

He said he did not identify big government with good government, rather he thought the level of government involvement should be determined by the job that needed to be done. "I am an internationalist . . . I think that peace is the most important unfinished business of our generation. I don't like doles. I don't like subsidies. I don't like any interference with free markets, free men, and free enterprise. I like freedom to succeed, or to fail. I also know that there can be no real freedom without economic justice, social justice, equality of opportunity and a fair chance for every individual to make the most of himself. And I know that there is little the man on the assembly line or the plow can do to affect the chain of events which may close his factory or foreclose his mortgage."

This sounds a lot to me like someone who would find common ground with those campaigning today for a living wage, for pension reform, for improving the lot of the man or woman whose job has moved to India, Mexico, or China. It sounds to me like a man who would think of war, not as a first resort, but as the last.

Half a century ago, Stevenson was concerned with the growing economic disparity in the United States. It bothered him, not just because of the sheer injustice of hunger amid plenty but also because he believed that Americans' obsessive consumerism was destructive both to our souls and to our image abroad. "The goal of life is more than material advance; it is now, and through all eternity, the triumph of spirit over matter, of love and liberty over force and violence," he said. That was 1952.

By 1960, he'd become more critical. "The contrast between private opulence and public squalor on most of our panorama is now too obvious to be denied. Yet we still spend per capita almost as much on advertising to multiply the private wants of our people as we do on education to enable them to seek a fuller, wiser, and more satisfying civic existence. The face that we present to the world, especially through our mass circulation media, is the face of the individual or the family as a high consumption unit with minimal social responsibilities—father happily drinking his favorite beer, mother dreamily fondling soft garments newly rinsed in a wonderful new detergent, the children gaily calling from the barbecue pit for a famous sauce for their steak. With the supermarket as our temple and the singing commercial as our litany, are we likely to fire the world with an irresistible vision of America's exalted purposes and inspiring way of life?"

As we then battled the Soviet Union for favor in smaller nations, Stevenson thought the outcome would turn on our ability to guarantee equality of opportunity, to reduce the gap between rich and poor, to make democracy, as he put it, "accord in practice with its premises and professions of faith. We won't resist the Soviet impact on the Western world with a schizophrenic society which protests its devotion to democratic ideals while it indulges in undemocratic practices. If Western civilization is to save its body, it must save its soul too."

While it might be said that we vanquished communism, it can't be said that we adequately delivered on the premises of the nation. Rich and poor are farther apart today than they were forty years ago. The education achievement gap between whites and blacks is growing again. The poor are increasingly isolated. Gated communities and long stretches of suburban highway divide us.

In Stevenson's time, much of the world equated the United States with the fundamental beliefs in which the nation was founded, with free speech, free thought, free movement. Today, sadly, much of the world equates the United States with arrogance, and they do so because that is what we give them. Our official plans for the world's future need no support—we can impose those plans by ourselves. International agreements can be discarded, though we are signatories, because no one can make us follow them. We seem to treat the UN as a party of our inferiors, people we visit from time to time in hopes of finding better kitchen help. Our allies of longstanding are seen as senile and irrelevant—Rumsfeld's "old Europe."

Would that the Guv were here. Writing in 1951, he said, "We should look at the UN, as we do other political instruments, see what it is *not*, disabuse ourselves of any illusions, and appreciate how useful it still can be." Writing in 1963, he pointed out that, on a daily basis, the UN "attempts to conciliate, mediate, discuss, compromise, or if need be, simply delay the conflicts which play, like earthquake tremors, across the frail political crust of our society." He could say the same today, and furthermore make the case, certainly more eloquently than I, that there is no other forum of its kind. In our arrogance, we cast it aside to go our own way in Iraq. We have paid for this with many Iraqi and American lives.

I wish that the Guv were here to check that arrogance, to remind us of what we should stand for. "Patriotism is not the fear of something; it is the love of something." Patriotism with us was not hatred of communism yesterday, nor is it hatred of Islamic extremism today. It should be, as Stevenson put it, "the love of this republic and of the ideal of liberty of man and mind in which it was born and to which this Republic is dedicated." A patriot who loves the ideal of liberty of man would not discard the Geneva Conventions, sanction the torture of those who oppose us, or suggest that a little humiliation, perhaps a dog collar around the neck, might help soften suspects for interrogation.

Stevenson again: "But now, as society and the world become more complex, some people . . . seem to yearn for the old simplicity, for the shorthand analysis, for the black-and-white choice, for the cheap-and-easy answer, for the children's guide to good and evil. The very color and diversity of our pluralistic society seem to confuse them. They want it plain and unitary. . . . The greatness of the issues calls out for greatness in ourselves, to validate democracy, to speak for freedom, and to make our profoundest affirmation of faith in the American way of life."

"The challenge to all of us is to prove," he said, "that a free society can remain free, humane, and creative, even when it is under heavy and ruthless fire; that it can combat poverty, injustice, and intolerance in its own midst, even while resisting a monstrous foreign despotism. . . . We shall be accused of idealism or some such crime for projecting so optimistic a vision. To which the only truthful answer is that we are guilty. This is not to say that we guarantee a happy ending; it is only to say that we retain our confidence in man's ability to achieve the triumph of decency and compassion in our lifetime."

Reading Stevenson today, I think he had a profound sense of American society and its probable direction. I am much taken with his welcome to the delegates of the 1952 convention. "Here, my friends, on the prairies of Illinois and of the Middle West, we can see a long way in all directions. Here there are no barriers, no defenses, to ideas and to aspirations. We want none; we want no shackles on the mind or the spirit, no rigid patterns of thought, and no iron conformity. We want only the faith and conviction that triumph in fair and free contest."

The Guv could see the dangers of an apathetic electorate, and he warned of its consequences. When citizens lose interest, he told the Princeton Class of 1954, a power vacuum is created, and it will be filled by "corrupt men, or incompetents, or worse." In ordinary times, he said, the corrupt and incompetent could be suffered for a while and then ejected, but 1954 was no ordinary time, and he believed the world's fate hung on how well or how ill the United States conducted its affairs. He had the courage to wonder if the American electorate was mature enough, "whether we have reached the awesome pinnacle of power we now occupy too soon, before we have sufficiently elevated our national mind to lead the world wisely." He warned that Princeton class that in times of crisis, when men of ideas waffled, they opened the door "to the strong dumb brute—the man on horseback."

The Guv lived before the days when candidates wrapped themselves in the flag, but, in 1952, he seemed to see it coming. "A campaign addressed not to men's minds and to their best instincts, but to their passions, emotions and prejudices, is unworthy at best," he told an audience in Chicago. "Now, with the fate of our nation at stake, it is unbearable." In a radio address to the Armed Forces, he said, "I don't know yet whether one can win an election with hard, distasteful truths, but this is the only way I want to win it." Imagine, today, a candidate saying he would rather lose an election than mislead the electorate.

Imagine, today, a candidate for the presidency ungoverned by polls and focus groups; unafraid of being far ahead of those he hoped to lead. That was Stevenson on nuclear disarmament. He spoke for a nuclear test ban treaty in 1956. Few embraced the idea, and he was bitterly attacked. He persisted and certainly influenced Eisenhower, who proposed a moratorium on all nuclear testing in 1958.

It was Stevenson who pressed President John F. Kennedy to move on the issue within months of his taking office, though JFK believed that the nation wasn't ready, that disarmament had value as a propaganda tool but was unachievable in the short term. That fall, Kennedy spoke to the UN General Assembly, challenging the Soviet Union, "not to an arms race, but to a peace race." By the spring of 1962, the Geneva Disarmament Conference was under way. In the summer of 1963, a limited test ban treaty was signed. Some of those who had vilified the Governor were now on the bandwagon, seemingly unaware that they'd given the driver a good lashing seven years earlier. He had had the stuff to overcome those attacks.

The Guv had a worldview we need now. I long for a president who sees that partnerships operate through consultation and persuasion. "There is no room for the 'Big Stick' or the ultimatum,"

Stevenson said, "be it the small or the medium size or even the large economy size. Ours must be the role of the good neighbor. The good partner, the good friend. Never, the big bully." I long for someone to make integrity and credibility a national asset, for a leader to speak of the need for humility and modesty, for someone who brings out the best in us, not the worst.

No man on horseback for me. No candidate wrapped in the flag. I want the man standing in the boat, saluting not American troops on foreign soil but children on a pier. I was afraid for him then. I wish he were here now. I'd carry his water bucket; even keep it dry for him, as he waded neck deep, in the turmoil of the day.

◦➤═◗◖═➤◦

EDITOR'S NOTE

Adele Simmons' recollections of her godfather, Adlai Stevenson, his feelings about what he saw and thought about America, its example and unfulfilled needs and its role in promoting and providing international understanding and assistance as a total achievement of the American dream, are eloquently reflected in his closing words to the New York State Democratic Convention on September 10, 1956:

> Our purpose this fall is to restore government to our democratic society—open government which includes the American people . . . [and] shows the peoples of the world by our deeds that democracy is the best hope of man.
>
> The challenge of our age lies in the long struggle for freedom, justice and abundance for all people. We in the United States have made great strides toward meeting that challenge. Yet even in our own overflowing land, there are areas of insecurity, areas of want, areas of fear. Our very wealth deprives us of alibis. When we tolerate insecurity, want and fear, it is not because of a failure of resources. It is because of a failure of will.
>
> In the United States, political and economic questions thus become moral questions—questions of directions and questions of leadership. . . . But we cannot satisfy our ambitions within our national frontiers. The ultimate American mission is to strive to help, not just ourselves, but all people everywhere. . . .

We need to recover once again our sense of purpose and our sense of hope. Armed with the power of our ideals, we cannot only save ourselves, but we can help save themselves. In our mutual salvation, through steadfastness and cooperation and sacrifice, lies the hope for mankind.

These are exalted objectives. They may seem far removed from politics in an election year. But politics, rightly construed, is itself an exalted occupation. It is the means by which free society realizes its purposes.

CHAPTER 3

STEVENSON: CONCERNED AND BRILLIANT—HIS FINEST HOUR WAS IN SEEKING A NUCLEAR TEST BAN

Ken Hechler

Ken Hechler, former White House research assistant to President Harry S. Truman and a longtime associate of Judge Samuel I. Rosenman in the joint assembly of the thirteen-volume *Public Papers and Addresses of Franklin D. Roosevelt*, was appointed Executive Assistant to Adlai E. Stevenson in April 1956. He accompanied the Governor throughout the presidential election campaign of that year. Some years before, he received a Ph.D degree in political science from Columbia University where he taught beginning in 1937 and on his return from the Army, at Princeton University. During World War II, he rose from the rank of private to major, heading up a four-man history unit that accompanied General Hodges' First Army's historic advance to the Rhine River at Remagen, gateway to Germany. He was recipient of five battle stars and a Bronze Star. In 1958, he began nine outstanding terms in the U.S. House of Representatives from West Virginia. From 1985 to 2001, he served four terms as West Virginia's Secretary of State. In addition to *The Bridge at Remagen*, he is author of the following books: *Insurgency, Personalities and Politics of the Taft Era; West Virginia Memories of President Kennedy; Working with Truman; Toward the Endless Frontier; Toward the Space Frontier; and Hero of the Rhine.* In 2002, he received the Truman Public Service

Award, given annually to "an outstanding public servant who best typifies and possesses the qualities of dedication, industry, honesty, and integrity that distinguished Harry S. Truman." He presently resides in Charleston, West Virginia, and frequently addresses school, college, and civic groups about Adlai Stevenson, Harry Truman, Remagen and other public issues. Email: fesenms@wvle.lib.wv.us

⊸⊱⩵⊚⊰⊸

When President Truman's former Secretary of the Air Force Thomas Finletter interviewed me for a presidential campaign position with Governor Stevenson in the spring of 1956, he warned: "If you go to work for this man, keep in mind that if Socrates were alive today, Stevenson would tie him in knots with his logic."

Having worked with Truman on his White House staff from 1949 to 1953, I observed a marked difference between him and Stevenson. Truman seemed to make quick decisions almost through his viscera; Stevenson made all his decisions with his fertile brain. Because Adlai Stevenson weighed decisions carefully, he was unfairly charged as being indecisive.

On January 22, 1952, Truman invited Stevenson to the White House to try to persuade him to be the Democratic nominee for President. Disappointed that Stevenson expressed a desire to run for re-election as Governor of Illinois, Truman argued: "Look, if a knucklehead like me can be president and do a fairly good job, look what a real smart, well-educated person like you could do in that job." Friction, however, arose between the two men when Stevenson later in 1952 replaced Frank McKinney with Steve Mitchell as the Democratic national chairman and moved his presidential campaign headquarters to a home base in Springfield, Illinois.

Looking at Adlai Stevenson's legacy, like Gaul it can be divided into three parts: international relations, politics and issues, and the incandescent brilliance of his intellect and concern. Of the three parts, Stevenson's vision shone brightest in the international arena. He had already played a key role in the establishment of the United Nations in San Francisco in 1945. Despite warnings from political advisors in 1956 that urging a hydrogen bomb test ban would cost him votes and the public would support Eisenhower simply because as a military man he argued against it (at that time), this, like the 1962 Cuba missile crisis, was clearly Stevenson's finest hour. His insistence during the 1956 campaign of the danger to civilization from the testing fallout from strontium-90 paved the way for future presidents—also Eisenhower two years later—to follow the path which he had pioneered.

Adlai Stevenson possessed a global vision of what Woodrow Wilson proclaimed as a decent respect for the opinion of other nations. He recognized the incipient revolution of rising expectations that was surfacing in so many other countries. He boldly took the position that the United States should exert its leadership to show and assist developing nations to rise and respond peacefully to these expectations as they yearned for justice, freedom, and economic betterment. If it were true that some subsequent leaders have strayed from this global vision, nevertheless, Stevenson's collaborative articulation is the inspirational standard destined to prevail.

During the presidential campaigns of 1952 and 1956, Stevenson always lived up to the pledge he had made in accepting the 1952 nomination to "talk sense to the American people"—regardless of the political risk, to tell them the truth. He never departed from his conviction that a campaign must be an honest educational experience. Even when Senator Estes Kefauver was handshaking and "corn-poning" voters to win over Stevenson in the 1956 Minnesota primary, Adlai insisted on stressing those policies which would produce a just economy at home and peace in the world.

In the course of two presidential campaigns, Stevenson inspired millions of Americans to rise above their cynicism about politics and play an active role at all levels of government. It is as important today as it was then. This legacy has had far-reaching effects beyond Stevenson's death in 1965 as a new breed of activists came forward to provide the yeast for progress.

One of Stevenson's significant legacies—reminiscent of his development of a "Bill of Particulars," underlying the challenge in his successful 1948 gubernatorial campaign, was the work that he and Finletter initiated to provide an informed background on the most important issues then facing the nation and the world. Although Franklin Roosevelt assembled a so-called brain trust for his presidency drawn primarily from Columbia University, Stevenson carried this concept light-years forward.

Much of the groundwork was laid by a young Rhodes Scholar named Dr. John Brademas, who preceded me as Stevenson's Research Director before he returned as planned to Indiana to run for Congress in the fall of 1956. Elected to the House of Representatives two years later, he served twenty-two productive years in Congress, where he authored a host of educational laws of continued importance. He then became President of New York University, and since 1992, its President Emeritus. Working with the greatest intellectual talent from colleges, universities, and other sources of expertise, he shepherded the assembly of far-reaching analyses and position papers reflective of Stevenson's thoughts and ideas on every issue, from agriculture to small business to taxation, to foreign and defense policy (naming only a few). These analyses were stockpiled as the grist for the Stevenson campaign of 1956.

The material produced by these experts and articulated by Stevenson, moreover, prominently figured in virtually every aspect of President Kennedy's "New Frontier" and what later came to be known as President Lyndon Johnson's "Great Society."

The most difficult area to assess in Stevenson's legacy is his intellectual brilliance. Very few faculty members remaining at Princeton University, where I taught for three years, could recall him scholastically as being much more than an indifferent, average student.

His initial foray into law at Harvard Law School was not different; he eventually received a law degree at Northwestern University in Chicago. How and when he achieved brilliance is somewhat of a mystery, but I agree with Finletter in his observation about Socrates. On one occasion, when I was asked to draft a speech for Des Moines, Iowa, my friends at the Des Moines *Register* advised me that if Stevenson would come up with a good speech on agriculture, Iowa's largest newspaper would give him an enthusiastic editorial.

So I produced a draft touting the family farm as the backbone of America. I quoted Thomas Jefferson's *Notes on Virginia* that "those who labor in the earth are the Chosen People of God." When I triumphantly presented this proud draft to the Governor, he fingered it with a frown and to my surprise said: "I don't know why I have to mouth all this stuff about the family farm. Think of all the consumers in this country. Wouldn't it be preferable to stimulate, support and encourage large agri-businesses who could produce farm products at lower prices which every consumer could afford?"

Of course, I immediately accused him of adopting Republican propaganda. My consternation rose as he continued to argue for lower-priced farm products. In desperation, I angrily blurted: "You're talking just like Herbert Hoover!" We continued to spar on for twenty more minutes. Then, he suddenly laughed and said: "Every afternoon about this time I have to get my intellectual exercise. Now, let's get back to the family farm."

I related this story to Stevenson's law partner Willard Wirtz, who commented: "That's very characteristic. He frequently poses as the devil's advocate to draw out the best arguments for his beliefs."

I honestly believe Adlai Stevenson was the most brilliant political leader we have had this past century. Others may point to others. But I would respond that politically it was Stevenson, who over thirty-five years was repeatedly seen from both private and public venues as the one honestly and courageously running the right idea—even a scientifically based one—down to the goal line for the sake of the public. I recall so well, in this regard, our four-hour flight to San Diego during the campaign. During the trip, the Governor constantly kept me busy back and forth with radio messages to leading scientific experts here and abroad, searching for data and answers to questions on the effect of nuclear fallout in meadows where cattle grazed and ate grass and thence produced the contaminated milk that would be consumed by tending mothers and others. He truly had an inquisitive mind that demanded a full-blown assembly of the scientific facts affecting the matter that would be the underpinning of his statements in the campaign.

One other difficulty in assessing the legacy of Adlai Stevenson on the personal side is one relating to my perception of the electorate. It seems to me they are more interested in issues when they vote for candidates for Congress, whereas candidates for U.S. President are often favored for their personality. Thus in 2004, voters rated John Kerry 20 percent smarter than George Bush but voted for the "Aw, Shucks" smile of Bush. Similarly, in 1952 and 1956, the tremendous popularity of the "I like IKE" slogan, plus the Eisenhower smile, were superior to the intellectual brilliance of Adlai Stevenson. As Stevenson himself remarked: "Running against Eisenhower is like running against George Washington," and in his classic address to the Gridiron Club in January 1953, Stevenson proclaimed modestly: "I was glad to even come out second."

Again, I would emphasize that the legacy of Adlai Stevenson in the areas of international relations and politics and issues is clearly recognizable. No defeated candidate for President has ever proved as influential. In addition, I believe that legacy will live on for generations to come. When a political legacy is defined, one customarily thinks of great and lasting influences on international and domestic policies. Yet, a legitimate definition I believe should also include the very personal influence that an individual has on others, by way of inspiration, encouragement, and helping to pave the way to their goals in life. There have been countless numbers of those whose lives have been so touched by Adlai Stevenson.

On many occasions in 1956, in Oregon, Florida, Minnesota, and other states, I went with Governor Stevenson to elementary schools far out in backwater communities where he sowed seeds of tolerance, justice, freedom, and other American ideals in intimate dialogues with those many times too young to vote. Stevenson lived by the Golden Rule, and he constantly went out of his way to inspire others to realize their potential and to direct that potential into channels to improve the lot of all mankind.

I also cite two experiences of meaningful personal support. In 1957, I had moved to Huntington, West Virginia, where, anxious to make friends in the community, I started a weekly television program commenting on current issues. I took a tape recorder over to Stevenson's office to see if I could get some quotable reactions for a future program. Before I could ask the first question, Stevenson spoke to the recorder as follows: "I just want the people of West Virginia to know that I have read the most remarkable book on World War II, written by my friend Ken Hechler and entitled *The Bridge at Remagen*. It is a saga of human courage involving the first assault crossing of the Rhine River since Napoleon. Many West Virginians were involved in this heroic story, and I hope everybody in West Virginia reads Ken Hechler's great book."

In 1962, during my second term in Congress, I contacted Stevenson at the UN for an appointment to get his advice concerning the apprehension felt by my constituents and others about the Cuba missile crisis. Though heavily involved as Ambassador at the UN, he readily agreed to make some time available, and I flew up to New York. We met late in the afternoon as dusk approached. He immediately buzzed for a photographer and said, "Let's get a photo in front of the U.N. building." Despite a drizzle of rain, we put on our topcoats, and it was done. The photograph not only turned out well but he suggested a caption: "Ambassador Adlai Stevenson confers with Congressman Ken Hechler on the Cuba Missile Crisis." He could not have been more responsive.

I have always been amazed at the time and effort that Adlai Stevenson expended to help so many others, unselfishly and joyfully. His legacy certainly includes these efforts, as well as his more public pursuits. They both have enriched the lives of countless human beings here and abroad and constitute his greatness.

CHAPTER 4

ABOUT THE H-BOMB

Adlai E. Stevenson II[1]

WHY I RAISED THE H-BOMB QUESTION

The echoes of the 1956 campaign are dying now. But many of the issues of that campaign are still unresolved. One of these is the hydrogen-bomb issue.

As the *Bulletin of the Atomic Scientists* said last month: "The H-bomb problem is by no means disposed of by Eisenhower's re-election. Scientists, in particular, cannot cease considering the world-wide danger of the nuclear arms race as the *most important challenge to man.*"

It was for precisely that reason that I spoke during the campaign about the urgency of halting test explosions of these thermonuclear superbombs. I was warned that it was unwise politics to raise such a complex question, that my position could be easily distorted and misrepresented, that it would cost votes. Probably all those things were true. Certainly, the issue was grossly distorted by my opponents. (As a result of these distortions, many Americans may be under the impression that I want to stop testing smaller nuclear weapons and other new devices—I want to stop all atomic research.

1. *Look* magazine published the following article by Governor Adlai E. Stevenson II in its February 5, 1957 issue.

This is *not* true. My proposal was for a suspension of the further testing of super H-bombs, in which, I understand, we already have a long lead.)

But the issue seemed to me so important to the survival of mankind as to demand the fullest discussion and debate. And if it isn't the responsibility of candidates for President to discuss the great issues that affect our country, then what are campaigns for?

So I think the question is not *why I* talked about the H-bomb, but why I thought it was important to talk about it, even at great political risk.

Now that I can speak as a citizen, and no longer as a candidate, let me set down some of the reasons that moved me to speak as I did. In time, these reasons will, I think, cause more and more people to agree that ways must be found to halt these explosions that poison our bodies, damage the position of America in the world and threaten our very existence.

My concern dates back ten years when I was an American delegate to the United Nations and we struggled in vain to control atom-bomb development. With the advent of the superbomb, many nuclear physicists, geneticists and others with access to the facts warned us that man now had the power to exterminate himself.

The frightening truth about the superbomb convinced me that America should take the lead in halting further test explosions. So last April, four months before the political conventions, I proposed that America take the initiative in this direction and strike a blow for humanity.

I made my proposal before the American Society of Newspaper Editors, without criticism of the Administration's policy and with no intention of making it a partisan issue. My proposal was virtually ignored by the White House then. But when I restated it before the American Legion Convention on September 5, *during* the campaign, the President chose to make this proposal a political issue, and on September 19 called it "a theatrical gesture." This was followed by a barrage of epithets and ridicule from Vice-President Nixon, Thomas E. Dewey and others. I confess I had not anticipated the curious ferocity of the Republican response. There was, indeed, reason to believe that the National Security Council itself *between September 5 and September 19* had voted "unanimously" in favor of a similar superbomb proposal; but this decision had then been set aside for obviously political reasons, and my suggestion for *strengthening* our position morally and physically in the world was grievously distorted and assailed by Republican campaign orators as a proposal to *weaken* our defenses.

I hoped that there would be time further to explain my views to meet this unconscionable attack. As it turned out, events in Hungary and the war scare in the Middle East during the last days of the campaign diverted our attention to more immediate dangers.

But we cannot forget about the super H-bomb. We can't sweep it under the rug. In fact, with politics suspended for a while, we should all take a fresh and more dispassionate look at this life-touching problem and decide what to do about it.

As I saw it last April, and as I see it today, there are at least three imperative reasons why we must take the lead in establishing a world policy of halting further test explosions of superbombs:

1. The survival of mankind may well depend upon it.
2. It would increase our national security.
3. It would strengthen our position in the Cold War.

Thus, on humanitarian, strategic and international political grounds, I believe this is a sound proposal. Here are the compelling arguments:

The Survival of Mankind

A 20-megaton H-bomb is a thousand times more powerful than the atom bomb which obliterated Hiroshima in 1945. One such superbomb could wipe out New York or London or Paris or Moscow.

Already, it has been predicted by Lt. Gen. James M. Gavin, the Army's chief of research, that a superbomb attack on Russia would result in several hundred million deaths, including many in either Western Europe or in Japan and the Philippines, depending on which way the wind was blowing. Force has now far exceeded the bounds of reason and morality and, probably, even military utility. When more than one nation can deliver such weapons to the target, any thought of "victory" in war is an illusion.

What's more, even the testing of such H-bombs in peacetime is dangerous to the whole human race. With every explosion, huge quantities of radioactive materials are thrown up into the air currents that circle the globe at all altitudes. For many years afterward, these materials gradually sift back to earth as dust, or in rain or snow. This radioactive fall-out carries many elements, including strontium-90. This is a new radioactive isotope, created by nuclear explosions, which may cause cancer and other dread diseases, and dangerously affects the reproductive processes. One tablespoonful of it shared equally by all members of the human race would endanger the lives of every one of us.

Prior to the atomic age, strontium-90 was practically nonexistent. Careful studies show that today all of us—all over the world—have some of it in our bodies. It enters our bodies through foodstuffs grown in soil on which the bomb dust has fallen. It enters through the meat and fish we eat and the milk we drink, since animals graze on land dusted with it and fish swim in water that absorbs it. It is everywhere. Since it has some of the characteristics of calcium, it is a "bone-seeker" in the human body. Children are particularly vulnerable. Further, it tends to collect in higher concentrations in those areas of the world where the soil is low in calcium—for example, the American Midwest.

The danger to health is twofold—genetic and pathologic. All the scientists appear to agree on the genetic dangers of any radiation. The report of the National Academy of Sciences on *The Biological Effects of Atomic Radiation*, released last June, states that all radiation is genetically harmful and enough of it will ultimately deform many of our children and our children's children. Certainly, the threat to our capacity to produce normal, healthy children and the danger to our posterity for generations to come should be clearly understood and not ignored.

But scientists are even more concerned by the frightening pathological damage that may be caused by strontium-90. It seeps into the human bones, particularly children's bones, and may produce blood changes and cancer—among other dread results. It has been steadily descending on the earth from the stratosphere ever since the nuclear tests began, and, even if no further tests are held, it will continue to seep down for another generation. While there is no conflict of opinion among scientists as to the danger to health—genetic and pathologic—from the fall-out, there is much controversy as to the actual damage we have suffered or will suffer.

In defense of his position opposing any moratorium agreement on further superbomb tests, President Eisenhower issued a so-called "white paper" toward the end of the campaign which was full of reassuring assertions. While, in my opinion, there were many omissions and misstatements in this official Government paper, evidently more calculated to mislead the reader about the things I had said than to answer them, it did contain this declaration on the subject of health:

"Four: The continuance of the present rate of H-bomb testing—by the most sober and responsible scientific judgment—does not imperil the health of humanity."[2]

This is not a scientific fact. Hundreds of our most outstanding scientists vigorously disagree. They emphasize that no one knows with certainty whether the present rate of superbomb testing will or will not cause significant damage to the health of millions of people who are alive today.

The report of the National Academy of Sciences, mentioned above, on which the President's white paper relied, itself said: "How much radiation will produce a given result, how much can be done to counteract the deleterious effects, these are largely unresolved problems."

The International Commission on Radiological Protection and the British Medical Research Council warn that the danger level for radioactive strontium should be set, not at the optimistic level used by our Atomic Energy Commission, but at *one tenth* that level.

Dr. A. H. Sturtevant of the California Institute of Technology, one of the authors of the Academy of Sciences report, has recommended that the conclusions on fall-out danger be "revised upward."

Members of the Atomic Energy Commission Research Project at the University of Rochester Medical Center have declared they fear that, if bomb testing continues, the levels likely to be reached "may not be safe."

The Federation of Atomic Scientists, with a membership of 2,100, has urged an end to tests of large nuclear weapons. And the Federation's Radiation Hazards Committee has declared: "It may well be true that in certain areas of the world, the strontium-90 hazard has already passed the danger point, to say nothing of the additional production of this material in further tests."

2. This is the first sentence only in Point Four of the President's "white paper."

Furthermore, according to an AEC publication (University of California Radiation Laboratory Report 2674), AEC Commissioner Willard F. Libby himself undertook to investigate methods for removing strontium-90 from milk and got cost estimates on large-scale milk purification.

Clearly, we don't know all the answers yet. What we do know is that the hazards to human health from superbomb testing are already considerable, and even the future of the human race itself may be imperiled.

Yet we must still ask ourselves whether these risks are not offset by advantages to our national security. That is, do we need to continue testing superbombs to maintain our freedom?

Our National Security

We are caught up today, along with the rest of the world, in an arms race that threatens us all with disaster.

We dare not tear down and abandon our defenses and our deterrents to war before we devise more effective safeguards to peace. Indeed, we must maintain and improve them; we must lead the race if we can.

But, likewise, we must never relax our efforts to impose progressive and effective brakes on this contest of destruction, because there can be no real security for anyone, now that the superbomb is within reach of any aggressor nation. Because we have no aggressive intentions; because we are not trying to scare anyone; because we want nothing save the peace, security and independence of everyone, the big H-bombs have no value to us except for retaliation following attack. Furthermore, we have the most to lose should these ultimate weapons ever be used.

So the real question is: Could we rely on a moratorium agreement with the Russians without inspection?

We could—because you can't hide a superbomb explosion any more than you can hide an earthquake. President Eisenhower said in 1955: "Tests of large weapons, of any nation, may be detected by long-range monitoring methods; universal adherence to the ban could be determined without resorting to roving international inspectors." And our own monitors could be double-checked if necessary by a United Nations monitoring system.

An agreement to end such testing would deprive us of none of the advantages we presently enjoy. We would not give up any weapons. We would not give up research and development on new and different types of weapons in the megaton range. We could go on manufacturing and stockpiling more of our present proved weapons. We would not be deprived of the power to retaliate in event of an attack.

Such an agreement would freeze the test situation of the three powers now possessing superbombs; it would go far toward preventing other nations from producing such bombs; and it would break the disarmament deadlock. Ultimately, our security—and the world's too—depends not on a balance of terror, but on effective arms controls.

Finally, in appraising the likelihood of violation, we should consider the political price Soviet Russia would have to pay. For years, the Russians have been telling the neutral nations with great success that their purposes are peaceful, that the United States is warlike, that they favor a ban on further tests of nuclear weapons—and that the U.S. opposes it.

Would they violate a ban at the risk of turning the uncommitted bloc of nations against them? And what of their own people? As most observers agree, the Soviet masses deeply dread a world conflict, and their memories of World War II are still vivid.

Soviet Russia would like to speak for or represent the majority of the world's peoples. It cannot afford to cut itself off from the majority, which is what would automatically happen the moment it lit the fuse to the big bomb in violation of an international agreement.

The Soviet leaders say they are willing to halt the testing of their super hydrogen explosives if we do. To that, I say: Thank God! I say that, not because the record of Communist promises is good, but because here is a place where we can safely begin. Only when the first step is taken, can we plan for the second step toward sanity.

I believe a moratorium on superbomb testing would endure because to violate it would represent a declaration of war against all mankind. In short, it would be a major breakthrough in the disarmament deadlock and a new beginning in our continuing search for peace.

Victory in the Cold War

Finally, I believe that the United States must take the initiative; that the great struggle for men's minds, which is the essence of the Cold

War, will be won not with bigger bombs but with better ideas. The battle for the uncommitted peoples of the world, for their friendship and respect, will go to the nation that is wise, compassionate and considerate, as well as strong.

Toward the end of the campaign, I had a letter from one of the most respected elder statesmen of Asia. Speaking of the superbomb tests, he said: "America cannot justly continue this aggression on the whole world and its health and yet talk convincingly of peace."

I wish we had taken this step earlier. But if we take it now, I am sure that it will reassure millions of people all over the earth who, even though they have been outraged by Russian brutality in Hungary, still are troubled by our reliance on nuclear weapons and talk of "massive retaliation."

I believe that the security of the American people consists of many things. It begins with the people themselves—their belief in themselves, the meaning they attach to their history, their faith in the future, the value they place on their freedoms, their ability to be inspired by the things that count, their readiness to think and to act. If we have this kind of strength, then military strength can have meaning. But let us not delude ourselves about what military strength *is* and what it is *not* in the present world.

The position that America holds in the world, where we stand with respect to the good will and support of the overwhelming majority of the world's peoples—this has a direct connection with true national security. We are preparing our military defenses in order to guard against the possibility of a military showdown. We pray there will be no military showdown.

One thing, however, is certain: Whether or not there is a military showdown, a *nonmilitary* showdown is coming up in the world. It is a showdown on the battlefield of world public opinion. And the side with the best ideas will win.

Our ideas must be concerned with the common security of people everywhere. Thus, we must come up with working ideas for the control of war itself and must never be separated from our moral leadership in the world.

A ban on superbomb testing is one of these ideas. That is why I talked about it during the campaign, and why I bring it up again today.

CHAPTER 5

HOW ADLAI STEVENSON HELPED TO END NUCLEAR-WEAPON TESTING

George Bunn

George Bunn was a Stevenson supporter in 1952, 1956, and 1960. As General Counsel of the U.S. Arms Control and Disarmament Agency created by Congress, based on a bill he helped draft in 1961, he supported negotiations to end nuclear-weapon testing during President John F. Kennedy's Administration from 1961 to 1963, when an international treaty banning all tests except those underground was negotiated. The original U.S. draft proposal for this treaty was prepared in Bunn's office. Earlier, in 1956, Adlai Stevenson had proposed an end to all tests of hydrogen bombs in the atmosphere. Later, as Deputy U.S. Representative and then Ambassador to the Geneva Disarmament Conference, Bunn helped negotiate the nuclear Non-Proliferation Treaty prohibiting countries without nuclear weapons who joined the treaty from acquiring them. Later, he taught law and then joined the Center for International Security and Arms Control at Stanford University. His book, describing test ban and other nuclear negotiations was published by Stanford University Press and is called, *Arms Control by Committee: Managing Negotiations with the Russians.*

I have supported efforts to control nuclear weapons since the end of World War II when, as I perceived it, my life was saved by the bombs dropped on Hiroshima and Nagasaki. Until those bombs were dropped, the rulers of Japan showed no signs of surrendering. This was true even though they had lost territory to American forces, including the islands of Okinawa and Iwo Jima. American troops were landed from small landing craft lowered into the sea off-shore from these Japanese islands by navy troop-carrying ships, such as the one I was headed for as a crew member in 1945.

These ships had become the favorite target of Japanese kamikaze suicide bombers, and some had been sunk in the battles of Okinawa and Iwo Jima. If there had been a battle to conquer the main island of Japan, those suicide bombers would have come out in great force, and my ship would have been one of their targets. Instead, my ship brought American troops home from Pacific islands after the war was over. Because of the atomic bomb, I never faced the kamikaze dive-bombers. I have been interested in preventing further use of the bomb in war ever since.

As Adlai Stevenson did, I learned about early efforts to control the atomic bomb from the Truman Administration's Acheson-Lillienthal Report and Baruch Plan—unsuccessful U.S. efforts to place all nuclear weapons under the control of the UN Security Council without veto. Combining my guilt about the thousands of dead at Hiroshima and Nagasaki (who had been killed while my life was saved) with my newfound interest in controlling nuclear weapons, I went to law school to learn about what national govern-ments did to regulate national and international affairs, and to learn about how law is created, including national regulations and statutes and international treaties. My first job was to have been at the State Department. However, when requests for funds for new employees were not approved by Congress, I ended up at the U.S. Atomic Energy Commission instead in 1950. I supported Adlai Stevenson in the 1952 campaign.

During the 1956 election campaign, with President Dwight Eisenhower in the White House, I was working for Arnold, Fortas, and Porter, a private law firm in Washington. From that period, my most vivid memory of Stevenson was listening on the radio to his speech to the American Legion Convention during the campaign. He advocated an end to testing of large nuclear weapons in the atmosphere above the earth. I was impressed.

Stevenson's criticism of nuclear tests above the earth was trig-gered by an American hydrogen bomb test over the Pacific in 1954 (called Bravo). This test had dumped radioactive fallout far beyond the area of the testing zone from which American weapon testers had warned people to stay clear. Unanticipated winds and a huge test, twice bigger than expected, spread radioactive fallout over a broad area of the ocean. Twenty-three Japanese fishermen on an oceangoing fishing boat suffered radioactive sickness; one of them died. A wave of protests against nuclear testing spread around the world.

Reacting to the worldwide concern about testing and radioactivity, Stevenson proposed an end to large, aboveground tests of hydrogen bombs, like Bravo. On April 21, 1956, before nomination again by the Democrats as their presidential candidate, he urged that the United States "give prompt and earnest consideration to stopping further tests of the hydrogen bomb." He said such an agreement on aboveground tests could be verified without inspections.

But the U.S. negotiators, at negotiations then going on with the Soviets and others, with the American position based on interagency-consensus agreement (including nuclear weapon testers who did not want a test ban), said the United States was prepared to agree to testing restrictions only if there was also agreement on onsite inspection for clandestine tests, as well as agreement on major reductions of nuclear weapons with inspections to make sure the weapons had been eliminated. Agreement on all this, said the United States, was necessary before nuclear weapon tests could be ended. This was clearly not negotiable with the Soviets at the time. Indeed, in several statements, representatives of the Soviet Union had argued that the issue of tests should be dealt with separately from a nuclear disarmament agreement.

On September 10, 1956, Stevenson, now the Democratic Party's candidate, appeared before the American Legion's annual convention and proposed U.S. agreement "to halt further testing of large nuclear devices, conditioned upon adherence by other powers to similar policy." (I remember this speech. By then, the Soviet Union had also tested nuclear weapons.)

The next day, Marshal Bulganin, then head of the Soviet Union, wrote Eisenhower proposing that nuclear-weapon testing be banned separately from the "general problem of disarmament" and that it be "the first important step toward unconditional prohibition of these types of weapons." Later, shortly before the U.S. election, Bulganin again wrote Eisenhower: "We fully share the opinion recently expressed *by certain prominent figures* in the United States concerning the necessity and the possibility of concluding an agreement on the matter of prohibiting atomic weapon tests" (emphasis added).

Eisenhower replied, that to be effective, a ban on nuclear tests would require a system of inspection, which the Soviets had refused to accept. He did not comment on Stevenson's idea, supported by Bulganin's letters, that banning tests aboveground could be done without inspections because the inevitable radioactive fallout and other signals from an atmospheric test could be detected from afar. President Eisenhower was clearly not prepared to negotiate seriously during his campaign for reelection, and the sincerity of the Bulganin offer—just before the U.S. election and supporting a proposal of Eisenhower's opponent—was open to question. But Stevenson had started the ball rolling, though it took a long time to reach its goal. The Soviets then, unlike the Russians now, were viewed as Cold War adversaries.

In 1957, the Soviets proposed a two- or three-year moratorium on tests, to be verified by monitoring stations (but not on-site inspections) located in the countries having nuclear weapons. This time, President Eisenhower was supportive of exploring this idea with the Soviets. However, some members of the U.S. Atomic Energy Commission and the U.S. Senate raised questions. The critics included the important Washington State Democrat, Senator Scoop Jackson, a Senate expert on nuclear weapons and a leader in the Joint Committee on Atomic Energy and the Senate Armed Services Committee.

This was the year of Sputnik, the first Soviet satellite to fly around the world, over the U.S. I worked for a while on the staff of a Senate Armed Services subcommittee headed by Lyndon Johnson to investigate the significance to the United States of Sputnik. Clearly, their space program was ahead of ours and that had military implications. I became quite aware of the difficulties the Armed Services Committee members could present to Eisenhower if he explicitly agreed with the Soviets to end all nuclear testing, even for only a few years. Moreover, leading members of the U.S. Atomic Energy Commission and of its nuclear weapons laboratories opposed the idea. So, Eisenhower's offer to the Soviets was to link an agreed three-year testing ban to another nuclear arms control measure that was clearly not popular with them.

The Americans and the Soviets both continued testing. After the Soviets had finished a major series of tests in 1958, they seized the

initiative by announcing that they would do no further testing provided other countries did not test. This time, to gain scientific advice
independent of the Atomic Energy Commission and its weapons
laboratories, Eisenhower had appointed a White House Science
Advisor and an advisory committee of prominent nongovernmental
American scientists. They reported that a control system, with monitoring posts but *not* onsite inspection within the Soviet Union,
could detect any Soviet tests except very small ones.

Eisenhower thus proposed, and the Soviets agreed, to a meeting
of scientists to assess these technical requirements. Knowledgeable
scientists from the Soviet Union, the United States and from other
countries with seismic or other relevant expertise participated. They
finally produced a consensus report on what could be detected *without* on-site inspections. This became the basis for negotiations when
the governments on all sides became ready for negotiations.

There was, however, no consensus within the U.S. government.
Both the Atomic Energy Commission and the Department of
Defense opposed a long-term ban on nuclear-weapon tests unless it
was linked to further steps, including significant nuclear weapon
reductions. The Soviets usually opposed U.S. disarmament plans
unless the United States, which still had more nuclear weapons, was
prepared to eliminate more of them in the agreement than the
Soviets would have to eliminate. Later, after further negotiations,
the linkage to nuclear-weapon disarmament was dropped. However,
at the same time, based on new seismic data from both earthquakes
and weapon tests, the U.S. demanded inspections and more monitoring posts in the Soviet Union to verify that no tests had been
conducted.

Eisenhower then wrote Nikita Khrushchev in 1959 proposing an
agreed ban on testing that started with weapons tests in the atmosphere up to the high altitude of fifty kilometers, halfway to outer
space and far above most atmospheric testing areas. He proposed
some control posts in the Soviet Union and in the United States
but did not demand on-site inspections (and did not propose a ban
on underground tests either). This was an elaboration, and a step
beyond the proposal Stevenson had made in 1956. This proposal
had been produced by interagency negotiations within the U.S. government. It required more verification (the control posts) than most
outside (usually academic) experts thought was necessary for a ban
on tests in the atmosphere above the earth and did not give the

Soviets the ban on underground tests that they had wanted. It was promptly rejected by Khrushchev.

Negotiations continued during the last of Eisenhower's years in office and the beginning of President Kennedy's in 1961. I had worked without success to gain a majority in the 1960 Washington, DC, primary election to draft Stevenson to be the Democratic nominee for President. We won in the precincts for which I was responsible but lost in the District of Columbia as a whole. Stevenson was very reluctant to be identified with this effort and with states where the draft movement had been active.

The draft had little impact at the 1960 Democratic Convention, which I attended in support of the Stevenson draft movement. John F. Kennedy and Lyndon B. Johnson were nominated at that convention. Later, after the election in which I worked for the Democratic candidates, I went to work as a special assistant to the Advisor to President Kennedy on arms control and nuclear reductions, John J. McCloy. Aside from drafting an occasional test ban suggestion, my first job was drafting legislation to create what became the U.S. Arms Control and Disarmament Agency. After we had managed to get that through the Congress, I became the chief lawyer for the new agency and had a hand in reviewing arms control treaty drafts.

Negotiations had continued during the last of President Eisenhower's term in office. The first Kennedy test ban position in 1961 was based on interagency consensus positions drawn initially from the last scientific review in the Eisenhower Administration.

In April of 1961, however, the United States for the first time produced at the U.S.-Soviet negotiations a draft test ban treaty that included an "uninspected" ban on all but relatively *small* underground tests. These smaller tests would usually be hard to detect with stationary manned monitoring posts some distance away, and would therefore require, for detection, on-site inspectors who could move around the countryside based on where various seismometers said that the seismic movement was greatest. Called a "threshold test ban treaty," our draft would have permitted these relatively small underground tests but no other underground tests.

The Soviets replied by demanding a moratorium (without inspections) even on the small underground tests. The United States refused. The test ban negotiations were stymied.

The reason for this hard Soviet line appeared evident as the Soviets resumed testing in a major way. In September 1961, after their testing had begun, President Kennedy, in a meeting with Prime

Minister Harold Macmillan of Britain, proposed for the first time a ban on all nuclear tests in the atmosphere (but not any underground), a ban that he said would not require any control posts or on-site inspectors in any country. A month later, the White House announced that the Soviets planned to test a fifty-megaton bomb. This was to be the climactic end of a test series they had started earlier that year despite an earlier test moratorium observed by both the Soviets and the United States (though there was no written agreement), a moratorium begun on the U.S. side by Eisenhower in 1958.

Stevenson had been appointed in 1961 by Kennedy to be the chief U.S. Ambassador to the United Nations. Our effort to draft him as the Democratic Party nominee had not prevented his appointment by Kennedy to this important post, which suited his great ability as an effective advocate so well. After the White House announcement about the Soviet fifty-megaton test in October, Stevenson made a very important statement to the General Assembly in the annual debate of its First Committee on disarmament:

> The Soviet Union is now nearing the conclusion of a massive series of nuclear weapon tests. Unless something is done quickly, the Soviet testing will necessarily result in further testing by my country and perhaps others. . . . [T]he United States is obliged in self-protection to reserve the right to make preparations to test in the atmosphere, as well as underground. But the United States stands ready to resume negotiations for a treaty tomorrow. . . . [U]nless a treaty can be signed and signed promptly, the United States has no choice but to prepare and take the action necessary to protect its own security and that of the world community.
>
> We have lived sixteen years in the Atomic Age. During these years we have ingeniously and steadily improved man's capacity to blow up the planet. But we have done little to improve man's control over the means of his own destruction. . . . [T]he hands of the clock creep toward midnight. . . .
>
> When President Kennedy took office, he ordered an immediate review of United States policy in order to overcome the remaining obstacles to a final agreement [to end testing]. . . . At Geneva, the United States and the United Kingdom submitted comprehensive treaty proposals aimed at ending the fear of nuclear tests and radioactive fallout. . . . But the representatives of the Soviet Union reacted

> very oddly. . . . They renounced agreements they had already made [concerning negotiations relating to these proposals]. . . .
>
> Now, in a single instant, the Soviet Union intends to poison the atmosphere by creating more radioactivity than that produced by any series [of tests] since 1945. . . .
>
> If nations can set up a collective system which abolishes nuclear tests, surely they can hope to set up a collective system which abolishes all the diverse and manifold weapons of human self-destruction.

Despite Stevenson's eloquence, the Soviets were not persuaded. The massive Soviet test went off, and the United States began testing again. The Soviets stopped for a while but then resumed testing before the U.S. stopped. Nevertheless, in October of 1962, a year after the huge Soviet test, the U.S. delegation at the Geneva disarmament conference offered proposed texts for two test ban treaties, two drafts that had been largely drafted in my office at the Arms Control and Disarmament Agency in Washington, with suggestions and criticisms from other agencies. One banned all tests, *including* those underground but required on-site inspections. The other banned all tests *except* those underground, but required no such inspections.

In New York at the UN General Assembly's First Committee, Stevenson made a statement about these two drafts to explain them to the many countries that were not members of the Geneva disarmament conference and had not heard the U.S. statements there. After describing the draft treaty banning all tests but requiring inspections, he described the "Limited Test Ban" that had been proposed by the United States in Geneva. He said it would be:

> an agreement to ban all weapons testing in the water, in the atmosphere, and in outer space, that is, all testing above ground. . . . [T]he United States would much prefer a comprehensive treaty banning all testing everywhere. But, if that is impossible, a half a loaf is better than none. And it is more than half a loaf, because at least 90 per cent of the force of all nuclear tests from the beginning has been exploded above ground.
>
> Again, I regret to say that the response from the Soviet side is negative. They have rejected even such a limited test ban agreement.

Next came the Cuba missile crisis. In his request to the President of the UN Security Council for a meeting on the Soviet deployment of missiles in Cuba, Stevenson said that the United States had:

> *incontrovertible evidence* that the Union of Soviet Socialist Republics has been installing in Cuba a whole series of facilities for launching offensive nuclear weapons and other weapons and installing the weapons themselves. . . . The establishment of bases for nuclear missiles capable of raining thermonuclear destruction throughout most of the Western hemisphere *constitutes a grave threat to the peace and security of this hemisphere and the whole world.* (emphasis added)

Paradoxically, the Cuba missile crisis produced a turning point for the test ban negotiations. The crisis was finally resolved by exchanges of letters between Kennedy and Khrushchev, by secret negotiations between the two sides, by the U.S. Navy preventing Soviet ships from going to Cuba, and then by withdrawal of the Soviet missiles. After sighs of relief on all sides, President Kennedy and Prime Minister Macmillan sent a "peace gesture" to Khrushchev. The letter offered to send senior representatives to Moscow to negotiate a test ban treaty.

A little later, in June 1963, Kennedy made his conciliatory American University speech outlining a "strategy for peace." He pointed to strong Soviet and American mutual interest to avoid nuclear war. He made several arms control and disarmament proposals that had earlier been developed by American arms control experts, including those at the Arms Control and Disarmament Agency where I was working. These included a ban on *all* nuclear tests (with inspections) and a ban on all *except* underground tests (without inspections). He also announced a moratorium on testing akin to Eisenhower's except that it only covered atmospheric tests. The United States "does not propose to conduct nuclear tests in the atmosphere so long as other states do not do so."

In July, Khrushchev responded by accepting, as the basis for negotiations, the American proposal for a ban on all tests but those underground, but rejecting, because of its inspection requirements, the proposal for a comprehensive ban on all tests. Kennedy chose a high-level delegation to be headed by the Assistant Secretary of State Averell Harriman, who had been the U.S. Ambassador to Moscow during World War II. The delegation included the Deputy Director of my agency and an advisor from the White House. Their instructions included negotiation of a treaty based on the U.S. "limited test ban" text that had been drafted in Washington by my office and by representatives of other interested agencies. This was essentially the draft that the U.S. delegation had presented at Geneva in 1962.

The 1963 test ban treaty resulted from the Moscow negotiations. It was called by the United States the "Limited Test Ban Treaty" because it did not ban underground tests. With major effort over several weeks in July–August of 1963, we were successful in gaining the necessary votes of two-thirds of the members of the U.S. Senate for the treaty. Based on that difficult experience, I don't think we could have achieved a two-thirds Senate vote for a treaty that banned *all* tests. I had, however, greater hopes in 1999 that the Clinton Administration would be more successful in gaining a two-thirds Senate vote for the Comprehensive Test Ban Treaty that had finally been agreed to at Geneva after many years of effort.

I was wrong in 1999. The Comprehensive Test Ban Treaty failed by a large vote in the Senate that year. It failed for many reasons, including a desire of some conservatives in the Senate to punish President Clinton for misdeeds for which they had been unable to remove him. But another reason was similar to the troubles we faced in the 1960s when we made concessions to make a comprehensive nuclear test ban possible; some experts responsible for designing, maintaining and improving American nuclear weapons were not yet prepared to cut off forever the useful information they obtain from testing. This includes information about whether U.S. nuclear weapons will work and, if so, how well.

Stevenson would surely have supported President Clinton's treaty in 1999. But some weapons experts were unwilling to give up all tests and did not support it. In addition, some moderates and conservatives in the Senate opposed it for that reason, not because of a desire to punish President Clinton.

⊷⊱⊜⊰⊷

To prevent the spread of nuclear weapons to ever more countries, we must somehow set a good example ourselves. Continued testing accelerates the nuclear arms race, as Stevenson, if he were still alive, would probably be the first to say today. At a time when we have worried about the possibility of nuclear weapons in Iraq, Libya, Iran, North Korea, and increasing numbers of other countries, we need to set a better example. If the United States, *with the most powerful conventional forces in the world*, needs its nuclear weapons so much that it wants periodically to be assured that they will work perfectly, how can we persuade other countries that they don't need nuclear weapons?

CHAPTER 6

STEVENSON AND THE COMPREHENSIVE TEST BAN TREATY TODAY

Sidney D. Drell and James E. Goodby

Dr. Sidney D. Drell is a professor emeritus of physics at Stanford University and a senior fellow at its Hoover Institution. For many years, he has been an advisor to the U.S. government on technical national security and arms control issues, including membership on the President's Foreign Intelligence Advisory Board (1993–2001) and the President's Science Advisory Committee (1966–71). He has led and participated in a number of studies for the government on nuclear testing and the safety and reliability of those weapons. Honors recognizing his contributions to both physics and national security include the Enrico Fermi Award, the National Intelligence Distinguished Service Medal, a MacArthur Fellowship, and election to the National Academy of Sciences.

Ambassador James E. Goodby joined the U.S. Atomic Energy Commission in 1954 and served during the early 1960s as Officer-in-Charge of nuclear test ban negotiations at the U.S. State Department and the Arms Control and Disarmament Agency. His most recent assignment in the government in 2000–01 was as Deputy to the Special Advisor to the President and Secretary of State for the Comprehensive Test Ban Treaty. He served as Ambassador to Finland in 1980–81. He is the winner of the Honor Award in Public Policy, the Commander's Cross of the Order of Merit of Germany, and the Presidential Distinguished Service Award and the holder of an honorary Doctor of Laws from the Stetson University College of Law.

Dr. Drell and Ambassador Goodby co-authored the book, *The Gravest Danger: Nuclear Weapons,* published by the Hoover Institution in 2003, from which parts of this chapter are drawn.

◆〰◌〰◆

During his second campaign for the presidency against Dwight Eisenhower in 1956, Governor Adlai Stevenson spoke out strongly and clearly for an end to the testing of thermonuclear H-bomb weapons. His call for such a ban came shortly after the first demonstration of a successful hydrogen bomb, or so-called superbomb, of such great destructive power that it released explosive energy equivalent to millions of tons of TNT, a hundred times more destructive than the primitive atom bombs that obliterated Hiroshima and Nagasaki. The hydrogen bomb triggered concerns about the very survival of civilization. Stevenson viewed a test ban to prevent their further development to be a small step "for the rescue of man from the elemental fire which we have kindled" (McGeorge Bundy, *Danger and Survival* [New York: Random House, 1988], 239).

Adlai Stevenson's position about "the urgency of halting test explosions of these thermonuclear super bombs" was, in his words, based "on humanitarian, strategic, and international political grounds." As he stated then, "there are at least three imperative reasons why we must take the lead in establishing a world policy of halting further test explosions of super bombs:

1. The survival of mankind may well depend upon it;
2. It would increase our national security;
3. It would strengthen our position in the Cold War."

The first of these three reasons referred to the dangers due to radioactive fallout contaminating large areas as a result of testing weapons above ground in the atmosphere. It would be an issue discussed intensely for the next six years during the Eisenhower and Kennedy Administrations, leading to a limited test ban treaty in April 1963. That treaty banned all nuclear test explosives in the atmosphere, in outer space, or under the seas. Only underground testing that did not disperse radioactive debris above ground was authorized under the treaty. This exemption for underground testing was based on an inability of the United States and the Soviet Union to agree on cooperative means for verifying compliance with the treaty.

President Eisenhower's decision in 1958 to propose a moratorium on all nuclear testing, not just thermonuclear, and to pursue for the remainder of his time in office a comprehensive ban on nuclear testing was certainly a vindication of Adlai Stevenson's stance. To the extent that Stevenson's advocacy of a partial test ban influenced Eisenhower, we can give Stevenson much credit for the successful negotiations that followed. The legitimacy that Eisenhower—a former general—gave to the idea of a test ban enabled President Kennedy thereafter to carry the plan forward. Without those debates and decisions of 1956–58, there would have been no limitation on testing until much later.

The Limited Test Ban Treaty was extended in 1974 to a Threshold Test Ban Treaty that banned underground nuclear explosions of weapons with yields exceeding 150 kilotons, or approximately ten times the yield of the Hiroshima bomb. For twenty years thereafter, there were abortive attempts to address the second and third concerns raised by Adlai Stevenson and reach agreement for a comprehensive or total test ban treaty.

Arguments with various degrees of intensity have continued to this day on issues of technological improvements, the limits of verification of a comprehensive test ban and alleged strategic needs in a world whose survival rested upon avoiding a nuclear conflict, without much progress being made. Lost in the noise of these debates were the words of President Eisenhower in May 1961 shortly after he returned to private life after eight years in the presidency, in which he said that "not achieving a nuclear test ban would have to be classed as the greatest disappointment of any administration—of any decade—of any time and of any party."

Following the fall of the Soviet Union in 1991, the possibility of a comprehensive test ban drew greater attention, and the second and third arguments of Adlai Stevenson as to the merits of a ban on testing super weapons, to "increase our national security" and to "strengthen our position in the Cold War," returned to prominence.

The Cold War was over, but strengthening the position of the United States in the world where the dangers of nuclear proliferation were growing and emerging powers without nuclear capability grew increasingly restive under the discriminatory restraints against them of the Non-Proliferation Treaty, brought into force in 1970, led to increasing pressures that the nuclear powers reduce their reliance on these weapons and terminate programs for their continued refinement and improvement. Arguments that had been made by

Stevenson more than thirty years earlier were viewed with renewed cogency and prominence.

A first step toward a full test ban treaty was taken by President George H. W. Bush in 1992, when he declared a one-year moratorium on testing and terminated a program to develop a new nuclear weapon with the observation that we had no need for new weapons following the collapse of the Soviet Union and its threat of worldwide domination. As the Non-Proliferation Treaty approached its fifth and final scheduled five-year review at the United Nations in 1995, the chorus of voices of the nonnuclear powers for a ban on continued testing grew louder. A comprehensive test ban treaty was increasingly viewed as a strong reinforcing mechanism for the Non-Proliferation Treaty, as well for helping to assure compliance with it.

Bringing a comprehensive test ban treaty into force would also fulfill the commitment made by the nuclear powers in gaining the agreement of 185 nations to extend indefinitely the Non-Proliferation Treaty in 1995. The Non-Proliferation Treaty remains the cornerstone now of the worldwide effort to limit the spread of nuclear weapons and reduce nuclear danger.

Many nations signed on to the indefinite extension of the Non-Proliferation Treaty in 1995 on the explicit condition that the nuclear powers would cease all nuclear-yield testing. This situation presented the United States and the other nuclear powers with a strong political and strategic incentive to formalize the moratorium on testing by ratifying and working to bring into force the Comprehensive Test Ban Treaty (CTBT) signed by the United States in 1996. It is obviously one of the critical cornerstones of the Non-Proliferation Treaty, which, as Secretary of State Colin Powell said in his testimony before the Senate Foreign Relations Committee on July 9, 2002, "is the centerpiece of the global non-proliferation regime."

A U.S. decision to resume testing to produce new nuclear weapons would therefore dramatically undermine the Non-Proliferation Treaty. Conversely, a U.S. decision to ratify the already signed comprehensive treaty and lead the effort to bring that treaty into force would be an effective way of strengthening the Non-Proliferation Treaty and, through it, worldwide antiproliferation efforts.

Bringing the comprehensive treaty into force would have the added technical advantage of allowing for the full implementation of the system described in the treaty to verify compliance. Full implementation would add to the worldwide remote-monitoring network a challenge-inspection protocol that would permit on-site inspections of suspicious events. Currently, the Bush Administration has declined to participate in the ongoing work in Vienna to develop the on-site inspection regime and is refusing to fund the U.S. share of that activity.

All U.S. allies in NATO, including Great Britain, Germany and France, have signed and ratified the Comprehensive Test Ban Treaty, as have Japan and Russia. Israel has signed the treaty and is participating energetically in the work of setting up a verification system. Others, including China, have indicated they will work to bring the treaty into force once the United States has ratified it. As of May 2006, thirty-three of the forty-four states that have built nuclear reactors, the so-called nuclear-capable states, and must ratify the treaty for it to enter into force, have done so. In all, 129 states have ratified the Comprehensive Test Ban Treaty.

Therefore, the White House and the U.S. Senate should enter into a serious debate to clarify the underlying issues, both the concerns and the opportunities. This debate was not adequately joined in 1999 when the comprehensive treaty first came before the Senate for its advice and consent and did not receive the necessary votes for ratification. Regrettably, the current Bush Administration has thus far refused to reopen the question.

Why is the United States reluctant? In addition to the dubious need to develop "concepts for follow-on nuclear weapons better suited to the nation's needs," including nuclear earth penetrations against hardened deeply buried targets, opponents of the treaty have raised two questions: 1) "How can we be sure that many years ahead, we will not need to resume yield testing in order to rebuild the stockpile?" and 2) "How can we monitor compliance by other treaty signatories with standards consistent with U.S. national security?"

The answer to the first question is that total certainty can never be achieved. But it is possible to ensure that there is a strong program in place with the necessary support of competent engineers and scientists who would sound a warning bell should a serious, unforeseen problem arise. With the enhanced, multifaceted, science-based program of stockpile stewardship established during the past eight years, the United States can have confidence in its ability to understand the character of the stockpile and the way in which special bomb materials age. As a result of the stockpile surveillance program, a number of flaws have been reported and dealt with appropriately. The flaws thus far uncovered within the nuclear devices themselves are related primarily to design oversights. That is, the flaws, or their precursors, were present when the weapons were put into the stockpile.

The United States can be assured that the Comprehensive Test Ban Treaty is consistent with the ability to retain high confidence in the reliability of its existing nuclear force for decades. This conclusion has been demonstrated convincingly by a number of detailed technical analyses. In 1995, a team of independent scientists working with colleagues from the weapons community, including technical leaders involved in creating the current nuclear arsenal, reached this finding ("Nuclear Testing," JASON 1995 report for the U.S. Department of Energy). It was that determination that led the United States to negotiate the Comprehensive Test Ban Treaty and sign it in 1996.

Most recently, in August 2002, a panel of the National Academy of Sciences published a comprehensive study on Technical Issues Related to the Comprehensive Test Ban Treaty. The study group, which included retired directors of weapons laboratories, bomb designers and technical and scientific experts, concluded that the United States can maintain confidence in its enduring stockpile under a ban on all nuclear-yield testing, provided it has a well-supported, science-based stewardship and maintenance program, together with a capability to remanufacture warheads as needed.

A similar detailed analysis that addressed strategic as well as technical issues, led by General John M. Shalikashvili, former Chairman of the Joint Chiefs of Staff was conducted in 2000–01 with government cooperation and authorization, and it reached the same conclusion. In his letter to the President, General Shalikashvili affirmed that the Comprehensive Test Ban Treaty "is a very important part of global nonproliferation efforts and is compatible with keeping a safe, reliable U.S. nuclear deterrent."

Concerning the question of compliance, there is a broad agreement that the United States could monitor comprehensive test ban compliance with standards consistent with its national security. Based on its technical analysis, the National Academy of Science study group concluded that:

the worst-case scenario under a no-CTBT regime poses far bigger threats to the U.S. security—sophisticated nuclear weapons in the hands of many more adversaries—than the worst-case scenario of clandestine testing in a CTBT regime, within the constraints posed by the monitoring system.

As noted by General Shalikashvili in his study: "Ironically the more testing expertise a country has, the better able it would be to conduct an evasive test and extract useful information—but the less difference that information would probably make in advancing the country's nuclear capabilities." Conversely, it is true that the less experience in nuclear weapons that a country has, the more difficult it is to carry out successfully a useful test without actually exceeding the low detection threshold of the fully implemented verification system.

When fully implemented under the treaty, the verification system becomes more robust and difficult to evade because it will then acquire challenge rights to check out data initially derived from remote sensors by conducting short-notice, on-site inspections of suspicious events. For a very modest cost, the international monitoring network could be improved—for example, by incorporating private or government seismic stations as full-time participants in the detection system.

A further strengthening of the sensitivity of the CTBT to detect covert, treaty-violating activities could be negotiated by adding appropriate bilateral transparency and confidence-building measures with the other nuclear powers, Russia and China in particular. These would permit on-site sensors to be introduced at their instrumented test sites to monitor for signals—seismic and radiological—from possible underground tests that are banned by the treaty. The current Bush Administration should clearly state its willingness to initiate such an arrangement, reciprocally with the Russians, at Novaya Zemlya and the Nevada Test Site. Bilateral forums that supplement, but cooperate with, the existing treaty organization would be needed to manage this process.

The Comprehensive Test Ban Treaty does not increase the requirements for the United States to monitor and identify underground testing. The United States will want all information on testing activities, with or without the treaty. However, it does add to the difficulties for a country to evade the treaty not only by strengthening the system but also by adding the inspection rights.

Furthermore, given that the United States has the most advanced and sophisticated diagnostic, analytical, experimental, and computation facilities, it is in a stronger position than other nations to maintain a deterrent under a test ban. As General Shalikashvili concluded in his study: "I believe that an objective and thorough net assessment shows convincingly that U.S. interest, as well as those of friends and allies, will be served by the Treaty's entry into force."

Pending entry into force, the United States should do whatever it takes to strengthen the present moratorium, which has now lasted thirteen years. This would involve stronger statements of no intention to resume nuclear testing than the Bush Administration has yet made. And it would include stronger support for the International Monitoring System (IMS) that the treaty has established, components of which already exist. The Administration should continue to support the IMS financially and begin to fund the development of the on-site inspection regime so that it could be implemented voluntarily, even before the treaty enters into force. It also should facilitate the addition of seismic research stations to the network, as mentioned earlier, and try to supplement them with bilateral monitoring agreements with other nuclear weapon states, especially China and Russia. Without question, the United States should maintain and strengthen existing national technical capabilities for verifying treaty compliance.

Adlai Stevenson was told that his support for a ban on thermonuclear testing would hurt him in the presidential campaign of 1956. Perhaps it did. He was attacked ferociously for proposing it. But this is the way it is with those who think of the long-term consequences of our actions. Only later does it become clear how right they were. Stevenson helped to create a constituency for a test ban. He helped to build political pressures that were felt by the Eisenhower White House. Today, he would be in the lead calling on the United States and nations around the world to ratify the Comprehensive Test Ban Treaty and working to bring it into force. And without a doubt, his eloquent voice would be heard urging America truly to move beyond the Cold War by cutting the numbers of nuclear weapons in our arsenal to levels more in keeping with the shrinking role for nuclear deterrence.

His courage and his vision still serve as an example for those who seek and occupy public office in our country.

Gov. Adlai Stevenson with Congressman John F. Kennedy and Stevenson's three sons before a speech during his 1952 presidential campaign
Source: Abraham Lincoln Memorial Library

Adlai Stevenson greets a supporter at presidential whistle-stop, with his sister Elizabeth (Buffy) Ives (l.) approvingly looking on
Source: Abraham Lincoln Memorial Library

Adlai Stevenson at the threshold of the Kennedy Administration, 1960
Source: Abraham Lincoln Memorial Library, Atlanta Const. by Baldy

PART II

HIS ROLE IN THE CREATION AND MISSION OF THE UNITED NATIONS

CHAPTER 7

ADLAI STEVENSON AND OUR TIMES

Brian Urquhart

Sir Brian Urquhart was the second member of the United Nations
Secretariat to be recruited and served as personal assistant to Gladwyn
Jebb, the Executive Secretary of the United Nations Preparatory
Commission, and to Trygve Lie, the first Secretary-General of the
UN. He first met Adlai Stevenson, U.S. representative, during the
UN preparatory meetings in London in 1945. From 1953 to 1971,
he worked with Ralph Bunche on peacekeeping, conflict control and
the peaceful uses of atomic energy. The period included the setting
up, deployment and direction of the first UN peacekeeping force
(UNEFI) in the Suez Canal Zone in 1956, and two periods of service
in the Congo—in 1960 as chief assistant to Bunche, who was the head
of the operation, and in 1961–62 as UN representative in Katanga. In
1972, Urquhart succeeded Ralph Bunche as UN Undersecretary-
General for Special Political Affairs. He retired from the UN in 1986.
Brian Urquhart was born in Dorset, England in 1919. He was edu-
cated at Westminster School and Christ Church, Oxford. He served in
the British Army from 1939 to 1945 in infantry and airborne units in
England, North Africa and Europe. Sir Urquhart's books include:
Hammerskjold (1972), a biography of the second UN Secretary-
General, *A Life in Peace and War* (1987), memoirs, and *Ralph
Bunche: An American Odyssey* (1993). He currently resides in New
York City.

I first met Adlai Stevenson during the meetings of the United Nations Preparatory Commission in London in 1945. The purpose of this commission was to design the actual structure of the new world organization on the basis of the Charter that had been signed in San Francisco four months earlier. Stevenson was the deputy to Edward R. Stettinius, the former Secretary of State who became the first United States Ambassador to the UN, but there was little doubt about who actually did the work.

The Preparatory Commission was a distinguished body, still to some extent animated by wartime allied solidarity. Its membership included among others, Andrei Gromyko, Lester Pearson of Canada, Jan Masaryk of Czechoslovakia, Wellington Koo of China, and Ernest Bevin of Britain. In my first civilian job, I was personal assistant to Gladwyn Jebb, the Executive Secretary of the commission. Jebb, himself a brilliant public servant, frequently consulted with Stevenson, an old friend, and it is no exaggeration to say that Jebb, Stevenson, and Lester Pearson were the life and soul of this extremely important group.

In London in 1945, Stevenson was in his prime. He had played an important part in the San Francisco Conference and was determined to build a lasting and effective world organization on the basis of the principles and objectives of the Charter. The principle of universality, the unprecedented authority of the Security Council, the goal of decolonization and an international Trusteeship System, the advancement of human rights, and the independence of the future UN secretariat were among the principles and goals that must be preserved and strengthened by the Preparatory Commission. The commission also decided that the headquarters of the new world organization would be in the United States.

Stevenson was a master of the highly complex subject matter, and his eloquence, charm and humor were almost irresistible, even to Gromyko. Although Soviet distrust of the West was already evident, Stevenson did a great deal to ensure that the proceedings of the Preparatory Commission remained courteous and constructive. The group finished its work and delivered its very substantive report in record time.

In those days, in strong contrast to the present time, the United States government was the main champion and protector of the United Nations Charter and of the fledgling organization itself. The members of the U.S. delegation were almost unanimously enthusiastic promoters of the new world organization. Most of them had been at San Francisco and they were intolerant of skepticism, let alone cynicism, about the future of the United Nations.

Stevenson had a rather different approach. Together with Archibald MacLeish he had, at the behest of President Franklin Roosevelt, run a yearlong, nationwide, public relations campaign to win the support of the American people before the San Francisco Conference. In April 1945, ninety-four percent of the American people were estimated to be in favor of the draft charter and its consideration at San Francisco. As a senior member of the U.S. delegation at San Francisco, one of Stevenson's tasks had been to explain the U.S. position to the large and distinguished group of American journalists each day. "I am the official leak," he told them.

These experiences had caused Stevenson to brood over the possible weaknesses of the UN as established in the Charter, and, although he had done so much to persuade the American people to support it, he was one of the first Americans to utter words of caution. For example, in June 1945, immediately after San Francisco, he told the Chicago Bar Association, *a propos* the UN Security Council, "Everything depends on the active participation, pacific intentions, and good faith of the Big Five [the permanent members of the Security Council]." The imminent onset of the Cold War and its paralyzing effect on the Security Council soon proved how right he was.

Although most of us followed his subsequent career with great interest and admiration, Stevenson only came back to the United Nations fifteen years later as President John F. Kennedy's, and later President Lyndon Johnson's Ambassador to the United Nations. The post of United States Permanent Representative to the United Nations is an important and unusual one. The Permanent Representative probably gets as much or more public exposure, especially in times of crisis, than any other public official. When Henry Cabot Lodge, who had also been a presidential candidate, was appointed by the Eisenhower administration, the post was upgraded to Cabinet level.

The list of United States Ambassadors to the UN is a distinguished one, including Henry Cabot Lodge, Arthur Goldberg, William Scranton, Charles Yost, George H. W. Bush, Daniel Patrick Moynihan, Andrew Young, Jeane Kirkpatrick, Thomas Pickering, William Richardson, Madeleine Albright, and Richard Holbrooke. Its less well known members were highly skilled and effective members of the Foreign Service. Adlai Stevenson certainly added great luster to this outstanding group, and, unlike any of his predecessors, he had played an important part in the founding of the United Nations.

I do not think that Stevenson was altogether happy in this job, which is, in any circumstances, a grueling one. His relations with the Kennedys were complicated and often unsatisfactory—he had withheld his support for JFK until the last moment in the presidential election—and he was sometimes tired and distracted. When he needed to unburden himself, he often came over to talk to his old friend, Ralph Bunche, the UN Undersecretary General for Special Political Affairs and by far the most respected official in the Secretariat.

In moments of crisis, however, Stevenson was an immensely effective representative of the United States. His finest and best-known performance in this period was his famous confrontation in the Security Council with the Soviet hatchet man, Valerian Zorin. Stevenson showed a spellbound Security Council blown-up aerial photographs of the Soviet missile sites in Cuba, the existence of which the Soviet Union had, up to that point, strongly denied. He then demanded that Zorin tell the Council whether he knew of the Cuban missiles, saying that he would wait for his answer "until Hell freezes over." Zorin complained that he was being treated as a defendant in a criminal court, which of course was basically true. This dramatic public demonstration of the threat to the United States was a vital launching point for United States policy in the most serious and potentially catastrophic peacetime crisis of the twentieth century. Stevenson's stature as orator and statesman allowed him to carry out this historic mission with the maximum public effect.

Stevenson's relations with Lyndon Johnson's administration were also complicated, not least by his views about the Vietnam War, and he often felt that he was being kept out of vital concerns by Washington, or that his performance of his task at the United Nations was being criticized or underestimated in the capital. Two episodes throw light on this situation.

The third UN Secretary-General, U Thant, made a spirited attempt to find a means of ending the disastrous Vietnam War. He evolved a plan for a cease-fire in place and for a meeting of all the parties in Rangoon, where all had diplomatic representation, to agree on how to negotiate a final end to the war. At the time, before the bombing of Hanoi started, this plan would have been acceptable to the North Vietnamese. U Thant gave Stevenson the outline of his plan and asked him to get Washington's reaction to it.

Nothing more was heard from Washington, and there is no written record of what Stevenson did about it, although it now seems likely that Secretary of State Dean Rusk, who distrusted U Thant's efforts on Vietnam, may have blocked it. In the last days of his presidency Johnson arrived unexpectedly at the UN to ask U Thant for help on trying to bring the Vietnam War to an end. U Thant was surprised to discover that Johnson had never heard of the plan he had given to Stevenson. Ironically, Johnson had come to urge U Thant to play an active role in the search for a negotiated end to the war.

The other episode occurred in San Francisco during the celebration of the UN's twentieth anniversary in 1965, ten days before Stevenson's death in London. The centerpiece of this affair was to be a speech by President Johnson. The press, allegedly prompted by Stevenson, had speculated that the President would announce a fundamental change in U.S. policy on Vietnam. This had infuriated Johnson, who deliberately arrived 45 minutes late at the Opera House and gave a markedly insignificant speech, hardly mentioning Vietnam. The President's deliberate lateness effectively sabotaged a lunch in his honor hosted by U Thant and the antiwar Mayor of San Francisco.

To be sure of further upsetting the lunch, Johnson sent a message asking to see U Thant immediately after his speech. Ralph Bunche and I were supposed to join U Thant for this meeting and, with some difficulty, made our way through the presidential security detail to the tenor's dressing room, Johnson's temporary office. As we arrived at the door Adlai came out, red in the face with anger. Bunche asked him where he was going. Stevenson replied that the President had thrown him out of the meeting. Bunche said that in that case we wouldn't join the meeting either, and we tried to cheer him up. It was the last time either of us saw him alive.

Ralph Bunche, Stevenson's faithful and affectionate friend, was one of the most remarkable, and least remembered, of the extraordinary generation of statesmen that the United States deployed on world problems and the future after World War II. He had drafted Chapters XI and XII of the Charter, on Non-Self-Governing Territories and the international trusteeship system. He was a notable member of Stevenson's team in London in 1945. In 1950, Bunche won the Nobel Peace Prize for negotiating the Armistice agreements between Israel and her Arab neighbors, thus putting an end to the war that had started with Israel's statehood.

Bunche admired Stevenson and cherished him as a personal friend. When he returned to the UN in 1961, they met or communicated almost daily. After Stevenson's death Bunche was one of the group of Stevenson's friends who flew to London on Air Force One to bring Stevenson's coffin back to the United States.

One can only speculate on Stevenson's reaction to the present state of affairs. The world organization that the United States so strongly and successfully championed and that Stevenson had helped to build came into existence in a world that had just experienced six years of total war. It was a world of great suffering, as well as a world of hope, idealism, and vision. Stevenson, with his pragmatic idealism and generosity of spirit, had been a major part of that world.

Stevenson believed that the unique position that the United States enjoyed in 1945 must be used for world leadership and cooperation and never for coercion or bullying. In those days, the United States gave an unprecedented example of how a great country might use its enormous power for the general good. Its aim, also unprecedented in world history, was to build a new world order rather than submit to the temptations of empire. As one of the original, and most realistic, builders of the United Nations, Stevenson had no illusions about the problems that the world organization would face in the future, nor about its vital importance in pioneering a new world of law, collective security, and cooperation. He also foresaw that it would be an essential safety net and last resort if the great powers once again chose a path of confrontation, as they all too soon did.

Adlai Stevenson had very much the same conception of the basic purpose of the UN as another of its great champions, Dag Hammarskjöld, who once defined the United Nations as "a venture in progress towards an international community living in peace under the laws of justice." Like Hammarskjöld, Stevenson was convinced that the world had to find its way to the international rule of law and to mutual responsibility for the great affairs and problems that humanity would undoubtedly have to face in the future and that any other course would sooner or later lead to disaster. He would certainly have been dismayed by the relatively recent ideological sabotage of the UN, symbolized by the nomination to the high responsibilities of United States Ambassador to the UN of John Bolton,

one of the most outspoken demolitionists of international organization and international agreements.

Stevenson would certainly have advocated the strengthening of
the Security Council and the Secretary-General and their capacity to
deal in a timely fashion with threats to the peace and humanitarian
disasters. Although it is still a forbidden idea in Washington and an
unpopular concept with some other governments, he would certainly have supported the idea of a UN rapid deployment force. He
would have recognized that the inability of the UN to react immediately with necessary force at the critical outset of a crisis was a
major failing of the UN and the Security Council—a failing which
has allowed many conflicts to metastasize into standing disasters like
the long-running nightmare of Africa's Great Lakes region that has
already taken an estimated four million lives.

In our uncertain and rancorous time, forty-two years after Adlai
Stevenson's death, both those in government and citizens interested
in our future and in the fate of the human race would do well to read
his speeches and especially those he gave at a time when the world
was recovering from an enormous disaster. It was a time when both
governments and peoples agreed that such calamities must never
happen again, and when United States leadership was a shining light
to the world.

U.S. Ambassador to the UN Adlai Stevenson (r.) and Assistant Secretary of State Harlan Cleveland (l.) attend Organization for Economic Cooperation and Development Conference in Paris, 1963
Source: "Sabine Wiess for OECD"

CHAPTER 8

ON A WORLD-SCALE ROLLER COASTER: ADLAI STEVENSON AT THE UN, 1961–65

Harlan Cleveland

Harlan Cleveland, political scientist and public executive, was closely associated with Adlai Stevenson during the four and a half years (1961–65) that Stevenson served as U.S. Ambassador to the United Nations in New York. During that time, Cleveland was Assistant Secretary of State for International Organization Affairs in the administrations of Presidents John F. Kennedy and Lyndon B. Johnson. In government, he has also served in the Allied Control Commission in Italy during World War II, as a UN relief and rehabilitation administrator in Italy and China, as a top official of the Marshall Plan, and from 1965 to 1969, as U.S. Ambassador to NATO. In academia, he has served as dean of two graduate schools of public affairs (the Maxwell School at Syracuse University and the Hubert H. Humphrey Institute at the University of Minnesota) and as President of the University of Hawaii. During the 1990s, he was President of the World Academy of Art and Science. He lives with Lois, his wife of 66 years, in Falcons Landing, Sterling, Virginia. His e-mail address is: harlancleve@falconresidents.org.

BEGINNINGS

I had long admired Adlai Stevenson from afar and voted for him when he first ran for President in 1952. I had even crossed his trail in the 1940s during World War II: after he had surveyed Italy's post-war economic needs for the Truman Administration, I became responsible for helping the Italian economy during and just after World War II—working first for the Allied Control Commission and then for the UN.

However, my first personal contact with him came in 1955. As the 1952 candidate, he was then naturally the front-runner in speculation among Democrats about the 1956 election. A few of his supporters, however, thought it might be wise for him to avoid being a candidate in 1956; running against President Dwight Eisenhower, the popular incumbent who had also been a military hero, was quite likely a lost cause.

I was then working in New York City, first as executive editor then also as publisher, of *The Reporter*, a fortnightly "magazine of facts and ideas," rated at that time as the nation's most successful liberal journal. (Canada's Prime Minister Lester Pearson, for whom what happened in the United States was of course "international affairs," famously rated our magazine as the world's best international journal.) Its owner and editor-in-chief was Max Ascoli, an Italian political philosopher who had escaped Mussolini's anti-Jewish pogrom in the 1930s, moved to the United States, and married Marian Rosenwald, daughter of Julius Rosenwald who founded Sears Roebuck.

Ascoli, a brilliant mind with an ego to match, had surprisingly offered to relinquish his editor-in-chief title if Adlai Stevenson would take it on. The idea was that Adlai could then decline to run against Eisenhower and become his natural successor by winning the 1960 election. Adlai was interested but reluctant to move away from his home in Illinois. So we cooked up a scheme to accommodate him: I would commute every two weeks to Chicago, where Adlai officed with a law firm, carrying with me a draft editorial that Adlai would edit; that writing would be his featured editorial in each issue of *The Reporter*. Adlai seemed comfortable with this part of the plan. He had apparently read a good deal of my writings, in the magazine and otherwise, and (as I later learned in working with him on UN policy) he was a superb editor who much preferred to start not with a blank page but with someone else's first draft.

This was far from an altruistic ploy on our part. With Adlai Stevenson's worldwide reputation for liberal eloquence, we were sure that our magazine's circulation, already growing healthily, would soar.

The offer was on the table for quite a while in 1955 as Adlai tried to decide what to do. Though I was slated for a ghostwriting role, I was not involved in the long negotiation. He finally decided that he had an obligation to the Democratic Party he couldn't in good conscience put aside. We were disappointed. In retrospect, I still think it was a pretty good idea.

RELUCTANT CANDIDATE

Despite a second, even-more-decisive defeat in the presidential election of 1956, Adlai Stevenson remained an immensely popular public figure. He was not only the titular head of the Democratic Party—a status that meant a lot more then than it has come to mean in recent decades—but he traveled widely and came to know the best-known leaders in many other countries, especially in Europe. He worked hard on his many public utterances and was often described as America's most eloquent public voice. (President Eisenhower had many estimable qualities, but eloquence was not one of them.)

As the 1960 presidential election drew near, a big question in the Democratic Party was: Will Adlai run? There were evident alternatives. Senate majority leader Lyndon B. Johnson of Texas was one. An attractive young senator from Massachusetts, John F. Kennedy, had announced his candidacy early. Several governors, from New Jersey to California, were "mentioned."

In New York State, a slate of delegates to the Democratic National Convention, with Mayor Robert Wagner of New York City as its chairman, was being assembled in Kennedy's support. Some notable New York delegates, including Eleanor Roosevelt and Thomas K. Finletter, were anxious to hold the door open for Adlai Stevenson to step through. But consistent with his attitude in previous elections—for governor of Illinois back in 1948 and for president in 1952—Stevenson wasn't reaching for the prize; he would accept it if he was drafted.

By this time, I was Dean of the Maxwell School of Citizenship and Public Affairs at Syracuse University. Though a lifelong Democrat, I was not very active in party politics. A university administrator with a taste for that sort of thing experiences more than enough politics just in building consensus within the nobody-in-charge polity of teachers and scholars, alumni, foundations, and business community, and the state and federal governments. But in upstate New York back then, visible Democrats were in rather scarce supply. So it required only well-placed hints for me to be chosen by the state committee to be a New York delegate (with half a vote) to the Democratic presidential convention in Los Angeles in 1960.

As soon as I was known to be a delegate, I began to hear from Stevenson supporters who (because of my previous association with *The Reporter*) considered me a dependably liberal voice on the New York delegation.

This would have been awkward if Adlai had been an active candidate for the nomination. No one had asked me to sign in blood as a Kennedy delegate, but Mayor Wagner and the state committee were obviously trying to put together a solid bloc of votes for Senator Kennedy. Besides, I was inclined that way myself; JFK was just a year older than I was, and in my early 40s, I felt that our generation's time had come.

Fortunately for my conscience, Adlai Stevenson kept saying he was not running. In those pre-e-mail days I spent a good deal of money, during the weeks just before the Los Angeles convention and during the convention itself, replying by telegraph to a flood of telegrams from Adlai enthusiasts by pointing out that their candidate, attractive though he was, didn't seem to be in the race.

To those contending for power and preferment, the Los Angeles Convention must have seemed an unruly zoo. As a junior member of a large state delegation already committed to a candidate, I wasn't expected to *do* anything except turn up on the convention floor and not object when the delegation chairman cast the state's vote.

For my wife Lois and me, the convention days and evenings were a continuous round of festivities put on by the various candidates. We listened to lots of speeches, some of them even eloquent, though drowned out by the continuous din of loud conversations on the convention floor. We were exposed to innumerable rumors, many of them fascinating and most of them false. We attended uncounted cocktail parties, where the kind, quality, and volume of the liquors served as some index to the self-image of the hosts, many of whom thought they were running for president or at least vice president. We heard many stories about whether Adlai Stevenson was running, none of them from people who had any more reason to know the answer to that question than Lois or I did.

On the day before the balloting for president, Adlai Stevenson entered the convention hall. The balconies were filled with wildly enthusiastic supporters—by no action of his, I'm sure, but organized on his behalf—with ready-made signs. There followed a huge pro-Adlai demonstration, unscheduled by the convention managers but quite well planned by his supporters.

Those nominally in charge of the convention proceedings couldn't do anything about it. There were too many people making too much noise to continue whatever was supposed to be happening on the podium. The convention managers simply waited it out, which took a long wait. But from where I sat on the convention floor, it was all too noticeable that the noise was coming from the balconies. Most of the delegates, who would be making the decision on the morrow, were sitting on their hands.

For me, the next act in this drama came when Lois and I were invited later that same evening to come to the penthouse suite of William Benton—who owned the *Encyclopedia Britannica* and became a vice president of the University of Chicago when Robert Hutchins was its president. I knew Bill Benton; we had discussed for some weeks in 1959 his offer that I become editor of the *Britannica*. I had passed up this tempting opportunity on the hunch that a favorable turn of the political wheel in Washington might provide another opportunity for me to work directly in international affairs, which was always my favored option.

When we arrived at Benton's sumptuous suite, the hidden agenda became clear. Several other members of the New York delegation were there at the same time; the purpose was evidently to introduce us to Adlai Stevenson. The ranking member of our New York group was the Democratic Chairman of Nassau County on Long Island. After Gov. Stevenson had said a surprisingly few words, this natural spokesman for the New York delegates stepped forward.

"Well, Governor," he asked, "what do you want us to do tomorrow?"

Adlai Stevenson looked a little discomfited, even surprised, by the question. Then he replied: "My friends, you'll just have to make up your own minds about that."

End of dialogue. The New Yorkers drifted away; most of them soon left the room. Lois and I stayed, whether from curiosity or the need for another drink, I no longer recall. A few moments later, we found ourselves isolated in a corner with "the Guv," as his early political friends still called him. I don't know whether he or we felt more keenly the strangeness of the brief encounter we had just witnessed.

Before I could think of anything useful or sympathetic to say, Adlai spoke up. "You know, Harlan, this is rather embarrassing. Bill Benton invited me up here this evening, but I didn't know it was supposed to be a pitch for votes!"

Dear Adlai, I said, fortunately only to myself. You've been the object just this afternoon of one of the great ovations in the history of political conventions. Tomorrow is the balloting for the presidential nomination. You didn't know this party was supposed to be a pitch for votes?

Since I no longer remember what I said out loud in reply, it evidently wasn't nearly as memorable as what I *didn't* say.

TRANSITION

The 1960 election was over. The Kennedy-Johnson ticket had won, by a nail-biting margin—a small fraction of one percent—of the popular votes nationwide. Now the question for Adlai Stevenson was—what next? That was the question for me, too. I had been chairman of Citizens for Kennedy in Central New York, the upstate region centering on Syracuse. We had done pretty well, helping JFK carry Syracuse and coming remarkably close even in Onondaga County—which had last gone for a Democrat named Franklin Pierce, in 1852. It was a time for waiting and wondering; you don't "apply" for the kind of presidential appointment I was hoping might happen.

What Adlai Stevenson had been hoping—to be Secretary of State—was blown away by the way his noncandidacy developed before and during the Democratic convention. The last opportunity probably passed him by the afternoon he received that loud ovation on the convention floor; the contrived noise didn't impress most seasoned delegates, but it must have been impressive in millions of living rooms around the country. I remember thinking at the time that if Adlai were to seize that moment, step to the podium, thank his supporters, and ask them to help make John F. Kennedy the nominee, a Kennedy nomination on the first ballot would be assured.

Of course many of his own supporters, including Eleanor Roosevelt, would have reacted with disappointment, even outrage. And as things turned out the next day, Kennedy did make it anyway on the first ballot, if only when the alphabetical call of the states got all the way to Wyoming. The scenario in my mind's eye was high risk and low probability. But certainly, by the time the convention was over the probability of Adlai Stevenson as Secretary of State in a Kennedy Administration had sunk to zero.

I don't know just when Adlai learned for sure that he wouldn't be Secretary of State. I learned later that, when he was asked to become Ambassador to the United Nations with Cabinet rank, he put that proposal on ice until he knew who would head the State Department.

The President-elect's search process was impressively broad and serious. He had not previously met either of the men—Dean Rusk, president of the Rockefeller Foundation, and Robert McNamara, president of Ford Motor Company—who became Secretary of State and Secretary of Defense.

After a good deal of bargaining, Adlai agreed to become the chief U.S. diplomatic gladiator at the United Nations. The bargain made him a member of the Cabinet and of the National Security Council, and thus potentially involved in all foreign policy decisions, even when there was no UN angle. The President-elect also promised that Adlai could propose the nominee for the State Department post who would serve as his primary "backstop" in Washington—the Assistant Secretary of State for International Organization Affairs.

Meanwhile, I watched as people I regarded as professional colleagues and personal friends were recruited into the foreign-policy-establishment-to-be. Dean Rusk had offered me a job in the Rockefeller Foundation in the 1950s, but as Dean of the Maxwell School, I was having so much fun spending foundation money on international projects that I didn't think it could be nearly as interesting to be giving money away. Rusk was announced as Kennedy's choice for Secretary of State—on the same Sunday, as it happened, that *The New York Times Magazine* published an article I had written titled "Memo for the Next Secretary of State." His two top deputies, it soon appeared, would be Chester Bowles and George Ball, both of whom I knew well.

Phone calls from friends close to the recruitment process kept me in touch with the rumor mill. Bowles had suggested I manage the foreign-aid program. Someone else (I never learned who) proposed that I become director of the U.S. Information Service, the post to which Edward R. Murrow was about to be appointed. Then, to my surprise, I got a phone call directly from Dean Rusk. He said there were two jobs he was sure I could do: foreign aid administrator and Assistant Secretary of State for the UN and other international organizations. There were also two people "mentioned" for both appointments: Harry Labouisse and myself. What did I think?

I had to think fast. I had assumed the Kennedy recruiters were just filling slots, not asking recruits what they would like to do. "If I were the Administration," I found myself replying, "I would put me in the foreign-aid business." I had worked on foreign economic policy and economic development for almost a dozen years earlier in my life, and thought I knew where most of those bodies were buried. "But if you're asking me what I'd like to do, I've never been on the political side of foreign policy, and I would opt for the Assistant Secretary assignment."

Rusk, who never wasted words, simply said, "OK, I'll try to make it come out that way." Earlier in his career, when the Korean War was framed from the start as a UN operation, Dean Rusk had headed what was then called the Office of UN Affairs; my guess is that I made the choice he wanted me to make.

Within days, I had a phone call from Adlai Stevenson: Would I come to Chicago and spend a day with him? I promptly did. Once again, he turned out to have read a surprising lot of what I had written, and we plunged into an extraordinary day of lively conversation—not only about the United Nations as such, but about U.S.-Soviet relations, China, arms control, human rights, world poverty, the pace of decolonization, the prospects for democracy. These were my bread-and-butter issues; my understanding of them had been honed both as a practitioner and as an academic. What impressed me was how substantive was his knowledge, and how up-to-date were his reactions on issues I hadn't thought would be so clearly on the radar screen of a fulltime politician.

Of course, I wasn't interviewing him; he was interviewing me. At the end of that intensive day of one-on-one conversation, I was very anxious to work with him. He prudently didn't say what he was going to recommend. But after a few days of nervous waiting, I learned that Rusk and Stevenson had both recommended that I be nominated as Assistant Secretary of State for International Organization Affairs in the new Kennedy Administration. I was asked to come to Washington as soon as possible after the January 20 inauguration. I started work on January 23, 1961.

As usual in politics, that wasn't the end of the story. President Kennedy had agreed, but his influential brother Robert was objecting. I was not surprised. "Bobby" had run a hardnosed JFK campaign, and he had developed the impression that the Citizens for Kennedy were insufficiently orthodox JFK loyalists. That was true, in a way. We were working hard to elect our common candidate, but the Citizens' task was to attract independents and liberal Republicans to vote for Kennedy, so we naturally talked and wrote in ways that differed from those more focused on keeping "base" voters active.

For about a month, therefore, I was sitting as a "consultant" (with a provisional security clearance) in what would be my office, getting the "IO" bureau organized and starting to handle policy issues. One day in February, Rusk dryly told me that "the President has overruled his brother." My nomination soon went to the Senate, and I was quickly confirmed and sworn in.

THE WORLD'S BEST-KNOWN AMBASSADOR

It was high time. UN issues were making the highlight news—especially in *The New York Times*, which covered United Nations happenings as exciting local news. Ambassador Adlai Stevenson's every public comment was a candidate for a front-page story. The UN Secretary General (UNSYG in our diplomatic cable traffic) was Dag Hammarskjöld; his personality—an intriguing mix of activist and philosopher—made him newsworthy, too. And the ranking American as UN Undersecretary-General was Ralph Bunche, a well-known African-American who managed peacekeeping and was often sent out to mediate disputes. One such mission, which produced an Armistice Agreement between Israel and its Arab neighbors, had already won him the 1950 Nobel Peace Prize.

Plenty was happening to make "UN affairs" a very active beat, not only for journalists but also for the U.S. government. The biggest issue at first—and for quite a while thereafter—was the Congo. That large country in the middle of the African continent had just been decolonized by Belgium and was rapidly coming apart. The tripartite wrestling match featured Communist-led secessionists in the north, more secessionists backed by Belgian mining interests in the copper-rich southern province of Katanga, and a central government unable to govern, lacking the force to assert its sovereignty.

With help from the Eisenhower Administration, the United Nations had ridden to the rescue in 1960 with its largest peacekeeping force to date; both peacekeeping and peacemaking missions were supervised by Ralph Bunche. For us, a first foreign-policy task was to decide whether to support the UN in trying to glue the Congo's parts together. At my first meeting to pull together a recommendation to the new President on the Congo, I looked around the conference table and spotted four former governors: Adlai Stevenson of Illinois; Chester Bowles of Connecticut, who had just become the No. 2 man in the State Department; Averell Harriman of New York, the new Assistant Secretary for the Far East (I had worked with him a decade earlier when he headed the Mutual Security Agency); and G. Mennen ("Soapy") Williams of Michigan, the new Assistant Secretary for Africa. "This is no practice session," I wrote in a note to myself. "The varsity is on the field."

The case for continuing what President Eisenhower had helped start was clear enough, and was speedily agreed. Governor—now Ambassador—Stevenson described forcefully how the sudden UN presence in the Congo had baffled and frustrated the Soviets in their effort to establish a foothold in the middle of Africa. We told the President that if the UN were not successful, the United States would find itself deeply embroiled there, probably with U.S. troops instead of the Indians, Malays, Scandinavians, and Canadians who made up the 15,000-man UN contingent operating under the political supervision of the wise and crafty Ralph Bunche.

The President quickly agreed to support the UN effort. Then he had to redecide it several times thereafter as the Congo crisis produced a major row among Democrats in the U.S. Senate, with Senator Thomas Dodd of Connecticut running interference for the copper-mining Belgian interests in Katanga and Senator Hubert Humphrey of Minnesota backing President Kennedy and the UN initiative. On two different occasions in the Oval Office, the President pointed at me and asked, "Didn't you tell me, Harlan, that if the UN fails in the Congo, we'll have to do it instead?" When I confirmed his memory, he would quickly reconfirm the policy: "Then let's keep on supporting the UN."

Not all the foreign-policy headlines were generated by the drama in the Congo. Just to the south, new leaders in Angola were trying to speed up their country's independence from Portugal—producing another tussle between an African colony and its European metropole, a corresponding tussle between the European and African bureaus in the State Department, and frequent meetings of the United Nations Security Council.

South Africa's policy of *apartheid* was a hardy perennial in the UN General Assembly, and of course interacted with U.S. domestic debates about race relations. The Cold War was unofficially banned from the UN's agenda; but East-West arguments about everything from disarmament to human rights seeped into every conference room at the United Nations in New York. And Dag Hammarskjöld's activism was costing a good deal more money than the UN had in the till—so a budget crisis was looming, too.

Thus it was that Adlai Stevenson, the chief American gladiator under the klieg lights in midtown Manhattan, became the cynosure of many political eyes at home and abroad—and even the envy of some of his political friends. Hubert Humphrey, who had also run for President in 1960, chaired the main Senate subcommittee that dealt with UN affairs. I will not easily forget bringing to Senator Humphrey a plan for a set of hearings on UN policy. Adlai Stevenson was of course first on my list of lead-off witnesses. Hubert Humphrey, a good friend of Adlai's, pulled no punches in reacting to my list. "The lead-off witness can't be Adlai," he said with finality. Then he gave me a memorable lesson in political dynamics.

"You've got to understand, Harlan," he said. "Last week I carefully prepared an important speech and delivered it on the Senate floor. The press gallery was full. The text of my speech was available in advance. Next day, what happened? What I had said was summarized in the *New York Times*—in two paragraphs, on page 25." With a cheerful grimace, he continued: "All Adlai has to do, up there [in New York], is walk across the street and come out against the Communists, and he's on the front page—*with a picture!*"

Adlai Stevenson's role as a publicity hero on New York's manic stage was also producing heartburn in the White House. The President's workways featured a good deal of bedtime reading—mostly of staff memos on what had just happened or was just about to happen. And his first reading in the morning would be several newspapers, including *The Washington Post* and *The New York Times*. The puzzle wasn't hard to decipher: Front-page stories would report public votes by Ambassador Stevenson, speaking for the new U.S. government. But the President of the United States hadn't given the order to vote that way; he had not even known the issue was up for decision. And especially in *The New York Times*, the two or three front-page stories about what the Kennedy Administration had done in Washington would be running alongside a couple of pieces of news that Adlai Stevenson had made at the UN that same day.

Most of the doings in New York were far from high policy decisions. In a typical week, 90 percent of the instructions to "USUN" (the symbol for Adlai's diplomatic mission across the street from the United Nations building in New York) were approved in my bureau—often requiring lateral consultation with other bureaus, but seldom requiring review on the State Department's seventh floor (the Secretary's office), let alone by the President. It was not hard for me to imagine a bureaucratic nightmare in which everything Adlai Stevenson said and did at the UN, high policy or not, would first have to be cleared with the White House.

Sensing the restiveness in the White House staff, I went over to visit with McGeorge Bundy, the President's national security advisor. Together we decided that the best antidote to the growing neuralgia would be, at the end of each day, for me to provide a very succinct summary of what the United States had done at the United Nations that day, and why—paying special attention to whatever Adlai had done personally. Secretary Rusk agreed to the plan, and was fortunately trusting enough not to require prior clearance of my daily summaries—of which "the seventh floor" of course got a real-time copy.

Thereafter these notes were routinely put into the President's nightly reading file—and when he read the newspapers the next morning, he could say to himself, "Sure, I knew that." The staff heartburn was promptly relieved.

"FIELD-HEADQUARTERS RELATIONSHIP"

In the political science of public administration, the relations between field staffs and their headquarters are always touchy at best. People placed closer to the problems are *supposed* to develop and defend a viewpoint different from headquarters policy makers— otherwise, they might as well have stayed at headquarters.

Making this traditionally difficult relationship work was greatly complicated in our case by unusual circumstances. The "field" mission in New York was headed by a world-famous personality, a Cabinet member who outranked every person whose job was to tell him what he could or couldn't say—except the Secretary of State and the President. Yet Adlai Stevenson needed staff support from (and lots of writing by) not only colleagues in his own New York mission but countless Washington experts on world politics, the global economy, the motives of each member of the United Nations, and all kinds of military, technological, and demographic trends he needed to know about and take into account—not to mention the daily flows of secret intelligence controlled in Washington.

This need for information and advice was particularly acute for Adlai personally because he had a deal with the President that he would be cut in on all aspects of foreign policy—including issues (such as Berlin) that couldn't be handled in the UN at all. This also made my job, and those of my IO colleagues, even more interesting, since it provided a passport to intervene in the internal affairs of the regional bureaus, and even in other departments of the government, in order to satisfy our New York client's need for up-to-date and often highly secret research and analysis.

On the "headquarters" side, there was also a political complexity. John F. Kennedy had won the 1960 election over Richard Nixon by only 118,574 popular votes, out of more than 68 million people voting. (The margin in the Electoral College was more comfortable, 330 to 219.) The President was acutely aware that if Adlai Stevenson were to become disenchanted with the Kennedy Administration and resign in a huff, an alarmingly large minority of liberal Democrats might defect with him and cause all sorts of trouble down the road— in Congress, in some states, and in the run-up to the reelection campaign in 1964.

I realized from the start that keeping Adlai happy was an unspoken part of my mandate. JFK also decided during 1961 to charge Arthur Schlesinger, a well-known historian and political liberal who served in the White House as a Special Assistant to the President, to keep a sharp eye on Adlai's morale and help mediate any perceived unhappiness.

When Adlai came to Washington, which was not weekly but frequently, we had no difficulty in arranging an Oval Office appointment on any issue that needed to be explained directly to the President. To the extent Adlai was available, the President seemed to be trying to cut him in on White House foreign policy discussions even if no "UN angle" was immediately apparent. He also was consulted about appointments, especially of judges—almost as if he were doubling as a Senator from Illinois. And when Jacqueline Kennedy went to New York to take in a Broadway show, Adlai Stevenson was often her escort for the evening.

The relationship was chronically strained, however, by Adlai's tendency to complain in jocular fashion to friends and dinner partners about how complicated and troublesome his job was—occasionally hinting that he might have to quit. The first couple of times I heard rumors of what he had said to someone at dinner the night before, I rushed up to consult George Ball who had known Adlai best, and longest, of anyone in the State Department. George just laughed. "Don't take it so seriously," he told me. "That's the way Adlai has always been. And it *doesn't* mean he's going to resign!" I derived some comfort from this assurance—though still worrying that the same rumors were reaching the White House. In the event, George Ball's prediction turned out to be accurate: Adlai was still Ambassador Stevenson when he died in London in 1965.

Part of what made this field-headquarters complexity work was the high quality of the staff at both ends of the line. The top Foreign Service officer at USUN in New York was Charles Yost, an experienced, warm-hearted professional who later himself became the top U.S. Ambassador to the UN. He served in effect as Adlai's deputy for diplomacy, and occupied the U.S. seat in the UN Security Council when Adlai himself wasn't there. Unlike some experienced professionals, he didn't take himself too seriously—and frequently exhibited a delightfully dry wit. I recall his criticizing Gross National Product as "a peculiarly undiscriminating indicator," with this remark: "Like Oscar Wilde's definition of a cynic, it knows the

price of everything and the value of nothing. It is true to its name—
it is gross."

Adlai had also brought into his mission three very high powered,
and wealthy, citizens from outside the government: Francis Plimpton,
an astute and skillful New York lawyer, as his overall deputy; Philip
Klutznick, a Chicago housing entrepreneur who had also headed
the Anti-Defamation League, to handle economic and social issues;
and Marietta Tree, a statuesque woman as bright as she was beautiful, to handle human rights. Clayton Fritchey, an experienced
journalist, served Adlai both as public relations advisor and personal confidante.

The special character of the New York mission was dramatized by
the fact that it contained not one but five officials with the rank of
Ambassador—Adlai Stevenson of course, but also Plimpton, Yost,
Klutznick, and Tree.

At the other end of the busy phone lines between New York and
Washington was the "IO" bureau. I had inherited a superb staff of
Foreign Service professionals. Joseph Sisco already had long experience in United Nations affairs and proved to be an indispensable
guide to the Byzantine politics of that complicated organization; for
most of my time in the Assistant Secretary job, he served as my principal deputy—and succeeded me when I was appointed Ambassador
to NATO in 1965.

A younger colleague of his, William Buffum, was also adept at
handling the convoluted policy-cum-procedural questions that multilateral diplomacy poses to those who have to maneuver in it; he
later became the American Undersecretary-General of the UN. We
were also lucky to have Walter Kotschnig, Austrian by birth and
American by passionate conviction, who was a walking encyclopedia
on the UN Specialized Agencies, which came together—with much
unnecessary noise and confusion—under the UN's Economic and
Social Council.

I needed to bring in from the outside only two major appointees.
One was another Deputy Assistant Secretary, Richard Gardner, a
postwar Rhodes Scholar and international lawyer who was able to
handle all the kinds of subject matter that had been outside normal
Foreign Service experience, such as Law of the Sea, trade and monetary issues, population policy, the law of outer space, and much else
that required his special combination of imagination and intellectual
rigor. Dick Gardner later served as U.S. Ambassador to Spain and to

Italy. The other was Thomas W. Wilson, a skillful writer with wide experience and great fluency. His title, Special Assistant, was unrevealing; the centerpiece of his job was to write speeches on an extraordinary variety of topics for Adlai Stevenson to use at the United Nations.

To make sure that the New York mission and the State Department stayed on the same wavelength, I made an early deal with Adlai. He would try to be in Washington for one day each week; we prepared a well-appointed office for him, right next to mine. As a member of both the Cabinet and of the National Security Council, his presence was often required in Washington anyway—but even so, he never managed the once-a-week schedule.

I undertook also to spend one day a week in New York, discussing whatever needed discussion—and making sure I understood, up close, all of what was happening at the UN. Adlai agreed that this rhythm would make sense—and kindly invited me to stay, whenever I was visiting, in his spacious top-floor suite in the Waldorf, which served as the "Embassy residence" for USUN—and where he was the only permanent resident. This provided time, valuable to me, for quiet conversations to learn about his thinking and brief him on developments in Washington he should know about; the arrangement also enabled me to get to know some of the many friends who streamed through Adlai's life at the top of the Waldorf Tower.

THE BAY OF PIGS

The intensely personal relationship I felt developing with Adlai Stevenson was put to an early test in April 1961, when the Kennedy Administration stumbled into the fiasco called the Bay of Pigs.

The story line is all too well known: In January 1961, Kennedy inherited from the Eisenhower Administration a clandestine CIA project to sponsor an invasion of Cuba by a group of Cuban exiles, operating from a base in Nicaragua. The plan was for them to establish a beachhead at the Bay of Pigs. A Cuban government-in-exile called the Cuban Revolutionary Council would then provide an instant alternative to Fidel Castro's government, to which it was assumed that large numbers of Cubans would rally.

Some of the planners evidently thought that U.S. forces would have to become more heavily supportive than President Kennedy thought, or ever signed on to. In any event, the "brigade" scheduled to invade numbered only 1,400 men, only one-tenth of whom were really soldiers; its slow-moving B-26s proved no match for a few faster Cuban T-33 jet trainers, which the planners had somehow not taken into account. It soon became clear that nothing short of major support from U.S. forces could make this pitiful operation effective. Moreover, the hoped-for internal rebellion didn't materialize.

Once the operation was public knowledge, the shroud of secrecy shredded fast, and there was no way to pretend that it had been anything but a failed CIA venture. President Kennedy quickly took public responsibility for the "mistake," and it went down in history as a fiasco.

Part of the plan was to catch the Cuban air force on the ground, with two advance strikes that would appear to have been carried out by Cuban defectors in planes painted with Cuban air force markings. One of the pseudo-Cuban planes flew direct from its Nicaraguan base to Miami, where the pilot said he was a Castro defector who had just bombed the Cuban airfields. Another developed engine trouble and made an emergency landing in Key West; the pilot told the same "cover story" about why and where he was flying that day.

By an irony of fate, the first of these strikes was planned for a Saturday in April 1961, just before the Monday when an old Cuban item charging the United States with aggressive intentions was scheduled to be debated in the United Nations General Assembly. My first inkling of the whole scheme came just a week before when, to prepare for this coincidence, Tracy Barnes, a high official of the CIA, and Arthur Schlesinger from the White House went to New York to brief Adlai Stevenson about the whole plan, and I joined them there.

Schlesinger describes the briefing, in his 1965 book *A Thousand Days*, as "probably unduly vague," adding that it "left Stevenson with the impression that no action would take place during the UN discussion of the Cuban item." Later, at a Century Club lunch with Stevenson, Clayton Fritchey, and me, Schlesinger remembers (as I do) that Adlai "made clear that he wholly disapproved of the plan, regretted that he been given no opportunity to comment on it and believed it would cause infinite trouble. But, if it was national policy, he was prepared to make out the best possible case."

As soon as the first strike on Saturday morning was known, Raul Roa, the Cuban foreign minister—who was in New York for the UN

General Assembly—got the old Cuban item moved up to an emergency session of the General Assembly's Political Committee that
very afternoon. We were meanwhile burning the phone wires to
find out—from the CIA, via the State Department's Inter-American
Bureau—whether the Cuban defectors landing in Florida were for
real. Word came back that they were indeed genuine. Without
knowing that all we had was the cover story, I authorized Adlai to
treat them as real.

Stevenson was already on the General Assembly floor, and
promptly advertised the cover story as the truth (with two unnoticed
caveats): "These two planes, to the best of our knowledge, were
Castro's own air force planes and, according to the pilots, they took
off from Castro's own air force fields." At that moment, a member
of his staff who had been monitoring the press wire handed him a
ticker item with more details from the CIA cover story; he promptly
read that into the UN record as well.

My recollection is that it took less than twenty-four hours for the
cover to blow off. By the next day, I learned that an enterprising
reporter had gone to the crash-landed plane, scraped at its surface
paint, and found U.S. Air Force markings underneath. In any case,
the cover was evaporating fast; and Dean Rusk, after talking to Adlai
Stevenson, "concluded that a second strike [from Nicaragua] would
put the United States in an untenable position internationally." It
could only appear to come from Nicaragua, Rusk told the President.
"I'm not signed onto this," was Kennedy's reaction. The second
strike from the Nicaraguan base was called off, and that was the
beginning of the end of this ill-starred invasion.

Adlai was naturally outraged. His government had abused his personal integrity and international credibility. I felt equally betrayed.
But for me, the extraordinary part of the fiasco's aftermath was that
I had been the Washington authority that instructed him to lie to the
world; yet, he never blamed his resulting predicament on me. For 99
people out of 100, the natural way to express his resentment would
have been to say, "That's what those clucks in the State Department,
led by Harlan Cleveland, told me I should say. It was a barefaced lie,
but it was their fault!"

Adlai Stevenson wasn't that kind of person. He knew that I, and
others in the State Department on whose word I was relying, had
been duped by the CIA's cover story (the bureaucratic synonym for a
lie told in a supposedly defensible cause). He certainly felt mortified

that he had been "used." He may well have felt that the White House owed him some kind of apology—which never came. Even so, he carefully avoided placing the blame on the nearest and most vulnerable target—his "backstop" in Washington.

As the operation called the Bay of Pigs came apart, I had a ringside seat at its disintegration. Adlai Stevenson was having to react in the UN from hour to hour. At the same time, the White House felt the need to keep its breathless press corps informed. So for two days, as the failure of the Bay of Pigs invasion became clear in the packed White House Cabinet Room—in the off-and-on presence of the Joint Chiefs of Staff, the CIA Director, Latin American experts, experts on the Soviet Union, the Secretaries of State and Defense, the Attorney General, the Vice President, and the President—somebody had to try to make sure that what was said to the press in Washington and what was said to the UN in New York sounded like the same government speaking. That task fell to Pierre Salinger, the White House press secretary, and to me.

I was also observing the scene in the Cabinet Room as a sometime political scientist. Two moments of special illumination stand out in my memory four decades later. One was when the Chief of Naval Operations was using a large magnetic map to show just where each of the Navy's ships was currently deployed in the waters near, but not too near, the Cuban beaches. President Kennedy was listening with close attention. At one point, he rose, made his way around the long conference table, picked up one of the little magnetized destroyers, and moved it farther away from land. Wouldn't it be best, he asked politely, if all our ships were out beyond the horizon?

I happened to be looking just then at the Admiral's ashen face; it was not hard to decipher the mixture of shock and awe it revealed. "Is this young former Lieutenant j.g. going to be slicing down through the chain of command and making *tactical* decisions like this?" He didn't say anything like that out loud, of course; I was just reading it on his face.

The President returned to his chair on the other side of the Cabinet table, and the policy question he had raised, about how far offshore it was prudent for U.S. forces to be deployed (since this wasn't supposed to look like a U.S. operation), was rationally discussed. But what stayed in my mind, and in my notes, was the cultural dissonance between a four-star admiral worrying about the implications of all this for command-and-control, and a political leader worrying about damage control in an operation that was going sour.

The other memorable moment came when President Kennedy was temporarily out of the Cabinet Room, but most of the other mourners of what the President was about to publicly call a "mistake" were still there, hoping that a rabbit could still be found in the empty hat. Attorney General Robert F. Kennedy spoke up from the end of the long table, in his capacity as chief defender of the President's reputation. I don't want to hear anyone claiming to have thought this was not a good idea, he said in effect, glowering around the Cabinet table at us all.

Adlai Stevenson wasn't present to hear this admonition from the nation's chief law enforcement officer, but his sound instinct in any case was not to go public with his earlier doubts. Friends of Chester Bowles, who had also thought the CIA plan should be put aside, were not so discreet. Soon, Bowles was no longer Undersecretary of State.

A decade after the debacle, I found myself by chance sitting in an airplane next to one of the military leaders who had also been there as the Bay of Pigs invasion so rapidly fell apart. Both of us were by then retired from government, so I asked him why the Joint Chiefs hadn't told President Kennedy that the CIA's military plan was for the birds. We felt we were out of our league, he responded.

There we were, in the presence of this bright new political star, and—though we were all a good deal older than he was—we felt like children, waiting to speak when we were spoken to. And he never really asked for our military judgment about the plan as a whole. So we gave advice about tactics, not really about the strategy. (It was not the kind of conversation in which I took notes, so I'm not using quotation marks. But the essence of that conversation is as vivid in my mind today as it was then.)

President Kennedy was even more acutely aware, after the Bay of Pigs fiasco, how important it was to keep Adlai Stevenson on his foreign-policy team. In the early summer of 1961, Adlai was dispatched on an eighteen-day trip to the ten capitals of South America, accompanied among others by Lincoln Gordon, who had already been named as U.S. Ambassador to Brazil. Dick Goodwin, an assistant to the President, told Gordon that this was part of a "campaign of assuagement of Adlai's bitter resentment at having been led to lie to the UN Security Council . . . without being told that he was lying."

Adlai and his team met in each country with the President, Foreign Minister, and Economic Minister. In most capitals, there was a public speech by Adlai, attracting a large crowd. Even before this trip, Adlai was widely believed to be an expert on Latin America; he considered that reputation to be wholly unwarranted, apparently (he thought) based on the one trip he previously made there, in company with Bill Benton, a couple of years before. But the 1961 "state tour" of South America established him as an official whose views on hemispheric relations should be taken seriously.

The Honey Fitz Policy

As we were gearing up for the UN General Assembly in the autumn of 1961, Adlai and I hoped that it would feature an opening speech by President Kennedy—which we could readily arrange since the United States is the UN's "host country." It was important in any case for the President to know the range of issues that would be debated there beginning in September. Early in August we were invited, together with Arthur Schlesinger, to visit the Kennedy compound in Hyannis Port to discuss them.

The weather was gloomy, but Kennedy was determined to have our little meeting aboard the *Honey Fitz*, a motor launch with just enough room in the cockpit for the four of us to sit, with Jacqueline and two of her sisters-in-law on the deck up forward in bathing gear.

First on our agenda was what Adlai proposed as the major theme for the U.S. presentation: advocating general and complete disarmament. The President listened to Adlai's argument with close attention, then commented: "But disarmament, isn't this a propaganda thing?"

Stevenson was clearly stunned by this casual comment on an issue he felt so strongly about. Abandoning for a moment the ritual form of address, he said, "Jack, you've just got to have faith!" That was hardly the way to persuade so pragmatic a mind and spirit as John Kennedy's. Even though I was a junior officer on this little cruise, I thought I really had to intervene.

"Look, Mr. President," I said. "The Soviets have been getting away with murder. They keep talking about 'general and complete disarmament,' and we respond by wanting to talk about 'next steps.' So lots of people around the world think the Soviets want disarmament, but we're dragging our feet. But if, as the new American voice in this forum, you come out in favor of general and complete disarmament, there'll be nothing left to discuss at that airy level of abstraction. What will be left to discuss will be 'next steps,' and here our specific proposals could test or expose the real Soviet desire for arms reduction."

I have treasured in my memory for four decades President Kennedy's next words: "Yeah, that makes sense." As I watched and sometimes worked on arms control issues during the rest of the 1960s, my personal name for our U.S. strategy was "the *Honey Fitz* policy."

The next issue we had to discuss was how to handle Communist China's nonmembership in the UN. Kennedy relieved the tension by calling toward the bow, "Jackie, we need the Bloody Marys now." I have visited the White House a good many times in my life, but that's the first and only time a bikini-clad First Lady has handed me a cocktail.

The conundrum was this: The China seat in the United Nations was still occupied by the Republic of China, which, since 1949, had governed only the Island of Taiwan. So mainland China, governed by the People's Republic of China, was not in the UN at all. One solution floating around was "two Chinas," which we were authorized to explore. But there was no way to finesse the question, which of the two would wield the Charter-endowed veto in the Security Council.

In the end, before the 1961 General Assembly convened, Kennedy asked Stevenson to do whatever he could to keep Communist China out of the UN for the next year at least—not, he made clear, because he thought that made sense but because to do otherwise would make so much trouble in U.S. politics. We were able to accomplish this by an intricate series of parliamentary maneuvers that, with the help of aggressive moves by the People's Republic of China, postponed the reckoning until it was no longer a scratchy issue in American politics.

The outing on the *Honey Fitz* took place on August 5. By mid-September, it was still uncertain whether the President would make our opening speech personally. What settled it was the news, on September 18, that Dag Hammarskjöld had been killed in a plane crash during a trip to Africa. The Soviets were just then pushing the idea that the UN Secretariat, its executive branch, should be managed by a triumvirate—which came to be called the *troika*, a carriage of Russian origin drawn by three horses harnessed abreast. A week later, Kennedy made the opening speech to the General Assembly, calling on the UN to reject the *troika*, which, he said, would "entrench the Cold War in the headquarters of peace."

The UN was needed more than ever, he declared, for "a nuclear disaster, spread by wind and water and fear, could well engulf the great and the small, the rich and the poor, the committed and the uncommitted alike. Mankind must put an end to war—or war will put an end to mankind. . . . Let us call a truce to terror." The goal of disarmament, he continued, "is no longer a dream—it is a practical matter of life or death. The risks inherent in disarmament pale in comparison to the risks inherent in an unlimited arms race. . . . Together we shall save our planet, or together we shall perish in its flames." The *Honey Fitz* policy was alive and well.

THE CUBA MISSILE CRISIS

President Kennedy's learning curve was steep. He had not asked enough questions, early enough, to expose the Bay of Pigs plan for the unworkable scheme it quickly turned out to be. He had trusted experts, such as the CIA planners (headed by a brilliant economist) and the Joint Chiefs of Staff, to make sure they had taken into account what they didn't know about as well as what they did. By the time the Cuba missiles came into view, he knew what I tried to describe ten years later, after watching Kennedy and hundreds of other executives at work:

> The executive leader must be something of an intellectual, not just by training but by temperament as well. The executive who isn't personally plowing through the analysis and reflecting on what it means is not making decisions but merely presiding while others decide. The obligation to think hard, fast, and free is the one executive function that can neither be avoided nor delegated to others. (*The Future Executive*, 1972)

That the Soviet Union was secretly bringing offensive missiles into Cuba literally came into Kennedy's view on the morning of October 15, 1962. A U-2 spy plane—dispatched to fly over Cuba because of growing rumors about Soviet military construction there—had come back the day before with photos of a launching pad and one actual missile at a base in San Cristobal. The President promptly assembled a secret *ad hoc* group (which later came to be regarded as an executive committee of the National Security Council, or ExCom), consisting of top officials who met more or less continuously during the thirteen days of the ensuing crisis.

The idea that the Soviets would sneak offensive nuclear missiles into an island 90 miles from Florida was so contrary to the prior guesses of expert Kremlinologists that the crisis required lots of new thinking in a short week. At first, there was some old thinking in the ExCom. From the hardliners, "surgical strikes" to take out the new missile bases—but of course that would start by our killing some Soviet citizens guarding and managing the missile sites. From those who wanted to bet on diplomacy, a trade of missile bases in Turkey (their decommissioning had already been decided, with no date set) for the elimination of the Cuban bases.

After several days and nights of argument, the President opted to start with an intermediate kind of power, adopting a suggestion by Robert McNamara to deploy a naval blockade of Soviet ships coming into Cuba. This was combined with a complicated diplomatic scenario—"quarantining" Cuba by sudden action of the Organization of American States and then taking our case to the UN Security Council. (The word "quarantine" was used because "blockade" is an act of war under international law.)

Adlai Stevenson was part of the ExCom from the outset. I was part of a second wave of people brought in toward the end of the week. We were needed to flesh out with concrete plans and timed scenarios the sense of direction decided by the President, after he had listened to the endless arguments among his senior advisors in the ExCom. (He was indeed participating personally in the staff work.)

With Lois, I was at a dinner with the Swiss ambassador when Secretary Rusk called to ask that I come in to the State Department right away. I already had a hunch that something big was up, so I asked the Secretary whether he wanted to stir the curiosity of the rest of the diplomatic diners by having me depart hurriedly in mid-meal.

On second thought he told me to carry on through the first cup of coffee, and then say I needed an early bedtime for whatever reason—and come direct to the Department.

So at 10 p.m. that Friday evening I learned from Secretary Rusk about the missiles in Cuba, and about President Kennedy's tentative decision to respond.

The President was going to go public the following Monday evening in prime time, with our discovery of the missiles and what we were going to do about them. In the State Department, the diplomatic scenario was quickly sketched in. While he was speaking, we would ask for an immediate meeting of the Organization of American States; its headquarters were in the Pan American building in Washington, with special ambassadors from each country (except Cuba) in the hemisphere. At the same time, in New York, Ambassador Adlai Stevenson would demand an emergency meeting of the UN Security Council. But we didn't want it to happen so fast that there wouldn't be time for the essential OAS consensus to develop.

The weekend was full of homework for all of us in the know. Arthur Schlesinger came over to my office from the White House to help write Stevenson's Security Council speech, working with our writer Tom Wilson, Joe Sisco, and me. Edwin Martin, the Assistant Secretary for Inter-American Affairs, worked in parallel on what Secretary Rusk would say to the OAS.

We decided early on that we just had to have some of the best photos of the Soviet missile sites to use in our UN presentation. The CIA predictably didn't want to reveal how good U.S. long-distance aerial photography was, so the declassification of photos became a major sticking point. The White House finally had to settle the argument—in our favor—by ruling that the nation's need for credible, internationally publishable evidence clearly outweighed the desire of the intelligence agencies to protect their secret technologies. However, we also decided to hold the devastating photos in reserve, for use in rebuttal if, as seemed likely, the Soviets denied that they were installing offensive missiles in Cuba.

Ironically, the rotating presidency of the UN Security Council meant that in October 1962 the Soviet Union's ambassador, Valerian Zorin, was the presiding officer. By Tuesday, our strategy was hardly a secret. Zorin and anyone else who cared knew that the OAS ambassadors were assembling Tuesday morning. With some difficulty, the U.S. Mission managed to get our emergency session of the Security Council scheduled for four o'clock that afternoon.

The draft of Stevenson's speech was completed over the weekend. Arthur Schlesinger took it to the White House where President Kennedy also did some editing. Arthur then flew to New York, as did Joe Sisco, to help Stevenson. I stayed in Washington to make sure our complex diplomatic choreography worked the way it was supposed to work.

Secretary Rusk personally handled the Tuesday morning meeting with the Latin American ambassadors. We had assumed the OAS action could be completed by midday, but several of the Latin Americans had to seek further instructions from their governments during an extended lunch hour. Thus it was that the meeting was only just reconvening in the Pan American building a few blocks from the State Department when, in New York, the UN Security Council was called to order promptly by the Soviet delegate.

Stevenson's opening speech was of course carried on network TV. I watched the show from my office with several members of our bureau—following the script as he spoke and noticing that our colleague Joe Sisco was seated right behind the ambassador. It was still crucial to present our naval blockade as the product of hemispheric, not just United States, outrage. Yet at 4:40 p.m., I still hadn't heard from Secretary Rusk.

Then the phone rang. It was Ed Martin from the Pan American building: all but Uruguay had agreed, and I could authorize Stevenson to speak for the hemisphere. (Uruguay's decision was delayed by a peculiar form of democracy: governance by a committee of multiple presidents, all of whom had to be consulted before anything could be done. Later on, Uruguay made it unanimous.)

We had stationed a young woman from our UN mission in a phone booth right next to the Security Council chamber, for just this contingency. I called and asked her to get Sisco to the phone right away. On our Washington television screen the breathless staff assembled in my office could see her tap Sisco on the shoulder and watch him hurry off the screen to take my call. I dictated a carefully worded paragraph to add to the Stevenson text and specified just where to insert it. Still watching the screen, I saw Sisco come back into view and lay a white sheet of paper on Adlai's desk.

The Ambassador, however, was in full rhetorical flight. Holding his manuscript off the desk with both hands, he did not appear to notice the precious addition to his speech. I watched with a sinking feeling as he swept on past the point where the hemispheric action should have been announced. Only a minute or two of text remained; there might not be enough time for another call to New York.

The phone rang again and my secretary Tess Beach, normally very calm and collected, rushed in to report, "The President is on the phone—I mean *personally.*" I reached for the phone, still watching my corner of the Cuba missile scenario come apart on the screen.

"I've just heard about the OAS action," said the familiar voice with the New England accent, speaking even more rapidly than usual. "Is there some way we can get it into Stevenson's speech before he finishes?"

For a giddy instant I wondered what I would have said if we had not thought to cover that base. "We've done an insert on that, Mr. President, and it's just been placed in front of him," I said. "But frankly, I'm not sure he saw it."

At that moment, Stevenson reached for the little rectangle of white paper, took it in at a glance, and cleared his throat. Before I could say anything more, President Kennedy, who was naturally watching the same TV show in his White House office, cut in. "Oh, I see. He's picking it up and reading it now. Thanks very much, Harlan."

The Cuba missile crisis was not over. But mine was.

The United States was now on full military alert. An armed force of 100,000 men was getting ready for action from Florida. Ninety ships of the U.S. Navy, sixty-eight aircraft squadrons, and eight aircraft carriers were moving into position to enforce the OAS quarantine. Allies in Europe were expressing solidarity. However, in Cuba, forty-two medium-range nuclear missiles were still being unpacked and prepared for launching, and the public noises from Moscow were still truculent: The weapons in Cuba were defensive; the American quarantine was unwarranted.

U Thant, the UN Secretary-General, proposed that the Soviets suspend their shipments and the United States stand down its quarantine. Although this wouldn't work for us—it did nothing about the missiles already in Cuba—Adlai strongly urged a reply that would "keep the diplomatic option alive." He was authorized to insist that the weapons be removed but to "continue discussions" on how to get this done.

Meanwhile, there was a growing chorus of private hints that the Soviets wanted to escape from the bind they were in. One of the most interesting was a judgment by Averell Harriman, who had been Ambassador to Moscow, that "we must give him [Khrushchev] an out." (The normal channels for advice to higher authority are often circuitous in a crisis. Harriman was Assistant Secretary of State for the Far East. His comment went to Arthur Schlesinger in the White House and thence to the President.)

The Security Council reconvened on Thursday. It soon became a famous confrontation between Ambassador Stevenson and his Soviet counterpart. Ambassador Zorin argued that it was American actions that had created the threat to the peace. "This is the first time," said Adlai in reply, "that I have ever heard it said that the crime is not the burglary, but the discovery of the burglar." After a further exchange, Stevenson said, "those weapons must be taken out of Cuba." Then, in Schlesinger's later account, "he turned on the Russian with magnificent scorn":

"Do you, Ambassador Zorin, deny that the USSR has placed and is placing medium and intermediate-range missiles and sites in Cuba? Yes or no? Don't wait for the translation. Yes or no?"

Schlesinger: "Zorin muttered something about not being in an American courtroom."

Stevenson, cold and controlled: "You are in the courtroom of world opinion. You have denied they exist. . . . I am prepared to wait for my answer until hell freezes over."

Just outside the door to the Security Council chamber, U.S. Mission staff had stationed several large rolling screens with a montage of aerial photos of the nuclear installations. Adlai gave the signal, and they were rolled into the room. The suddenly declassified pictures produced, as we had hoped, a worldwide drama of demonstration—not just in that place at that time but globally, through the still miraculous novelty of television. It proved to be a classic case of world opinion playing a role in defusing a peace-and-security crisis.

Adlai Stevenson ended the debate this way, still addressing his Soviet colleague:

> We know the facts and so do you, sir, and we are ready to talk about them. Our job here is not to score debating points. Our job, Mr. Zorin, is to save the peace. And if you are ready to try, we are.

Defusing the crisis got complicated, of course—and lasted several months longer than most people realized. The immediate crisis featured a remarkably indirect channel of communication through John Scali, an ABC reporter, and the confusion of two letters from Khrushchev, one surging with anguished personal passion for a way out (if the United States would refrain from invading Cuba), the other written later by unknown Soviet hardliners (who wanted the United States to remove its missiles from Turkey).

Which letter to answer was a turning point in the complex diplomacy. Robert Kennedy is credited with the idea of answering the earlier, more personal letter and ignoring the other one. (That idea probably came from several people; I remember phoning in a similar suggestion from New York, after a discussion with Adlai and his associates about the two-Khrushchev-letters puzzle.)

The essence of the deal was that the Soviets would remove all their missiles under UN inspection if we promised not to invade Cuba. The noninvasion pledge was not hard for us; invasion hadn't really been on the U.S. agenda anyway since the Bay of Pigs. But UN inspection would require Cuban cooperation, and that turned out to be a nonstarter. With our help, Secretary General U Thant tried three different inspection formulas on Fidel Castro's government, to no avail.

So, in the end, the missiles were removed and the United States didn't invade Cuba—but a noninvasion promise was not formalized until the early 1970s when Richard Nixon was President, and the inspection was carried out not by the UN but by unannounced American photo reconnaissance, reinforced by an unannounced Soviet decision not to shoot down the high-flying U-2s. In an ironically fortunate twist, the Soviet SAMs (surface-to-air missiles) which could shoot that high were tightly controlled by the Soviets in Cuba; so we actually wanted the Soviet military there while the missiles were being removed.

The incoming Soviet vessels turned around to avoid challenging the quarantine. The "thirteen days" of the Cuba missile crisis were over. That's what history seems to record. But under cover of the U.S. Mission to the UN in New York, a long secret negotiation ensued between John J. McCloy and Vassily Kuznetsov on a range of U.S.- Soviet arms control and other issues. It was not a UN negotiation, but its venue meant the messages from McCloy were signed "Stevenson," the replies to McCloy (from the White House or wherever) were signed "Rusk"—and this two-way traffic consequently passed over my desk. Much of that story has yet to be exhumed.

But it's clear that the Cuba missile crisis led to a renewed arms race that ultimately impoverished the Soviet Union. Weakened also by its own incredible inefficiencies, plus the erosive impact of the Information Revolution, its empire collapsed a quarter of a century later.

From the perspective of Adlai and his many admirers, there was an unhappy postscript to the Cuba missile crisis. In December 1962, the *Saturday Evening Post* ran a story by Charles Bartlett and Stewart Alsop that accused Adlai Stevenson of advocating appeasement in the ExCom meetings. The metaphor used was a Caribbean "Munich." The article charged that Stevenson alone "dissented from the Executive Committee consensus" and was ready to trade Guantánamo and "the Turkish, Italian, and British bases for the Cuban bases." Nobody had tossed British bases into the equation. Stevenson had indeed discussed, in ExCom, the missile bases in Turkey and Italy but so had others; those bases had already been downgraded by the Pentagon as militarily dispensable. But, in the end, no one was advocating that their withdrawal, or a change in the status of Guantánamo, be associated with the Soviet missiles in Cuba.

The most damaging thing about the article was that Charles Bartlett was known to be such a close friend of President Kennedy that it was bound to look like an indirect White House attack on Stevenson. That conspiracy theory didn't make sense, Kennedy complained to Arthur Schlesinger: "Of course I don't want Stevenson to resign. I would regard his resignation as a disaster. . . . [F]rom a realistic political viewpoint, it is better for me to have Adlai in the government than out. [I]f I were trying to get him out, Charlie Bartlett is a good friend, but he's the last medium I would use."

Later testimony from Robert Kennedy and Stewart Alsop nevertheless confirms that in this case the Executive Branch was indeed a bottle that leaks from the top. "I think it came from a conversation between President Kennedy and Bartlett," Robert Kennedy is quoted in Porter McKeever's book as saying. "But the article was misinterpreted and out of context. What developed was not what was intended." Alsop added that the President did not inspire the article. "But it is true that Kennedy read the piece for accuracy and proposed a couple of minor changes."

Despite Kennedy's prediction that this would prove to be "a forty-eight-hour wonder," the story kept building. Schlesinger told Adlai what the President had said and got a quick reply: "That's fine, but will he say it publicly?" In New York, the *Daily News* ran a big headline: ADLAI ON SKIDS OVER PACIFIST STAND ON

CUBA. I spent a day in New York and reported both to Secretary Rusk and to Schlesinger and others in the White House that some kind of public presidential action was essential—to restore not only Adlai's morale but also his effectiveness in the UN.

Finally, President Kennedy sent Stevenson a public letter that didn't mention either the ExCom discussions or the leak in the Bartlett-Alsop article, but strongly reaffirmed his confidence in Ambassador Stevenson, declaring that his work at the UN was of "inestimable" national importance.

TRANSITION TO LBJ

The assassination of President Kennedy, in Dallas, Texas, in late November 1963, must have been a shock to Adlai Stevenson, but it did not come without warning.

Four weeks before, Adlai had been in Dallas for a United Nations Day meeting. This from *A Thousand Days*: "While Adlai spoke, there was hooting and heckling; placards and flags were waved, and noisemakers set off. When the police removed one of the agitators from the hall, Stevenson, with customary poise, said, 'For my part, I believe in the forgiveness of sin and the redemption of ignorance.' At the close, he walked through a jostling crowd of pickets to his car. A woman screamed at him, and he stopped for a moment to calm her down. The mob closed in on him. Another woman crashed a sign down on his head. A man spat at him. As the police broke through to him, Stevenson, wiping his face with a handkerchief, said coldly, 'Are these human beings, or are they animals?'"

As soon as he saw the report of this incident, Kennedy sent Adlai a message of sympathy. When Schlesinger delivered the message, Stevenson was pleased, then added, "But, you know, there was something very ugly and frightening about the atmosphere. Later I talked with some of the leading people out there. They wondered whether the President should go to Dallas, and so do I." Later, Stevenson didn't want his reservations expressed to the President. I discussed his experience with him when he returned to New York. He didn't feel he should be trying to tell Kennedy where he should and shouldn't go; the President obviously had more than enough professional advice about his personal security.

On Friday, November 22, 1963, the President of the United States was shot. Like most people on the Eastern seaboard at the time, Adlai learned about it at lunchtime. Hurrying back to his office he could only, like most of his fellow-citizens, sit in front of the television watching the reports from Dallas. But Adlai had something special to say: "That Dallas! Why, why, didn't I *insist* that he not go there?"

The new President was promptly sworn in. Lyndon B. Johnson was a very different person from John F. Kennedy, but his initial instinct about the transition was "Let us continue." He asked JFK's Presidential appointees to stay on, and set about to make happen what he judged Kennedy would have wanted to make happen.

With leaders coming from everywhere to mourn John F. Kennedy—and also take the measure of his successor—Adlai Stevenson was suddenly caught in a diplomatic maelstrom. At the big State Department reception where the new President could meet leaders of other countries, it was my job to squire Adlai Stevenson and Ralph Bunche.

Since both of them knew so many of the guests from five continents, I found that they were introducing lots more of them to me than I was introducing to them.

I didn't know Lyndon Johnson well, but I had occasionally consulted the Vice President on our congressional relations. When we thought we were in trouble on getting Senate approval of a UN bond issue to help fill in the peacekeeping deficit, he brought in his longtime Senate aide Bobby Baker and went through the whole list of 100 Senators, forecasting what each Senator would think of the proposition and why, and then suggesting what we might do in each case to get another vote for the UN bonds. I understood from that one session why he came to be called "Master of the Senate."

I was not sanguine about the new President's attitude toward Stevenson. While he was leader of the Senate, as biographer Doris Kearns later wrote, Johnson was scornful of "those intellectual liberals who supported Paul Butler and Adlai Stevenson. After all, their method of campaigning—with their search for big issues and big fights with the Republicans—was tried twice and it failed twice, producing the greatest defeat ever suffered by the Democratic Party." But here the context was international affairs, and the relationship might change.

Adlai's attitude, however, was upbeat. His initial reaction to the transition, expressed to me on several occasions, was that with Lyndon Johnson as President he, Adlai, could expect to be dealing with someone of his own generation, someone he understood and who understood him. "I've known Johnson for years; it'll be quite a different relationship." He expected his relationship with the White House to be more informal, and closer, than had been possible with the "younger generation" represented by the Kennedy White House.

From where I was sitting, I didn't see that happening. The rapport, in the end, was not nearly as good with Johnson as with Kennedy. McGeorge Bundy put it more bluntly: "After Johnson came in Stevenson was deceived. He thought he was going to be heard at last. He wasn't."

The UN General Assembly was still in session, and President Johnson agreed without hesitation to go to New York on December 17 and speak at the UN. When he flew to New York, he asked me to come along not only to help edit his speech but also to brief him on the many people from around the world that he would be meeting for the first time. He was naturally ill at ease in this new environment; if he needed my help he was reaching for help well beyond his normal circle of advisors—which, as President now, he obviously had to do.

In 1964, Adlai's life was a constant obligation to handle something at the UN. Every time he went away, even just for a long weekend, he would be brought back—for another eruption of the Greek-Turkish dispute about Cyprus, for an unanticipated Panama Canal crisis, for another crisis in the Congo or Kashmir. At the UN, a constitutional crisis was brewing about Article 19 of the Charter, which says any Member that is delinquent for more than two years in paying its assessments would lose its vote. In 1964, the Soviet Union and several of its Eastern European satellites were close to this Charter guillotine, and France was not far behind.

In persuading Congress to vote for the UN bond issue, we had said we would stand behind this Charter provision; "We shall be extremely stubborn about this," Adlai had told a Senate committee. The negotiation, especially with the Soviets, dragged on through the year, came to a head only in 1965, and wasn't resolved until after Adlai died.

Meanwhile, Lyndon Johnson was running for reelection, against Barry Goldwater, as it turned out. The President juggled possible

vice-presidential candidates, and Adlai briefly toyed with the possibility he might be tagged as a candidate. My guess was that he did-
n't take it seriously—which was just as well, since it was clearly not in
his horoscope. LBJ did want a northern liberal as his running mate,
but from his point of view, Senator Hubert Humphrey of Minnesota
was a more practical politician and a more dependably loyal choice.
In any case, Johnson decided—as a formula to rule out Robert
Kennedy, who was still Attorney General—that he didn't want a running mate who was a current Cabinet member. That ruled out Adlai
Stevenson as well.

In the spring of 1964, the not-yet-quite-a-war in Vietnam briefly
came to life in the UN. Adlai, brought back from London for the
occasion, provided the UN Security Council with the first full-dress
rationale for what would become a major U.S. war in Vietnam. The
United States had "no national military objective anywhere in
Southeast Asia," Ambassador Stevenson told the UN Security
Council. Moreover, the United States was involved "only because
the Republic of Vietnam requested the help of . . . other governments to defend itself against armed attack fomented, equipped, and
directed from the outside." There was no follow-up. The White
House and Secretary Rusk didn't want this to become a UN issue.

At the same time, Adlai was trying to think through a new foreign
policy—and, primarily with the help of Charles Yost who had been
Ambassador to Laos, he produced a long memo for the President. As
Porter McKeever summed it up in *Adlai Stevenson: His Life and
Legacy*, Adlai was "arguing for a basic shift in emphasis from Europe
to Asia—a concept that would not be fashionable until a quarter of
a century later." McKeever asked McGeorge Bundy whatever happened to Adlai's memo. Bundy replied "its fate was like all after the
election. . . . Everybody assumed that there was a mandate for
Johnson to do as he pleased."

UN ISSUES, 1964–65

The task of selecting those parts of Adlai's UN experience to highlight in this essay reminds me of a comment he sometimes made
when he spoke in public about the world organization. "Talking
about the United Nations," he would say, "is a little like being the

fan in relation to the fan dancer. You can't possibly cover the subject; all you can do is call attention to it."

Working at the UN on a dozen different issues at the same time, consulting constantly with colleagues from other countries, spending lots of time each week explaining the United Nations to as many audiences as he could fit in—all this was taking its toll not only on Adlai's body but also on his spirit.

Ambassador Stevenson had more than his share of unwarranted optimism, one of the key ingredients in the mix of talent and training that we call leadership. His irrepressible sense of humor certainly helped him carry the unusual burdens and contain the unusual excitements of his unique job. But his biographer Porter McKeever noticed a crack with a pessimistic twist that Adlai used with increasing frequency in the final months of his life: "Man is a strange animal. He doesn't like to read the handwriting on the wall until his back is up against it."

Two issues arose during Adlai's last year at the UN, which left him with a growing sense of futility. In both cases, his own hand was less than artfully played. But he projected his resentment onto the actions of others, particularly Secretary Rusk and President Johnson.

Vietnam

One of the most tangled webs in our UN policy during 1964–65 came from the Secretary-General's effort to get the United States and North Vietnam talking directly with each other. It started with a U Thant visit to Washington in August 1964, where he floated the idea of direct bilateral talks and apparently thought he had been encouraged to see what he could arrange. He took soundings through his Russian undersecretary, and got back a favorable response from Hanoi.

At first, the idea was held in abeyance until after the U.S. election, but during the winter, Adlai's conversations with U Thant started up again. In January 1965, though he had no instructions to go ahead, Adlai asked where the talks with the North Vietnamese might be held. U Thant suggested Rangoon and later reported that the Burmese had agreed—as long as they would not be directly involved.

Sometime in early February Adlai reported his conversations to Secretary Rusk, who (in McKeever's reconstruction of this imbroglio) "made it clear that the bilateral meeting [between the United States and North Vietnam] had never been seriously considered because the United States could not possibly meet secretly behind the back of our ally." Thereafter, Adlai sent a memo of his conversation with U Thant, followed up with a personal letter, directly to the President (via Bill Moyers), with a copy to Rusk.

During all this time, Adlai didn't tell either Plimpton or Yost, his two closest associates at the U.S. Mission in New York, what he was discussing with U Thant or what he was trying to accomplish. I was equally in the dark; neither Rusk nor Stevenson apparently thought the bureau responsible for UN affairs had a "need to know" about discussions with the UN's Secretary-General. This lapse led to a hugely embarrassing incident.

Adlai went to Jamaica on February 19 for some vacation time. He certainly needed a vacation; he was working hard, playing hard, gaining weight, and neglecting the medications his doctor insisted he should be taking. While he was away, Plimpton and Yost were talking one day with U Thant on some other UN business when the Secretary General suddenly asked them why he had never heard back from the United States about his proposal for face-to-face bilateral peace talks with the North Vietnamese. The two senior U.S. ambassadors were astonished by the question, looked quizzically at each other, and then said they knew nothing about it but they would check into it right away.

Two conversations quickly followed, which would have seemed funny if the subject hadn't been so serious. First, Charlie Yost phoned me in high dudgeon—"How can we do our job if you don't tell us anything?"—then cooled off when I told him I had also been told nothing. Secretary Rusk was away, so I charged up to George Ball's office—he was acting Secretary of State that day—and asked him, in a similar tone of injured indignation, the same question Yost had asked me a few moments before. Ball was as surprised as I had been; he had not known about the conversations with U Thant either.

I promptly got on the phone to Jamaica and asked Adlai what was going on. He rehearsed for me the whole story—over an open telephone line, so the story was no longer secret if, as seems probable, anybody else was listening in. I wrote it all up, of course, but by that time, a heavy fallout of mutual misunderstandings was foreordained.

At a press conference a few days later, U Thant charged that Washington was withholding from American citizens the possibility of peace talks. "I am sure," said this normally quiet Burmese Buddhist, "that the great American people, if only they knew the true facts and background to the developments in South Vietnam, will agree with me that further bloodshed is unnecessary. The political and diplomatic method of discussions and negotiations alone can create conditions which will enable the United States to withdraw gracefully from that part of the world. As you know, in times of war and of hostilities, the first casualty is truth."

Rusk found that comment offensive. So the Secretary of State took the unusual action of phoning U Thant personally. Rusk asked me to listen in on another phone, so there would be a record of the call. The Secretary-General thought he had made a "peace proposal," but Rusk gave that short shrift, characterizing it as "just procedural."

What had gotten under Rusk's skin, probably because it had also annoyed the President, was U Thant's charge that the truth was being withheld from the American people. Rusk asked U Thant to correct that impression, but U Thant simply repeated his belief that most Americans did not know the true facts about Vietnam. At one point in the argument Dean Rusk, whom I had always known as exceptionally mild-mannered, asked U Thant in exasperation, "Who do you think you are, a *country?*"

In his press conference, U Thant had mentioned Burma as the venue for the proposed bilateral (U.S.–North Vietnam) talks, saying that Burma wasn't getting any military assistance and was therefore "nonaligned." So Rusk said to him, do you really not know that we are giving military aid to Burma? Apparently, U Thant did not know this; Yost was promptly instructed to tell him all about it.

The conversation got nowhere fast, except to heat up the already overheated relations between the United States and the UN. Shortly afterward, the reason we did not take seriously the idea of bilateral face-to-face discussions with Hanoi was for the first time put on paper (in an instruction to Yost that he was to convey to the Secretary-General): The United States had no indication through any channel that either Hanoi or Peking [Beijing] is interested in discussing a peaceful settlement in Vietnam on a realistic basis.

The White House fed the misunderstanding further. Asked to comment on U Thant's accusation, George Reedy, the President's press secretary, may have asked the President what to say; the trouble was that he didn't consult the people who were following UN affairs—that is, my bureau in the State Department. Therefore, Reedy told the world that the President had never seen a peace proposal from the Secretary-General. What he meant was that there was no *substantive* peace plan—that, as Rusk told U Thant, it was "just procedural."

Adlai found increasingly distasteful his need to mollify U Thant in New York and defend him in Washington. At one point President Johnson, in a speech at Johns Hopkins University, responded favorably to a call from seventeen uncommitted nations for "unconditional discussions" with North Vietnam—and added a proposal some of us had been pushing, for a billion-dollar Southeast Asia development program in which North Vietnam could participate.

U Thant, even though the United States had been criticizing him publicly, hailed Johnson's speech as "positive" and "forward-looking." But there soon turned out to be a catch—the discussions could only be among governments, and Hanoi would not agree to talks without the Vietcong, which was not officially part of the North Vietnamese government but was doing much of the most effective fighting.

At one meeting with Johnson and Rusk, about how to respond to a Vietnam cease-fire proposal from U Thant, I was witness to what amounted to an open break between Adlai Stevenson and Secretary Rusk. Adlai gave the President a memo criticizing Rusk's position on Vietnam: "I think the conditions that Sec. Rusk has attached to any talk about peaceful settlement is [sic] unrealistic and unsupported by the illustrations he uses."

Years later, reflecting on this whole brouhaha, I summed it up this way: "The basic problem (I think) was that Stevenson did not like the answer he got from Secretary Rusk, hoped it would be moderated in time, and therefore did not pass it along to U Thant in a timely manner. This produced a growing resentment in U Thant, which finally boiled over in his February 24 press conference."

The net result was to confuse the American people, sour the relations between the United States and the UN Secretariat, and further deepen Adlai's discouragement about his inability to play an influential role in the foreign policy of the Johnson Administration.

Dominican Republic

Adlai was in the White House only by coincidence—at a meeting with President Johnson and others on how to respond to the Vietnam cease-fire proposal—when an urgent message arrived from Tapley Bennett, the U.S. Ambassador to the Dominican Republic. A rebellion led by Juan Bosch—some in the U.S. government thought his victory could lead to a Communist victory—was creating anarchy and endangering American lives. The Ambassador asked the President to send in the U.S. Marines. President Johnson did so immediately, announcing his action on television and radio that night. He was not about to have a Latin American country go Communist on his watch.

To my later surprise, Adlai did not object at the time to this uni-lateral invasion with 23,000 Marines. As soon as I learned about the decision, I discussed it with Ellsworth Bunker, the U.S. Ambassador to the OAS (the Organization of American States, established by the Rio Treaty). Bunker and I concluded right away that we should use "the Lebanon ploy": When President Eisenhower sent the Marines into Lebanon in the 1950s, their mission was described as peace-keeping, and there was a simultaneous call to the UN to authorize and organize a peacekeeping force—which it did with some delay.

In other words, the *framework* wasn't unilateral: the United States acted fast but was just holding the fort for the UN. That oper-ation goes down in history as multilateral—like the earlier Korean War, unlike the later war in Vietnam.

I have a vivid memory of an argument that week, about this "Lebanon ploy," with Dean Rusk and George Ball. At the beginning of our discussion, Rusk told us that this was a rescue mission, and therefore there was no need to consult others. My response, and Bunker's too, was that it may look like a rescue mission tonight, but by tomorrow, it will turn out to be a peacekeeping mission, which should have been internationalized from the start. So, we asked, "Couldn't we plan at least 24 hours ahead?"

Later the Secretary accepted this analysis and must have sold it to the President. The following weekend, Johnson was speaking to a business group in downtown Washington, and he described our mis-sion in the Dominican Republic as holding the line for an interna-tional peacekeeping force—using (to my surprise) some of the language from the memo in which I had argued that we should begin that way. But this after-the-fact rationale didn't help us much in the UN Security Council debate that was already in progress.

Adlai was caught in a bind. He had to face a Cuban protest in the UN Security Council. Then the Soviet Union asked for an urgent Security Council meeting to consider "the armed interference by the United States in the internal affairs of the Dominican Republic." In the Security Council, the Cuban and Soviet charges were so violent that their demand for an immediate U.S. withdrawal was defeated without our having to use the U.S. veto.

In the end, we signed onto a resolution expressing concern "at the grave events in the Dominican Republic," calling for a cease-fire, and asking the Secretary-General to send a representative to observe and report on the "present situation." Adlai had to address this subject in the Security Council on fourteen different days in less than a month.

"Nothing has caused me as much trouble since the Bay of Pigs and it goes on and on," he wrote to Arthur Schlesinger at the time. Later he added, "if we did so badly in the Dominican Republic, I now wonder about our policy in Vietnam." But Adlai was there as the unilateral invasion was being decided. If it should have been done otherwise, someone should have said so, in real time.

"THE SEEDBED OF WORLD DISORDER"

"I'm getting so sick of this place & this job and 'public life.' I don't like watersheds; I've had too many in life and now I'm on another one—blinded by the sunset and groping for the path down." Adlai wrote this note during a late night meeting of the Security Council, and added it to a letter to Marietta Tree in August 1964. By then he was determined to move to some other kind of activity. The only problem, a big one, was how to grope for the path down.

The day after his Inauguration in January 1965, President Johnson had asked Adlai to come see him, heaped praises on him for his "brilliant" job at the UN, and asked him to stay at the UN for the next four years. While expressing appreciation, Adlai told Johnson that he would really like to resign after the next General Assembly, which would have meant the end of 1965.

After the UN, what would Adlai do? All sorts of opportunities were opening up. He already had a tentative arrangement with a law firm, and proposals had also come from Columbia University and New York University, for appointments that would be compatible with the part-time practice of law. But nothing had been tied down by the time he flew to Geneva after the Fourth of July 1965 to speak at the UN's annual meeting of the Economic and Social Council (ECOSOC).

Economics was not Adlai's favorite field of study, so the ECOSOC session was often handled by Phil Klutznick or me. I had spent a dozen years, earlier in my life, in various kinds of foreign aid programs, including the Marshall Plan, so I always welcomed the chance to catch up on the field that had come to be called "development." Although Adlai didn't share this professional bias, he tackled with enthusiasm whatever subject required words of analysis or advocacy from him.

Moreover, the fight against poverty, which he called "the seedbed of world disorder," had become part and parcel of his political thinking. In our interdependent world, he had said, "there is no longer any line of demarcation between social problems and political problems." He was also deeply impressed that science and technology had created new chances to do something comprehensive yet practical about world poverty.

He arrived in Geneva overnight, short of sleep, exhausted, and facing a full schedule: a meeting with U Thant about Vietnam (and a phone call to Rusk about it), lunch with the Australian ambassador, editing his speech text (a task he always took very seriously), an Embassy reception in his honor, dinner with William Benton, a walk in the rain, and finally to bed at 11:30—facing a similar schedule the following day and evening. On the Friday, he was listening and talking in ECOSOC. A Stevenson speech was never ordinary, whatever its topic. This one showed clear signs of his editing, which sometimes favored long sentences for effect:

> Already science and technology are integrating our world into an open workshop where each new invention defines a new task, and reveals a shared interest, and invites yet another common venture. In our sprawling workshop of world community, nations are joined in cooperative endeavor: improving soils, purifying water, harnessing rivers, eradicating disease, feeding children, diffusing knowledge, spreading technology, surveying resources, lending capital, probing the seas, forecasting the weather, setting standards, developing law, and working away at a near infinitude of down-to-earth tasks—tasks

for which science has given us the knowledge, and technology has given us the tools, and common sense has given us the wit to perceive that common interest impels us to common enterprise. Common enterprise is the pulse of the world community—the heartbeat of a working peace.

The closing passage was pure Adlai: "Just as Europe could never again be the old, closed-in community after the voyages of Columbus, we can never again be the squabbling band of nations before the awful majesty of outer space."

THE END—AND A CONTROVERSY

He was leaving next morning for London, so we had a quiet supper together, talking about an enormous range of subjects. The war in Vietnam was inevitably one of them.

Paradoxically, Adlai's unhappiness about the way the Vietnam War was escalating was constrained by his reluctance to do what many of his liberal friends wanted: resign in a huff, coalesce the growing antiwar sentiment, and lead a "public crusade" against the Johnson Administration and the war. A similar ambivalence seemed to have held him back from pressing within the government his skepticism about the bombing of North Vietnam in retaliation for attacks on U.S. ships in the Gulf of Tonkin. This was authorized by the famous Congressional resolution named for that gulf but would have been hard to justify under international law.

The rapid drift toward major war in Vietnam saddened rather than activated Adlai. He was, moreover, repeatedly miffed by not being cut in more on the making of foreign policy. In one later oral history, I described Adlai as "a proud man who if not asked his opinions did not go out of the way to offer them to men who did not go out of their way to seek his views."

During our Friday evening discussion in Geneva—the last time I was with him—Adlai didn't mention his draft letter to peace advocate Paul Goodman, of the group called Artists and Writers Dissent. My strong impression from what he said to me that evening and on other occasions was that he did intend to resign but not until the end of the year and not as a protest.

Adlai had met with the Artists and Writers on June 1 and listened to their plea that he resign—and thus assume leadership of the peace movement. His thoughtful letter of reply was still a draft when he died; he had left copies with friends, asking them for their comments. His son Adlai III later released the letter (which he had received from Phil Kaiser, Minister at the U.S. Embassy in London), making clear that it was a draft-in-progress.

The draft letter was evidently an effort to respond seriously to Goodman and his colleagues, providing a rationale for his not resigning just then (even though, as they presumably didn't know, he was already planning to quit at the end of the year) that could appeal to the intellectual community. It declared the "purpose and direction" of American foreign policy to be "sound. Our overriding purpose must be to avoid war."

He was arguing, as his friend and biographer McKeever puts it, for two parallel lines of policy: to stop the extension of Communist power and influence and to build an international system that would "turn our small vulnerable planet into a genuine economic and social community." One paragraph gives the flavor:

> My hope in Vietnam is that relatively small-scale resistance now may establish the fact that changes in Asia are not to be precipitated by outside force. This was the point in the Korean war. This is the point of conflict in Vietnam. . . . I believe we must seek a negotiated peace in Vietnam based upon the internationalization of the whole area's security, on a big effort to develop, under the UN, the resources of the Mekong River and guarantees that Vietnam, North and South, can choose, again under international supervision, the kinds of governments, the form of association and, if so decreed, the type of unification of the two states they genuinely want to establish.

The effort to squeeze all these policy elements into one paragraph can't have been easy for the writer; they would have been even harder for the doers to make happen in the real world. But that's why this paragraph is a useful snapshot of Adlai's thinking just before he was yanked off the policy stage by a massive heart attack in London's Grosvenor Square on July 14, 1965.

Eric Sevareid, a well-known CBS correspondent, was with Adlai in London the evening of July 12. Just after Adlai's death he reported as broadcast news his judgment that the Ambassador was about to resign; another "name" correspondent, David Schoenbrun, said so too. Months later, in a long November article in *Look* maga-zine, Sevareid made clear that Adlai's resignation would not have been a protest. "Governor Stevenson died of exhaustion; he just wore himself out. I don't know how else to put it. Of course, the gathering frustration was part of this, but he did not die of a broken heart. If others regarded him as a 'tragic' figure, I don't think he thought of himself that way . . . "

In the perspective of history, I would venture a more nuanced way of thinking about Adlai and the Vietnam War. In the early sum-mer of 1965, U.S. involvement in Vietnam was still justified by the notion that we were advising the South Vietnamese government, not prosecuting an American war. The next huge step in escalation, sending 100,000 U.S. combat troops to Vietnam, was announced by ironic coincidence the same week that Adlai's funeral was held. Within two years, nearly half a million Americans would be deployed in a war that came to be seen in the United States as much more American than it was Vietnamese.

If Adlai had lived to resign at the end of 1965, he could hardly have reconciled the war with his own arguments about "relatively small-scale resistance" and avoiding war as our "overriding pur-pose." So he would probably have entered the antiwar fray in American politics—drafted once again, nearly always his preferred path to political leadership. His international standing and storied eloquence might even have led him to challenge President Johnson directly, as Senator Eugene McCarthy of Minnesota successfully did in the New Hampshire Democratic primary of 1968. What years of political drama we may have missed when Adlai Stevenson died at what would now be regarded as the early age of 65!

For me, historian Henry Steele Commager best summed up the whole Adlai phenomenon in an eloquent article written for the *London Observer* after he died: "Adlai Stevenson presents us with a spectacle rare in American, and probably in modern, history—a man whose public career was crowded into a few short years, whose every foray into large politics was marked by defeat, and who exercised immense authority wholly without power, an authority whose sanc-tions were entirely intellectual and moral. . . . [He] managed, by sheer force of intelligence and moral distinction, to lift the whole level of public life and discourse, and to infuse American politics with a dignity, a vitality, an excitement it had not known since the early days of the New Deal."

AUTHOR'S NOTE

This is more a personal memoir than a work of scholarship. I therefore have not intruded footnotes into the narrative. For background on the presidential year of John F. Kennedy, other than what I observed myself, I have found much nourishment in Arthur Schlesinger Jr.'s *A Thousand Days: John F. Kennedy in the White House* (New York: Houghton Mifflin, 1965, reprinted 2002). For background on the later period of Adlai Stevenson's service in the presidency of Lyndon B. Johnson, I have used a good many insights and quotes from Porter McKeever's *Adlai Stevenson: His Life and Legacy* (New York: William Morrow, 1989).

CHAPTER 9

THOUGHTS OF STEVENSON'S
UN DEPUTY CHARLES YOST

*Felicity O. Yost**

Charles W. Yost had a long global career in the U.S. Foreign Service
and key positions with the State Department beginning in 1930 in
Alexandria, Egypt. From 1961 to 66, he served as Ambassador Adlai
Stevenson's diplomatic deputy at the UN. From 1971, when he left
his post as U.S. Permanent Representative to the UN, to the time of
his death in 1981, he continued to be active in matters of foreign policy as President of the National Committee on U.S.-China Relations,
a Senior Fellow at the Brookings Institution, Senior Fellow at the
Council on Foreign Relations, President Johnson's envoy to the
Middle East, 1967, Special Advisor to the Aspen Institute, a member
of the Woodcock delegation to Vietnam, and Co-Chairman of
Americans for SALT. His wife, daughter, and two sons traveled and
resided with him during his various government assignments. His
books include: *The Conduct and Misconduct of Foreign Affairs*
(Random House, New York, 1972) and *History & Memory* (W. W.
Norton, New York, 1980).

   Ambassador Yost's daughter, Felicity O. Yost, has served in the
UN Secretariat's Office of Public Information since 1973, during
which she was a UN electoral observer in Namibia (1989), Haiti
(1990), Angola (1992), El Salvador (1994), and Mozambique (1994).
Ms. Yost was co-author of a United Nations Study Group Report,

* Charles W. Yost's daughter, a long-time member of the UN Secretariat.

Suggestions for Personnel Reform, sponsored by the Carnegie Endowment for International Peace, and illustrator and designer of the first United Nations children's book, *Marie in the Shadow of the Lion.* She is currently writing a biography of her parents, Charles and Irena Yost.

⊷⊷☰◎☰⊷⊷

"It was of Eleanor [Roosevelt] that Adlai Stevenson said: 'she would rather light a candle than curse the darkness.' They were a pair. One can no more write a thumbnail sketch of either of them than one can describe a smile or the touch of a hand. No one is perfect, but they came closer, without trying, to 'loving thy neighbor as thyself' than most people do, trying hard. Have you seen that photo of their profiles together, serene, simple, and human? They were both great and very simple—a rare, refreshing combination. . . . I think I am better for having worked with Adlai for four years. At least I should be."[1]

So wrote my father, Charles Yost, about Adlai Stevenson whom he first met at the San Francisco Conference when my father served as Secretary of State Edward Stettinius' assistant. At the time a rising young star, Stevenson, was also serving as an assistant to Archibald MacLeish, an Assistant Secretary of State.

Having already attended the Dumbarton Oaks Conference, my father's involvement and dedication to the ideals of the United Nations developed, as they did for Stevenson, at its birth. In 1946, their paths crossed again at the first UN General Assembly at Lake Success, while three years later my father also attended the Fourth Regular Session of the General Assembly in the company of Eleanor Roosevelt. Finally, in the 1960s, they would be reunited at the UN. Before that was to occur, however, my father fulfilled various assignments abroad, as Foreign Service Officer, where he continued to encounter Stevenson who would show up on various fact-finding missions.

In the twenty-first century, I feel my father and Stevenson would remember those who had joined them in San Francisco. They were determined to create a forum where governments could whisper before they shouted, a world where "nations shall not lift up sword against nation, neither shall they learn war anymore." Although it is true that the founders may have been naive about its potential, its critics have been blind to its accomplishments. Though well aware of its imperfections, my father and Stevenson were firm believers and

U.S. Ambassador to the UN Charles W. Yost (cen.) attends discussion between U.S.
Permanent Representative Adlai Stevenson (l.) and French Representative Armand
Barard (r.) on Chinese Representation, December 1, 1961
Source: UN photo, by M. B.

indefatigable champions of the United Nations. My father likened
the UN to a hearing aid. It amplified the world's problems and
allowed the United States and others to hear them. It was also, he
and Stevenson often emphasized, the only such forum available to
work with and thus what kind of forum it evolved into, or did not,
was our responsibility.

The end of 1960 found the Yost family in Morocco where my
father was serving as U.S. Ambassador. Despite the time difference,
in November of 1960, we had gathered in our living room in North
Africa and listened to the returns and heard that John Kennedy had
become our new President. Little did we know at the time that only
two months later, while on home leave, the new UN Ambassador,
Adlai Stevenson, would ask my father to be his deputy at the U.S.
Mission to the United Nations. Their relationship would now come
full circle to be solidified into a dynamic working team and deep
friendship.

When one assumes the position of U.S. Ambassador to the UN
one joins a community of diplomats representing, and defending,

the interests of their own countries but also representing far more. Each ambassador to the United Nations is the voice of all nations, where children are orphaned by AIDS, women are raped for their ethnicity, warring parties are seeking an intermediary, fishermen are faced with depleted oceans, and people are seeking redress for crimes against humanity.

My father and Stevenson often despaired that Americans did not realize that, for most parts of the world, the UN *does* work. Nations despair when the UN pulls out its peacekeepers or is unable to provide them in the first place. Americans do not see the UN on their doorsteps building roads, conducting elections, or setting up roadblocks between warring communities. In their ongoing efforts to change these perceptions, Stevenson and my father regularly participated in "Model UNs" and gave speeches across the country that explained the importance of the UN for all of us.

My father had always maintained that despite their different styles, which would most assuredly have clashed and perhaps cut short the relationship, Kennedy made a mistake in not naming Stevenson his Secretary of State. He felt that some of the early mistakes of the new administration could have been avoided. If Stevenson had been in that position "and had been listened to," he felt sure that the Bay of Pigs debacle would not have occurred.

My father also felt that with Stevenson as Secretary of State, the President might have been encouraged to withdraw the U.S. missiles from Turkey after the Soviet withdrawal from Cuba. By thus helping the Soviets to "save face," the Russians might not have felt the need to embark on their subsequent massive military buildup. Part of the problem for the new administration, as Stevenson and my father perceived it, was that Dean Rusk was too much of a Cold Warrior to serve the new President and seize the opportunities of the new era. Once he accepted, however, Stevenson enthusiastically plunged into his new assignment.

Those were heady days at the UN when Dag Hammarskjöld served as Secretary-General and Ralph Bunche and Brian Urquhart set the bar for the definition of "international civil servant." The White House, with Harlan Cleveland of the State Department and occasionally historian Arthur Schlesinger as its liaison with the U.S. Mission, set another bar and tone for how the United States was to involve itself in the UN. At the U.S. Mission, Stevenson had assembled a team of top professionals in various fields to deal with the myriad of issues that would soon explode onto the world stage.

The variety, intensity, and length of the workdays at the UN were unmatched. Stevenson's job, as U.S. Ambassador to the UN, was thus far more complex than any other posting in the foreign affairs field. During the General Assembly, the pace, which is normally hectic, becomes even more grueling as the delegations meet in Plenary session as well as on seven principal committees and numerous other groups.

In the 1960s, Adlai Stevenson's staff worked with over seventy countries while also representing the United States before the UN Secretariat and before the various UN agencies, the Security Council, ECOSOC (the Economic and Social Council), the Trusteeship Council, as well as negotiating with the Secretary-General. In between meetings, Stevenson and his staff had to make appearances in the lounges and corridors, as well as the nightly round of cocktail and dinner parties.

Many of these informal contacts, which took place in the hallways or at receptions, would offer insight into how a country might vote or what changes might be occurring on the ground in a particular country. Negotiations were often launched and differences worked out on these occasions and certainly Ambassador Stevenson was a welcome, and useful, master at "working" the corridors of the UN.

An added mix was thrown in when members of Congress came to New York, during the General Assembly, to represent the United States on various committees. Many of them, who had been fierce opponents of the UN, came away with a newfound respect and understanding for the volume of work that is tackled as well as of the benefits of daily contacts with so many countries.

Our move to New York was something of a financial shock for my parents. There were doubts, with three children in school and life in an expensive city, that my father could afford it. Stevenson had come to depend on my father and was determined that the question of money would not split them up. Springing into action, Stevenson got his old friend Bill Benton to contribute funds while also approaching other friends and financial backers:

> The man I spoke to you about is Ambassador Charles W. Yost . . . a lifetime Foreign Service officer, whom I enlisted to help me. . . . Yost is one of those really able, indeed brilliant, Foreign Service officers of whom we have too few. . . . Unfortunately, he is without means except what he earns, and after a life mostly abroad, finds New York together with the entertaining almost beyond his limited insurance.

I am genuinely fearful that after another year he may feel obliged to
ask for another Embassy abroad . . . [2]

The following year my father was able to repay Stevenson for his support when President Kennedy offered my father the post of Ambassador to Yugoslavia. Stevenson was eager for my father to remain in New York as his deputy and so, to the great annoyance of the President, my father agreed to stay on at the UN.

The 1960s were often tense times at the UN as one crisis followed another and as decolonization saw the UN grow from a small fraternity to a large organization. The Congo, the Middle East, South Africa, the India-Pakistan war, and Cyprus were among the flare-ups that meant Stevenson and his staff maintained a frantic pace, putting in long days. Security Council meetings often went on till all hours of the night and into the early hours of the following day—and the day did not end there.

Telegrams to the White House and to Harlan Cleveland, Assistant Secretary of State for International Organization Affairs at the State Department, would then have to be drafted so that a response on our negotiating position could be agreed upon and be received back by the Mission before the meetings were resumed the following day. While some joked or criticized Stevenson for being so often in the news in those days, he was key in making the United Nations newsworthy and the place to be for all the major newspapers. His staff knew what a tremendous asset he was and, though sadly things changed at the end, in the early days they had to urge him into socializing more.

In dealing with the many crises of the 1960s, the issue of a permanent UN military force often arose. My father, for whom this matter had always been of paramount importance, worked with Stevenson in their attempts to show how this idea could and must work. In writing about some of the UN's peacekeeping "failures" my father commented, "the fault lay not with the UN or the Secretary General but with the weakness of the *ad hoc* peacekeeping procedures which had been improvised when the great powers were unable to agree on the implementation of Article 43 [whereby members 'undertake to make available to the Security Council, on its call . . . armed forces, assistance and facilities' to deal with threats]."[3]

This issue, which continues to be debated in the twenty-first century, is one that involves the willingness of the nations involved to allow the Blue Helmets to cross their borders while also agreeing to allow the peacekeepers to remain until their mission is accomplished. My father believed that only by assuming this responsibility and having a well-trained, mobile force could the Security Council effectively implement its peacekeeping mandate and help serve as the "world's gendarme." Furthermore, as was proved in the Congo during the Stevenson years, it just made better sense. If the UN was allowed to extinguish a fire when it was small and localized, it could avoid having to deal with a major disaster down the road.

Much new information has come to light, concerning the history of the Cuba missile crisis, since the recent declassification of American and Soviet documents. In reviewing Stevenson's role, the historical record reveals that he participated and helped determine U.S. policy far more than was admitted at the time. From the outset, the perception by the White House was that Stevenson would not be "tough" enough, and so John McCloy was dispatched to assist in negotiations. My father, who attended the Security Council meetings and a majority of the meetings among McCloy, Stevenson, the Secretary-General and Soviet First Deputy Premier Vassily Kuznetsov commented, "actually the curious thing was that McCloy was a good deal softer in the conversations than Stevenson."

Time and again Stevenson would have to defend himself when news leaks painted negative pictures of his part in negotiations at the UN or would reveal details of ongoing talks. Time and again he would convey to the President, "We are at the point here [the U.S. Mission to the UN] where no one sees anything but Yost and me" and neither of *them* was leaking information. For the second, or third time, that month Stevenson would threaten to resign before being, again, talked out of it. This was a matter of mirth for many but in retrospect is more of a reflection on those who sought to belittle or denigrate him. Stevenson was after all trying to do the best job he could for an organization that he profoundly believed in.

Of great concern to all those who were there at the UN's founding, as well as to the current keepers of the flame, is the UN's ongoing health and survival. Adlai Stevenson and my father were among those who gave a good deal of thought to the issue of reforms and of how they might be implemented. The initial problem that they perceived was the failure on the part of the member states to carry out their obligations laid out in the UN Charter. The commitment must be, my father wrote, "an act of will on the part of its strongest members" to use the UN as it was intended. The member states need to enforce the Charter so that the UN is allowed to undertake and fulfill its mandate on the issues "affecting the peace of the world."

In analyzing the "central problem" of the United Nations, which is "maintaining international peace and security," Stevenson and my father considered the Security Council and the ongoing issues of its membership as well as the veto that was often used in those years. My father saw the veto, for obvious reasons, as "both the strength and weakness of the Council." Perhaps, my father wrote, nations could agree to use the veto sparingly but in the end it is only if member states are willing to work together that such will determine the outcome of an "enforcement action" and not the use, or lack of use, of the veto.

Membership on the Security Council has been an issue for years with various nations knocking at the door of what they perceive as a private club founded in another era. With an increased membership and thus increased exercise of the veto, any attempt to take swift action might be seriously compromised my father opined though the "act of will" by the strongest nations could help circumvent this. Further reforms that were discussed had to do with increased use of the machinery already in place. In the economic field, for example, the United Nations Development Program and the Economic and Social Council need to be given more authority, resources and be used more efficiently. ʼ

The issue of the financial health of the United Nations has been a perpetual problem and an ongoing issue for the U.S. Ambassador who must often go before the U.S. Congress begging them to allocate or restore much needed funds:

> Mankind's paramount instrument for survival, its only impartial and comprehensive institution for maintaining peace and security, runs a perennial financial deficit . . . so outrageously have governments . . . confused and ignored rational priorities. . . . There should be no further delay in taking the necessary measures to clean up the deficit, to ensure a steady income for approved administrative purposes, to set up a . . . 'peace-keeping fund' to be available in emergencies, and to increase substantially contributions to the principal UN agencies engaged in economic development.[4]

Since Stevenson and my father's time, the UN has been faced with scandals, some of which are of a financial nature. I would imagine that both of them would agree that while the UN is certainly in need of reform and housecleaning, it also must receive ongoing support, both moral and financial, during this period. One of the greatest concerns in our day is that the UN act honestly, justly, and efficiently. Having worked on Chapter VI and VII of the UN Charter, my father was well aware of ideals that had been conceived at the UN's inception that, when put into practice, did not work as intended or as desired. He and Stevenson realized that in order to keep the Organization current and vital there was always work to be done.

As to the Charter, like all such documents, it must at times be reviewed and, perhaps, amended. I would hazard a guess that both Stevenson and my father would also dedicate themselves to working against those who would simply revile the UN without offering any suggestions and those who would dismantle the UN without offering an alternative. Without the UN, they would both agree, there is no hope; there is no chance for peace.

This brings me to the perception, on the part of the public, about the UN. Far too often we hear of the UN's failures on the front pages of our newspapers. Why is the media so shy about trumpeting its success? Namibia, Mozambique, East Timor, and Iraq, to name a few, are part of the UN's roster of electoral monitoring successes. As Sir Brian Urquhart recently pointed out, "Who do people think ran the election in Iraq? Who do they think set up the polling stations and provided the ballot boxes?"

In discussing Adlai Stevenson's legacy one might consider what he could have accomplished had he been President or had he been Secretary of State. One also might contemplate how different the world might be had his advice been taken on various critical issues of the day. My father, for example, felt that Stevenson would have been bolder and more creative, in the late 1950s, in our attempts to confront the Cold War, while also more responsive "to the openings toward detente and to the more productive summit which Khrushchev seemed to offer."

The record is clear that Adlai Stevenson was often ahead of his times on such issues as the missiles in Turkey, the admission of mainland China to the UN, the Nuclear Test Ban Treaty, and Vietnam. It took years for many to catch up with him. Some felt that he was not bold enough in action. He was a bold and forward thinker who inspired many others to fulfill their potential. While he longed for higher office, the fact that he did not succeed in attaining it did not make him bitter nor diminish his dedication to whatever endeavor he moved on to. His mantra seems to have been perennial optimism, and I feel that in that spirit we all have a lesson to learn from Adlai Stevenson.

> For those who did not know Adlai Stevenson I would say:
> His words were often pure poetry and merit a second reading.
> His thoughts were often visionary and merit renewed consideration.
> His friendship was always precious and to be longed for.
> His sense of purpose was always simple and still inspires.

On the occasion of his last birthday, Adlai Stevenson wrote me a letter wherein he commented on gift-giving and offered me the essential Stevenson: "Loyalty and friendship are so much more precious and I am enriched by this."

NOTES

1. Charles W. Yost, *History & Memory* (New York: W. W. Norton, 1980), 241.
2. Walter Johnson, ed., *The Papers of Adlai Stevenson: Ambassador to the United Nations, Volume VIII, 1961–65* (New York: Little, Brown, and Company, 1979), 207–8.
3. Charles W. Yost, *The Conduct and Misconduct of Foreign Affairs* (New York: Random House, 1972), 185.
4. Ibid., 222–23.

CHAPTER 10

THE PRESIDENCY AND OUR ROLE IN
AND WITH THE UNITED NATIONS

William J. vanden Heuvel

William J. vanden Heuvel served as Deputy U.S. Permanent
Representative to the United Nations and as U.S. Ambassador to the
European Office of the UN in the 1970s. He was a supporter of Adlai
Stevenson for President in the 1950s and was supported by Stevenson
in his race for Congress in New York City in 1960. He is Co-Chair
of the Franklin and Eleanor Roosevelt Institute and of the Council
of American Ambassadors, Vice-Chair of the World Federation of
United Nations Associations and a member of the Council on
Foreign Relations. Ambassador vanden Heuvel is of counsel to the
law firm of Stroock & Stroock & Lavan in New York City, and Senior
Advisor to Allen and Company, a New York investment banking firm.
He has served as President of the International Rescue Committee,
Chairman of the Board of Governors of the United Nations
Association and Chairman of the New York City Board of
Correction. A graduate of Cornell University Law School, he was
Editor-in-Chief of the Law Review. He also served as Executive
Assistant to General William J. ("Wild Bill") Donovan, Special
Counsel to Governor Averell Harriman, and Assistant to Attorney
General Robert F. Kennedy.

   He is author (with Milton Gwirtzman) of *Robert F. Kennedy: On
His Own, 1963–68,* published by Doubleday, 1971, and also authored
The Triumph and Sorrow of Hungary, 1957 and numerous subsequent

articles on refugee matters; various articles on prisons, including *Attica: Analysis of a Crisis (1971)*, *Death of a Citizen*; and *How to Report Prisons*, Columbia Journalism Review; various commentaries on criminal justice, public law, and matters relating to the history and contemporary agenda of the United Nations; *America and the Holocaust*, American Heritage Magazine, July 1999; the Foreword to *The Future of Freedom in Russia*, the Templeton Foundation Press, 2000; and editor, along with historians Arthur Schlesinger Jr. and Douglas Brinkley, of the St. Martin's Press Series on *American Diplomatic and Political History* (now 22 volumes).

⋯⟐⟐⋯

I was a young man about to enter the military as the 1952 presidential election approached. Franklin and Eleanor Roosevelt and Harry Truman had defined the principles of the politics that I believed in. As the Republicans chose a national hero of immense popularity, General Dwight Eisenhower, to be their candidate, Democrats were generally discouraged, believing that no candidate could successfully oppose him. The Democratic Convention convened in Chicago. The delegates were welcomed by the Governor of Illinois. He gave an electrifying speech. In a few short minutes, he restored a sense of hope, gave purpose to our history, and seemed prepared to lead us to Armageddon.

In fact, Adlai Ewing Stevenson was a reluctant candidate. Many thought that America was ready for a respite from the dramatic leadership that had led us through the nation's worst economic depression to the triumph of World War II and into the leadership of a new world where, in a confrontation that defined the Cold War, we sent our armies to save the independence of South Korea and supported the Charter of the United Nations of which America had truly been the founder.

Governor Stevenson was nominated and gave an unforgettable acceptance address. It established him as the foremost orator of the nation. He used the power of words to reach out to new generations. His accomplishment was remarkable. He was never elected to the presidency, but he had greater influence and a more profound impact on the young citizens of our nation and on the Democratic Party than many in our history who have occupied the White House.

Just before joining the Air Force, I went to an American Legion convention in New York City where Adlai Stevenson spoke. He was not warmly received. The heart of the American Legion belonged to

General Eisenhower. But Governor Stevenson used the occasion to remind his audience of the meaning of American democracy, of the threat of McCarthyism, and the need for us to remain a united nation as we were obliged to accept the mantle of international leadership. To the astonishment of the reporters, he quoted Shakespeare: "Out of this nettle, danger, we pluck this flower, safety" (Henry IV, Part 1, Act 2, Scene III).

We did not expect him to win the election but we knew that he had saved the Democratic Party and had inspired millions of Americans and young people worldwide to aspire to public service and responsible participation in democracy.

On Election Day, 1952, I hitchhiked from Scott Air Force Base to Springfield, Illinois, where Governor Stevenson was receiving the election returns. I was a young Lieutenant in uniform, standing in the lobby of the hotel where the Governor had arrived for the evening's results. Humphrey Bogart and Lauren Bacall came through the lobby on their way to the election night event. Ms. Bacall, getting into the elevator, saw me and said: "Hi soldier—are you here for the Governor? Come with us—come with us." So I found myself on the elevator going to the election night party where Adlai Stevenson acknowledged his defeat and held all of us in thrall as he quoted Abraham Lincoln: "I am too old to cry, but it hurts too much to laugh." It was an occasion no one present would forget.

President Eisenhower asked his friend, General William J. ("Wild Bill") Donovan, the legendary hero of World War I and the founder and director of the Office of Strategic Services in World War II to be his Ambassador to Thailand with special responsibilities in Southeast Asia. General Donovan asked me to be his Executive Assistant, having been a young lawyer in his office before joining the Air Force. The French armies were still in Indochina. The Bandung Conference convened in Indonesia where the Third World found its voice. A truce was negotiated in Korea and the people of South Korea began the extraordinary period of building a democracy that has become a dynamic force in the world. It was an unforgettable opportunity to observe the beginning of the end of the colonial era and at the same time observe Vietnam and the origins of the struggle that wounded America so profoundly in the decade to come.

We returned to New York, and I became involved as a young lawyer in Democratic politics, coming to know Eleanor Roosevelt quite well and joining forces with the reform movement that she led in the Democratic Party. As candidate for Congress in the Silk Stocking District in the heart of Manhattan in 1960, it was my privilege to have Adlai Stevenson campaign with me on three different occasions. He pulled large, adulatory crowds. His appearances gave special attention to a difficult Congressional race. He loved New York and had many friends who were among my supporters, like Marietta Tree, Ruth Field, and Mary Lasker. It was in response to their interest that he was so generous in his support in a contest that held little prospect of victory. His telephone calls and personal notes made the whole effort worthwhile for me.

The New Frontier began. John F. Kennedy became President, and I was invited by Attorney General Robert F. Kennedy to be his special assistant. Adlai Stevenson was the U.S. Permanent Representative to the United Nations, an organization to which I even then was deeply committed. In 1962, we arranged to have lunch at the UN. It was before the missile crisis in Cuba gave Ambassador Stevenson the dramatic opportunity to galvanize world attention as he addressed the Security Council.

At our meeting, he expressed a sense of being "left out" of the major foreign affairs decisions that were being made in Washington. It was, he said, as though there had been a skipping of generations and the young tigers who controlled the White House looked at him as a senior statesman, a sage counselor, but not as a general of the New Frontier. He regretted that. After all, he was only 62, and he felt by experience and background he had much to give to a Democratic Administration confronting a tumultuous world. From my vantage point, he was immensely respected and his political power was not to be treated lightly, but the Kennedys never thought of him as part of the Inner Circle, in large part because in 1960, he resisted to the very end opportunities to support the nomination of John Kennedy, keeping alive the alternative of his own candidacy which the Kennedy politicians would neither understand nor forgive.

On the evening of November 22, 1963, a day that needs no further description, I was part of a small group, including Arthur Schlesinger Jr., John Kenneth Galbraith, and Adlai Stevenson, which came together at the home of Averell Harriman. As I recall it, Lyndon Johnson, the new President, called both Governor Stevenson and Averell Harriman during those hours and arranged to see them separately the next day at the White House.

Governor Stevenson talked with us at length about his recent trip to Dallas, just days before the President's assassination. He had been accosted by placard-bearers spewing messages of hate and violence against him and the government. He was so concerned about the President's safety that he talked to someone on the White House staff to tell of his own experiences and to caution regarding the abusive welcome that might be in store for the President. As I recall a later discussion of Adlai Stevenson's meeting with Lyndon Johnson, the new President said to him that the chair he was now occupying should truly have been Governor Stevenson's—but fate had decided otherwise and now the President needed him more than ever.

Adlai Stevenson was a remarkable Ambassador to the United Nations. He brought stature to the organization and an understanding of its history and its hopes. Although not an intimate of the Kennedys, he certainly had total access to them so that when he spoke to the Security Council or to other UN audiences, it was clearly understood that he spoke with the voice of the United States. He understood that part of the obligation of leadership is to give a vision of hope and confidence and courage. Having lived through the Great Depression and World War II, he had perspective regarding the threats to America and to the world that the Cold War represented. He understood that the founding of the United Nations was a singular act of political creativity, a significant and successful step in history's long journey to fulfill Mankind's quest for a just, compassionate, and peaceful world. Adlai Stevenson understood the limitations as well as the possibilities of the UN. For example, he knew that the UN is not a sovereign entity, but rather an association of sovereign member states. The United Nations is not a government. It is not an executive; it is not a legislature that can command the peoples of the world. It is not a court that can adjudicate and then enforce its decisions. It has no standing army, no air force; no, not even arsenals kept ready to support its missions. The United Nations is a mirror of a very imperfect world; it can only do what its 192 members permit it to do. The national interests of the United States can be advanced if our government has the will and skill to do so but because of our veto and our power, nothing significant can happen in the UN that adversely affects us. Ambassador Stevenson understood this reality.

In 1962, during our luncheon we talked about the world that might be if the Cold War had not intervened, forcing confrontation instead of coalition, thereby preventing the UN from playing an effective role in many international crises and making the institution itself a pawn in the East-West struggle. Many times in the intervening years, especially during those years when I myself was the American Ambassador to the United Nations both in Geneva and in New York, I asked myself about "the world that could be." As the Cold War ended, I asked what would the UN and the world be like if the American government, now the world's only superpower, truly wanted the United Nations to succeed? What would a President do who wanted the UN to be effective and successful? As every public opinion poll shows, there is a clear majority of Americans who want the UN to be successful and want the United States to be the leader in that effort. I have often wondered what an American government led by someone with the vision and pragmatic discipline of Adlai Stevenson would do today if our policy was to use the UN as an instrument of international governance in our quest for a better world. Here are some thoughts:

1. We would not begrudge the sum that we pay as our assessed obligation, recognizing that the $300 million annual obligation is probably the most cost-effective dollar that we spend in terms of American defense and foreign policy objectives. We would never stop reminding our countrymen that the UN is not a sovereign body, that it has no power or resources beyond what its members give to it, and that U.S. leadership is indispensable to the UN's success.

2. We would not degrade the character and quality of the international civil servants who serve the United Nations and its specialized agencies. Instead, we would recognize the high standard of their performance and do everything possible to motivate and encourage them to still greater achievements. And we would mourn with them the loss of the hundreds of brave men and women who have been killed in peacekeeping operations over the years.

3. We would acknowledge the extraordinary good fortune of having had a Secretary-General of the character, integrity, intelligence, and experience of Kofi Annan. We would welcome his successor, Ban Ki Moon, and support him in his leadership in furtherance of democratic objectives in the United Nations.

4. We would understand that the world has witnessed immense changes since the founding of the United Nations, that the UN

has been the midwife to many of those changes, such as the peaceful end of the colonial era, but that changes in structure and procedure which are never easy in national or in international organizations should be considered. For example, a crucial objective in the years ahead is a capacity to recognize and respond to the needs of nation-building.

A special Authority should be created for the purpose of nation-building so that the UN, with the assistance of the United States and other member states, could train and have available civil administrators, development experts, teachers, police, firemen, and security experts to assist nations disintegrating because of civil strife in negotiating and enforcing a social contract that would give them the possibility of peace and social justice.

5. We would recognize the difficulty in reforming the Security Council as witnessed by the discussions and proposals of the last decade. Instead of being discouraged by political roadblocks that are not easy to resolve, the United States could insist upon closer coordination and communication between the Security Council and the other member states. Close coordination and communication with all member states and regional groups should be the order of the day. In an age of instant communication, such a working procedure is clearly possible.

   Security Council proceedings should be open and televised whenever possible to allow a sense of public participation. Adlai Stevenson's statement to the Security Council when he admonished the Soviet Ambassador that we would wait "until hell freezes over" to hear the Soviet answer regarding the presence of their missiles in Cuba is not forgotten by anyone who saw it. Too much of the UN, like the Congress, is behind closed doors, and public apathy is a result.

6. We know that civilization needs a police force just as every one of our communities looks to its local police for security and protection against the lawless. If thugs control the streets, forget the hopes and dreams of civilized society. Adolf Hitler and his Nazi hoodlums brought the world to the precipice of destruction. The tinhorn dictators who challenge democratic values today when they carry out ethnic cleansing and assault innocent people, destroying their lives and their hopes, are in the same gangster tradition.

The United States does not want to be nor should it be the Policeman of the World. But for the United Nations to have the ability to enforce its moral authority, the United States must participate and lead. We should encourage the creation of forces that would be available to the Security Council to allow for timely peacekeeping and peacemaking interventions. It is not difficult to organize forces that would be available to the Security Council for specific purposes which its permanent members would have to approve. After the Suez crisis in 1956, both Secretary of State John Foster Dulles and the Congress stated their support for the principle of organizing a Rapid Deployment Force.

The armed forces of the United States could lend their extraordinary ability and experience to the creation and training of such a force as well as peacekeeping forces. We could invite young American men and women to volunteer for a special unit in our armed forces, which could be made available for peacekeeping or peacemaking missions. We would show the world how the idealism and courage of our young men and women can serve the purposes of peace and social justice as well as war.

7. Understanding the crucial role of the United Nations in the fight against AIDS and other threatening plagues and epidemics, we would constantly remind Americans that the World Health Organization, one of the specialized agencies of the United Nations, is a major force in protecting our country. We would be proud of the extraordinary achievements of WHO, which we have helped bring about, such as the elimination of smallpox and the near eradication of polio—and we would tell Americans that the World Health Organization is indispensable to the international cooperation necessary to fight the plagues and diseases that threaten the world and leave no nation immune.

8. We would use the United Nations as a forum to stand up to tyrants and to lead the world in recognition of the Rule of Law. There is no greater benefit to the national interest of the United States than to have a world that recognizes the Rule of Law. It should be our special mission to encourage the United Nations by every means possible to fulfill this objective. The progress that has been made in the creation of international law in the past sixty years because of the UN is stunning. The United States

has helped make that progress possible. We should be leaders in extending the concept of the Rule of Law.

We should welcome the International Court for Criminal Justice, for example, and if for whatever reason we could not promise ratification of the treaty that has created it, we certainly should not stand in the way of other nations carrying out its mandate. We would use the United Nations and instruments like the ICCJ to make it clear to tyrants that international legitimacy requires the consent of the governed and that all rational means will be used to end their oppression.

We would take pride in Eleanor Roosevelt's role in the creation of the Universal Declaration of Human Rights. Recognizing the limitations of the UN Human Rights Commission, we would work to make it more effective, inviting the nations of the world to join with us in making human rights a priority consideration on the international agenda. We would recognize the unique possibilities of the UN in mediation, arbitration, and conflict resolution and would move to strengthen those procedures in every possible way.

9. We would recognize the indispensable role of the United Nations in achieving a most urgent objective, namely, nuclear nonproliferation. We would strengthen the International Atomic Energy Commission and find the diplomatic means to accomplish the purposes of the nonproliferation agreement while at the same time making it clear that a civilized world cannot tolerate nations threatening the use of nuclear weapons. We would remember the bargain that we made in asking the nations of the world not to pursue the development of nuclear weapons—a bargain that obligated the United States to lead the international effort to reduce armaments and nuclear weapons.

10. We would work to give credibility to our commitment made at the Millennium Summit to help the less developed nations in terms of strengthening their civil societies and their economic prospects.

11. We would reaffirm our commitment to collective security as envisioned in the UN Charter. It was clear before the invasion of Iraq and it is abundantly clear now that we would be in a much stronger position in pursuit of our legitimate objectives if the United Nations, and through it, the nations of the world were

with us, strengthening our efforts to bring peace and a representative government to the people of Iraq.

Adlai Stevenson understood that a peaceful and prosperous world cannot be organized without the active engagement and leadership of the United States. Presidential leadership is absolutely vital to our role in the United Nations. The Congress can be hostile, the extremists can continue their rhetorical explosions, but if the President is clear in his purpose and willing to exercise the necessary political will, the United States can inspire the world by making the UN a powerful, effective instrument in the governance of a world that pleads for our leadership. Adlai Stevenson would have been such a President.

If history is our guide, we know that the window of opportunity for the beneficent exercise of our power will not remain open forever. Other nations will emerge in this century that will rival us and challenge our dominance. The American dream is not empire; it is constitutional democracy that assures personal freedom, equal opportunity and social justice. Our destiny is to create a better world where democratic values are fundamental. In that quest, the United Nations can be a crucial partner.

These are Stevensonian principles, ideas, and commitments. As we espouse them today, we continue to be inspired by the memory of his presence among us. He inspired young Americans to believe in an America that was not afraid to lead, to discuss, to negotiate, to be confident of our strength in the fulfillment of our quest. Adlai Stevenson died in London on July 14, 1965. As President, he would have added to our greatness. His legacy of integrity, eloquence, and commitment to the commonweal is remembered by everyone who knew him. It lights our path in defining our own lives.

-→=◎⊂=←-

U.S. Ambassador Adlai Stevenson (seated r. of center) leads UN Security Council Debate on Cuba Missile Crisis, October 25, 1962
Source: Courtesy of the UN, photo by M. H.

UN Secretary-General U Thant (l.) visits Pres. and Mrs. Lyndon Johnson in Washington with U.S. Ambassador Adlai Stevenson, Ambassador Charles Yost (l.), and UN Undersecretary-General Ralph Bunche (r.), August 6, 1964
Source: U.N. photo

PART III

HIS INTEGRITY AND HIS POLITICS

Gov. Adlai Stevenson (r.) attends Notre Dame football game with Sen. John Kennedy (l.) and campaign research assistant Dr. John Brademas (cen.) in 1956
Source: Dr. John Brademas

CHAPTER 11

STEVENSON: HIS IMPACT ON EDUCATION, INTERNATIONAL AFFAIRS, NIXON, AND POLITICS

John Brademas

Dr. John Brademas is President Emeritus of New York University (NYU) and served as President from 1981–92. During that time, he led the transition of NYU from a regional commuter institution to a national and international research university. In 1955–56, he was Executive Assistant to Adlai E. Stevenson, in charge of research on issues during Stevenson's second presidential campaign. An Indiana Democrat, Dr. Brademas served as U.S. Representative in Congress for 22 years (1959–81), the last four as House Majority Whip. In Congress, he played a leading role in writing federal legislation to assist schools, colleges, and universities; libraries and museums; the arts and the humanities; and to provide services for children, the elderly, and the disabled. Former Chairman of the President's Committee on the Arts and the Humanities, the National Endowment for Democracy, and the Federal Reserve Bank of New York, he is today President of the King Juan Carlos I of Spain Center of New York University Foundation. He is a fellow of the American Academy of Arts & Sciences and National Academy of Education (USA) and member of the Academy of Athens, European Academy of Sciences and Arts, and National Academy of Education of Argentina.

A B.A., *magna cum laude* graduate of Harvard University, John Brademas was a Rhodes Scholar at Oxford University where he earned a D.Phil. degree in social studies. He has been awarded honorary degrees by fifty-two colleges and universities, most recently

(2003) by Oxford University. The degree citation described him as "a man of varied talents and extraordinary energy, the most practical of academics, the most scholarly of men of action." Dr. Brademas is author of *Anarcosin-dicalismo v revolucion social en Espana (1930-1937)*, published in Barcelona by Ariel in 1974. He is, with Lynne P. Brown, author of *The Politics of Education: Conflict and Consensus on Capitol Hill*, published in 1987 by the University of Oklahoma Press. He is also author of *Washington, D.C., to Washington Square*, published in New York in 1986 by Weidenfeld & Nicolson.

INTRODUCTION

In 1952, while a student at Oxford University in England, on the eve of the presidential election in the United States that year, I joined several other Americans to put on a mock "National Convention" at Rhodes House where I nominated Adlai Ewing Stevenson as the candidate of the Democratic Party for President. I also wrote, for a student journal at Oxford, an essay entitled, "Why I'm voting Democratic in November," in which I sharply criticized the candidacy of Dwight D. Eisenhower, praised Stevenson, and went so far as to predict a Democratic victory. So politically intense was I and so greatly did I admire Stevenson that I had reprints of my article made and sent to, among others, Paul M. Butler, a lawyer from my hometown of South Bend, Indiana, who was the Democratic National Committeeman for the State, and William McCormick Blair Jr., a Chicago attorney who was Stevenson's law partner and close associate.

Only eight months after leaving Oxford in the summer of 1953 and returning to South Bend, I became the Democratic Party nominee from Indiana's Third District for Election in 1954 to the United States House of Representatives. Just 26 years old when I announced my candidacy, I won the congressional nomination in a contested primary. Indispensable to that victory was the endorsement of Paul Butler and the Democratic Party organization of St. Joseph County, my home county.

On September 18, 1954, I attended a dinner in Indianapolis to kick off the Democratic congressional campaign. I took a tape recorder with me and secured endorsements for use on radio from the Speaker of the House of Representatives, Sam Rayburn, and the titular leader of the Democratic Party, the presidential nominee in 1952, Adlai Stevenson, who was accompanied by Bill Blair.

I lost my first race for Congress, with 49.5 percent of the total vote, a margin of some 2,000 votes, to the incumbent Republican. A third candidate, of the Prohibition Party, won 700 votes.

In December 1954, in New Orleans, Paul Butler was elected Chairman of the Democratic National Committee.

Having come so close to victory in my initial plunge into politics, I naturally decided to run again in 1956. I thought it prudent to get some experience in Washington, DC, and joined the staff of Senator Patrick V. McNamara, a Michigan Democrat. Not long thereafter, I was invited by Congressman Thomas Ludlow Ashley, a Democrat from Toledo, Ohio, to become his Administrative Assistant, the top position in a Capitol Hill office. I accepted.

Several months later Bill Blair telephoned me from Chicago. Recalling my earlier enthusiasm for Adlai Stevenson, Blair said that "the Governor" was going to run for President again, in 1956, and asked me to come to Chicago to take charge of organizing Volunteers for Stevenson across the country. I replied that I was flattered but thought I was not the person for that job. I urged Blair to find someone who had been active in the 1952 campaign and so would already have a network of contacts.

Blair agreed but said there was another position in the campaign that might interest me, to be in charge of research on issues. I immediately said, "Yes." Having myself been a candidate for Congress, I was familiar with framing campaign issues. Already planning to run again, I would, in Chicago, be less than two hours by car from my home district. Most important, I was a dedicated champion of the candidacy of Adlai Stevenson for President of the United States.

My assignment led to one of the most fascinating, and valuable, years of my life. As Stevenson's Executive Assistant—my title—I had an office in the Continental Illinois Bank Building, where his law offices were located. His partners—in law and politics—were Blair, W. Willard Wirtz, and Newton N. Minow. Blair later served as United States Ambassador to the Philippines and to Denmark, Wirtz as Secretary of Labor and Minow as Chairman of the Federal Communications Commission.

In addition to developing position papers for Stevenson and collecting relevant newspaper and magazine clippings, I served as liaison, at the direction of Wirtz in Chicago and former Air Force

Secretary Thomas K. Finletter, in New York, with Stevenson's "Brain Trust," his policy advisors. This group included such persons as John Kenneth Galbraith, Seymour Harris, and Arthur M. Schlesinger Jr., all of Harvard; E. Cary Brown and Paul Samuelson of the Massachusetts Institute of Technology; Richard Musgrave of the University of Michigan; and Joseph Rauh, a Washington, DC, lawyer.

My fellow Hoosier, one of Stevenson's speechwriters in the 1955–56 campaign, later President John F. Kennedy's Ambassador to the Dominican Republic and author of a splendid biography of Stevenson, John Bartlow Martin, observed: "Grounded in the Finletter Group's work, which had drawn upon some of the best Democratic minds in the country, the research material had been built up mountainously by John Brademas and his associates."[1]

The writer with whom I worked most closely in Chicago was Harry S. Ashmore, who left his position as editor of the *Arkansas Gazette* to arrive in late September 1955. I was later joined by Ken Hechler, a former professor of political science who also later ran, successfully, for Congress. The two of us drew up a list of around 180 issues, then worked with the speechwriters, who prepared policy positions on each, "raising all the questions likely to be asked, setting forth the Administration's position, Congressional proposals, other positions, and Stevenson's position if he had one and a recommendation for a position if he did not. The papers were to be used for speeches and in briefing Stevenson for press conferences."[2] (Hechler and I kept the papers in a set of books we called the "Adlaipedia"!)

On November 5 and 6, 1955, at the home of Bill Blair on Astor Street in Chicago, the Finletter Group met, with Finletter in the chair, to discuss what the issues in Stevenson's campaign for President should be. Present for this strategy session were the editor of *Harper's*, John Fischer, Blair, Wirtz, Arthur Schlesinger, longtime friend Jane (Mrs. Edison) Dick, Ashmore, New Dealer Benjamin Cohen, Washington, DC, lawyer George Ball and his young colleague, John Sharon, and a former press secretary to President Truman, Roger Tubby, and I.

Schlesinger recalled that at this meeting the main thrust of the campaign would be on "qualitative liberalism," single-interest government and Republican deceit in speaking to the American people. As our talks broke up, into Blair's house walked Humphrey Bogart

and Lauren Bacall, strong Stevenson supporters. At Blair's invitation, Sharon and I joined him, Bogart, and Bacall for a memorable
lunch at the Ambassador East Hotel.[3]

The tone that had characterized the 1952 campaign, a kind of
high-level discussion of issues, was to some extent turned aside during the 1956 presidential primary wars with Senator Estes Kefauver
of Tennessee. Although Stevenson had the endorsement of Senators
Hubert Humphrey and Eugene McCarthy and Governor Orville
Freeman in the March 1956 Minnesota Democratic presidential primary election, Kefauver won. At a press conference the following
day in the Continental Illinois Bank Building, everyone on the staff
was gloomy, but Stevenson was rather jaunty, indeed, combative.
A reporter asked, alluding, of course, to Kefauver's campaign
style, "Well, Governor, now do you think it pays off in politics to
shake hands?"

Stevenson fired back, "Well, I do think it tends to establish a sense
of identification between the shaker and the shakee!" And he shook
a lot of hands after that.

I made a visit for Stevenson to Florida during the presidential primary there and, in light of my Greek ancestry—my father was born
in Greece—spent some time in Tarpon Springs, famed as home to
Greek sponge fishermen and site of an annual event when the local
Greek Orthodox priest would throw a cross into the waters, which
young Greek-American men then dived in to recover. After the 1956
election, I told Stevenson, "Governor, it's a good thing you lost. I
made a commitment to the people in Tarpon that if elected, you
would return on Greek Cross Day!"

I served on the Stevenson staff from the summer of 1955 through
the August 1956 Democratic National Convention in Chicago,
chaired by my political godfather, Paul Butler.

After the convention, I returned to South Bend and my own campaign for Congress. That year I faced a new Republican, the incumbent who defeated me in 1954 having decided not to run again. Not
only had his margin of victory that year been just half a percent, but
in the 1955 municipal elections in Indiana, Democrats had won
every mayoral contest in my District. Yet such was the attractiveness
of President Eisenhower at the top of the Republican ticket that he
defeated Stevenson by a larger margin in 1956 than in 1952. Also
caught in the Eisenhower sweep was I. So Stevenson and Brademas
both lost a second time. I thought, "Well, Brademas, here you are,

not yet 30 and twice defeated for Congress. You're a has-been before you've started."

But still convinced I could win, I became a one-man department of political science at Saint Mary's College, the women's college across the road from the University of Notre Dame, and waited to run again.

In my third campaign, in 1958, a year when Democrats gained forty-nine new seats in the House of Representatives, I was first elected, then ten times reelected, serving, therefore, for twenty-two years and during the Administrations of six Presidents: three Republicans—Eisenhower, Richard M. Nixon, and Gerald R. Ford; and three Democrats: Kennedy, Lyndon B. Johnson, and Jimmy Carter.

As I reflect now on the legacy of Adlai Stevenson, I think of four particular themes that characterized his leadership in American public life and that also proved significant concerns of mine, as legislator and university leader: education, international affairs, Richard Nixon, and, finally, the vocation of politics.

I do not wish to assert that the career of Adlai Stevenson was the sole influence in shaping my work in Congress. Even before learning of him, I found my interest in politics strongly encouraged on both sides of my own family. But Stevenson's example of political leadership I took as a model, one that contributed in serious fashion to my own commitments in Congress, at New York University, and in other positions of responsibility.

EDUCATION

My late maternal grandfather, William Chester Goble, was an Indiana school superintendent and college professor of classical history. Indeed, my mother was named Beatrice Cenci, after the young sixteenth-century Roman noblewoman whose tragic life and death inspired poems, plays, novels, and an opera. My brothers and sister and I spent summers with my grandparents in the tiny central Indiana town of Swayzee where my grandfather told me of his experience as a delegate to Indiana State Democratic Conventions and of his correspondence with Senators and Congressmen in Washington. If my grandfather thought politics important, it must be!

My Greek immigrant father reminded me, "We Greeks invented politics, and some of us should practice it!" And my mother showed me photographs of herself as a young woman with other young women wearing Woodrow Wilson banners as they campaigned for their candidate for President.

At the age of 8, from the front porch of my house at 701 North Michigan Street in South Bend, I waved enthusiastically at President Franklin D. Roosevelt as he passed by in an open car on his way to Notre Dame and an honorary degree. Little did I think that nearly twenty-five years later, I would, as U.S. representative in Congress of the Third Indiana District, go to the local airport to greet President Eisenhower *en route* to the same campus for the same honor.

At my request and with the support of letters from Paul Butler and Adlai Stevenson to Congressman Wilbur Mills of Arkansas, Chairman of the House Ways and Means Committee, the Democratic members of which at that time determined committee assignments of newly elected representatives, I was named to the House Committee on Education and Labor. Thus, I came to hold the same seat that, as a Massachusetts Congressman, John F. Kennedy had occupied, second-ranking member of the Subcommittee on Elementary and Secondary Education.

Central to my life in Congress was service on that committee.

Although when elected President in 1960, John F. Kennedy declared education among his legislative priorities, he encountered difficulty winning approval of his proposals.[4] The reasons were three: race, religion and Republicans.

Four years earlier, in the 1956 presidential campaign, Stevenson had, on October 2, issued a statement, "The New America: A Program for Education," in which he declared, "The passport to a better society is better education—for one and for all," and urged, at a time when federal support for education was controversial, action by the national government. He listed several "great problems in American education today"; he called them "shortages"—of buildings, teachers, talent, facts, and policy.

In his prescient October 1956 position paper, Stevenson sharply attacked the stratagem by which ninety-six Republicans in the House of Representatives first voted for an antisegregation rider to the 1956 school aid bill, then once the amendment was adopted, voted against the bill on final passage, the same device I years later, as myself a member of Congress, saw House Republicans, joining Southern Democrats, employ to defeat school-aid measures.

In words that could characterize debates over federal support for elementary and secondary schools today, Stevenson warned that local property and state taxes were no longer adequate to support public schools. He then explicitly endorsed federal aid for school construction, with particular attention to "reducing the severe educational handicaps presently suffered by youngsters who, through no fault of their own, happen to live in economically underprivileged communities," a harbinger of Title I of the Elementary and Secondary Education Act of 1965, which I helped write.

Stevenson went on to call for "a limited number of federally supported undergraduate scholarships or loans to students who want to go to college, are qualified to make good use of a college education, and will otherwise be denied this opportunity" as well as "fellowships, on the basis of merit and need, to specially qualified students who are prepared to commit themselves to service in teaching or in other fields of particularly acute shortage." Again, these proposals presaged the Pell Grant, Guaranteed Student Loan, and College Work Study programs enacted during my own years in Congress and to the writing of all of which I contributed.

Stevenson also asserted that "The rapid pace of change in the world and the prospect of increased technical development and a shorter work week" justified providing opportunities for continuing and adult education, and he endorsed as well strengthening the existing federal program of assistance for vocational education. And, a reflection of his abiding interest in the wider world, he urged expansion of exchange programs "to enable Americans to study abroad and foreign students and scholars to visit the United States."

Only days after his statement of early October 1956, in a sharp assault on Republican opposition in Congress to a federal school aid bill then under consideration on Capitol Hill as well as on President Eisenhower's indifference, Stevenson, on October 24, 1956, in White Plains, New York, declared, "I have said in the South and the North, and I say again tonight: we must carry out the Supreme Court decision on segregation in our schools," an explication of his earlier, October 2, declaration: "It is essential . . . that education be available equally, to all, without distinction or discrimination based on race or creed or color or economic condition."

Stevenson's strong endorsement of the use of federal tax dollars to support education found resonance just two years later, in August 1958, in the passage by Congress of the National Defense Education Act (NDEA), a measure that provided loans to college students and funds for the teaching of science, mathematics, and modern foreign languages—a significant advance.

In January 1958, Senator John F. Kennedy introduced legislation to authorize federal aid for schools and school construction, but the proposal died in the Eighty-fifth Congress.

The Democratic National Convention in 1960, at which Senator Kennedy was nominated for President and the Majority Leader of the U.S. Senate, Senator Lyndon B. Johnson of Texas, was nominated Vice President, and to which I was a delegate, adopted a plank calling for federal grants for classroom construction and teachers' salaries as well as for building academic facilities and dormitories at colleges and universities. The platform also pledged further federal support for vocational and adult education, libraries, educational television, and exchange of students and teachers with other nations. The education plank clearly echoed Stevensonian objectives.

Even as the Chairman of the 1960 Convention was my mentor, Paul Butler, Chairman of the Platform Committee was another United States Representative first elected in 1958, my colleague, Chester Bowles of Connecticut, who asked me to assist him in writing the Democratic Party Platform. I did so, working with a brilliant young professor from the Harvard Law School, the late Abram Chayes. Among the other members of the Platform Committee were the redoubtable Senator Sam Ervin of North Carolina and another potent figure on Capitol Hill, Chairman of the House Government Operations Committee, grandson of a slave, and Democratic leader of the South Side of Chicago, William Dawson.

As President, Kennedy called for legislation to implement most of the promises in the convention's 1960 plank on education. Disagreements, however, over aid to religious schools and to racially segregated schools blocked action on his 1961 proposals.

In January 1963, his third year in the presidency, in his "Special Message to the Congress on Education," still unsatisfied with progress on the issue, Kennedy proposed a comprehensive program, the National Education Improvement Act of 1963, to extend and expand the National Defense Education Act Student Loan and Fellowship program and to authorize funds for building college and graduate facilities, public community junior colleges, and college-level technical institutes. His plan also called for federal funds to aid elementary, secondary, vocational, continuing, and special education as well as libraries.

Declared Kennedy, "Education is the keystone in the arch of freedom and progress."

John F. Kennedy's 1963 proposals for federal aid to education were in large measure foreshadowed by those advocated by Adlai Stevenson in 1956 and pressed by Lyndon Johnson when he, after the assassination of President Kennedy on November 22, 1963, became President. Indeed, it was in December 1963 that the new President signed into law the higher and vocational education measures Kennedy had urged. Johnson had greater success in winning approval of his education program not only because of a wave of sympathy following the assassination but also, especially following Johnson's landslide victory over Barry Goldwater in 1964, there were substantially larger Democratic margins in both the House and Senate than Kennedy had enjoyed.

President Kennedy's dedication to education as an essential component of his "New Frontier," combined with President Johnson's skill in dealing with Congress meant, as William O'Hara concluded, that "Education [was] among . . . the highest accomplishments of the Kennedy Administration."[5]

The commitment to education that ran from Adlai Stevenson to John F. Kennedy continued with Lyndon Johnson's Great Society.

Although only in my second term in the House of Representatives, I had an unusual opportunity to contribute to greater attention to education when in 1961, the Chairman of the Committee on Education and Labor, Adam Clayton Powell Jr., appointed me Chairman of an Advisory Group on Higher Education and said, "Tell me what the federal government should do to help colleges and universities." The others in the group were among the ablest members of Congress: Democrats Robert N. Giaimo of Connecticut and James G. O'Hara of Michigan and Republicans Albert H. Quie of Minnesota and Charles E. Goodell of New York.

Every one of the recommendations of our Advisory Group in the January 1962 report, unanimously agreed to, *Congressional Action for Higher Education*, was subsequently written into law during the Administrations of Kennedy, Johnson, and, then, Richard Nixon.

I note that our advisory group's recommendation for encouraging "special attention to ways of fostering high-quality basic research on the learning process with a view to improving effectiveness of teaching and learning at all levels" antedated by eight years President Nixon's 1970 Special Message on Education, which included his proposal to create, to support research into teaching and learning, a National Institute of Education (NIE).

Although I found it easy to control my enthusiasm for most of the policies of Richard Nixon, I strongly favored this part of his education package. The federal government had earmarked for research substantial sums of budgets for defense, agriculture, and health, but the nation was investing very little in generating thoughtful, objective analysis of and evidence on how people teach and learn. I pressed the Department of Health, Education, and Welfare official in charge of legislative relations to write the bill to authorize an NIE in such fashion that it would be referred to the Select Education Subcommittee, which I chaired. I told him, "I'll pass it for you." I note that the proposal for a National Institute of Education was drafted by Daniel Patrick Moynihan, then a domestic policy advisor to Nixon and later, of course, a distinguished United States Senator from New York State.

As a member of both the Subcommittees on Elementary and Secondary Education and on Higher Education of the Committee on Education and Labor, I was an enthusiastic and active participant in shaping the education bills that became law during my twenty-two years on the Committee.

I was a co-sponsor of the Elementary and Secondary Education Act of 1965, which featured the Title I Program to channel federal funds to schools and communities where there were large numbers of children from low-income families, and of the Higher Education Acts of 1972 and 1976, which focused on such student financial aid programs as the Pell Grants, College Work-Study and Guaranteed Student Loans.

INTERNATIONAL AFFAIRS

If eloquent advocacy of federal support for education was a commitment of Adlai Stevenson, so, too, was his profound concern about the conduct of the foreign policy of the United States. Adlai Stevenson won recognition and respect throughout our country and abroad as one of America's leading voices in international affairs. Certainly, I was stimulated by his interest in travel and desire to learn about other peoples and cultures.

Both Stevenson and I were Midwesterners, from neighboring states, but neither of us drank from the isolationist cup that had nurtured so many political figures from our region. Indeed, in the summer of 1949, following my graduation from Harvard, I served, at Lake Success, by appointment of the Department of State, as an intern at the United Nations, in the Section for Non-Governmental Organizations of the Department of Public Information. The UN Secretary-General was Trygve Lie, and I still remember watching Ralph Bunche deliver to the Security Council his report on his mediation efforts in Palestine.

Stevenson had been engaged with the United Nations from the start, having been involved with preparations for the founding conference in 1945 in San Francisco, where he served as spokesman for the United States delegation. In 1960, he was appointed United States Ambassador to the UN by President Kennedy.

One of my own first acts as a freshman Congressman, after my election in 1958, concerned appropriations for foreign aid. I drafted a letter, to which I secured signatures of fifty House Democrats, to President Eisenhower, declaring that although he was a Republican and we were Democrats, we wanted to assure him of our support of his foreign assistance proposal, no more popular then than now.

The foreign policy issue with which I personally became most deeply involved during my service in Congress was Cyprus, an issue with which Stevenson also had to deal at the United Nations. The first native-born American of Greek origin elected to either the United States Senate or House of Representatives, and, in 1967, the only American of Greek descent in Congress, I strongly opposed the coup by a group of Greek colonels that brought the overthrow of young King Constantine of the Hellenes. I sharply attacked the colonels' action, refused to visit Greece or go to the Greek Embassy in Washington, and testified against United States military aid to Greece. I argued that Greece was a fellow member of NATO, the North Atlantic Treaty Organization, formed to defend democracy, freedom and the rule of law, none of which values the colonels respected. We should not, I asserted, provide weapons to such a government.

In the summer of 1974, the colonels attempted to oust the President of Cyprus, Archbishop Makarios, an act that not only caused their downfall but also triggered two invasions of Cyprus by Turkish armed forces, equipped with weapons supplied by the

United States. I led a small group of members of the House of
Representatives to call on Henry Kissinger, then Secretary of State,
to remind him that the Turks, using American weapons for other
than defensive purposes, were in violation of the conditions under
which they were provided the arms. Accordingly, we told Kissinger,
he was obliged to enforce the law and terminate further arms shipments to Turkey. We reminded him that the reason Richard Nixon,
who resigned the presidency the same week, was on his way to exile
in California was that he had not respected the laws of the land or
the Constitution of the United States.

Because, however, the Executive Branch refused to enforce the
law, we in Congress did so by voting an embargo on American arms
to Turkey. Years later, over my opposition, Congress voted to lift the
embargo and even now, three decades on, Cyprus remains a thorn in
the side of the European Union and a problem in United States relations with Europe.

Having a father born in Europe and having for three years studied in England and while there traveled to several European countries, I was, like Stevenson, keenly interested in learning about other
lands and cultures and as a member of Congress made a number of
trips abroad.

Before my marriage, in 1977, I usually spent two weeks in the
summers of nonelection years at my old Oxford College, Brasenose,
seeing friends and traveling to the European continent. While in
Congress, I visited the Soviet Union as early as 1961, Germany,
Romania, Poland, Czechoslovakia, Hungary, Yugoslavia, France,
Mexico, Panama, Peru, Kenya, Israel, and, of course, Greece.

In 1961, for example, with Congressman Robert Giaimo of
Connecticut, I went to Argentina to inquire into the potential contributions that Latin American universities could make to President
Kennedy's Alliance for Progress. Giaimo spoke Italian, I Spanish. We
talked with the Frondizi brothers, one the President of the Republic,
the other the Rector of the University of Buenos Aires. Giaimo and
I produced a report with recommendations for U.S. policies to
strengthen higher education in South America.

Thirty-seven years later, in 1998, I returned to Buenos Aires to be
inducted into the National Academy of Education of Argentina, an
occasion on which I delivered an address, in Spanish, recalling our
suggestions of nearly four decades earlier, indicating the changes I
understood had taken place and said what I thought needed to be

done now to enhance the capacity of universities in Latin America to assist in the economic and social development of the region.

In 1966, working with the thoughtful Secretary of Health, Education, and Welfare, John W. Gardner, and having been appointed by my committee chairman, Mr. Powell, the Chairman of a task force on the subject, I introduced, and Congress passed, the International Education Act, which authorized grants to colleges and universities in the United States—it was not a foreign aid bill—for the study of countries and cultures other than our own. Unfortunately, Congress failed to appropriate the funds to implement the statute. In my view, among the reasons—I do not say the only one—the United States has experienced calamities in Vietnam, Iran, Central America, and now Iraq, has been ignorance, ignorance of the histories, languages, and religions of those societies.

When, in 1981, I became President of New York University, I continued my commitment to international education. I established a Center for Japan–U.S. Business & Economic Studies in the Leonard N. Stern School of Business, a Casa Italiana Zerilli-Marimo, the Skirball Department of Hebrew and Judaic Studies, the Remarque Institute of European Studies, Alexander S. Onassis Program of Hellenic Studies, and, of particular interest to me, the King Juan Carlos I of Spain Center.

I must note that one of the finest persons I ever came to know in public life, whom I first met during my service on Adlai Stevenson's 1955–56 campaign staff, the late Paul Simon of Illinois, was a forceful and articulate advocate of international exchanges. Paul and I served in the House of Representatives together, and, of course, he was later elected to the United States Senate.

RICHARD NIXON

Although the focus of my legislative energies in Congress was the Committee on Education and Labor, I also served on the House Administration Committee where I took part in writing the post-Watergate campaign finance reform laws, and on the Joint (House-Senate) Committee on the Library of Congress.

It was as chairman of a subcommittee of House Administration that I wrote another law, in no small part affected by my having served on the staff of Adlai Stevenson.

It was thirty-three years ago, in the summer of 1974, that Richard
Nixon resigned the Presidency of the United States and Vice
President Gerald R. Ford became President. When the new
President decided to turn over to Nixon all the records of his
Presidency, including the tape recordings, under conditions that
could have led to their ultimate destruction, I was outraged. I
remembered Nixon's scurrilous attacks on Congressman Jerry
Voorhis of California in his first campaign for the House of
Representatives, in 1946, and on Helen Gahagan Douglas in the
1950 campaign for the United States Senate from California. Still
more vividly, I recalled Nixon's having in 1952 spoken of "Adlai the
appeaser . . . who got a Ph.D. from Dean Acheson's College of
Cowardly Communist Containment."

Beyond those recollections, I had been named, to the envy of my
fellow Democrats in Congress, to the Nixon "White House Enemies
List." Moreover, I was serving, by appointment of Speaker Carl
Albert, as member, for the House of Representatives, with Claiborne
Pell of Rhode Island from the Senate and Justice William Brennan
from the Supreme Court, of the National Historical Publications
and Records Commission, the entity that also contained a few eminent American historians and was chaired by the Archivist of the
United States.

Finally, I thought, in reaction to the Ford White House decision
on the Nixon records, "*Nazis* burn books; *Americans* don't burn
books!" Accordingly, I introduced in the House of Representatives a
bill, on which I conducted hearings in the Subcommittee on
Printing, which I chaired, of the House Administration Committee.
The bill ultimately became the Presidential Materials and Recordings
Preservation Act of 1974. This is the statute that annulled President
Ford's Executive Order and declared that all the Nixon records
belonged to the people of the United States. This is the law that
makes possible occasional publication of transcripts of the Nixon
tapes. In an address in 2001, I discussed the history of this legislation at a conference at the Lyndon B. Johnson Library in Austin,
Texas on "The Future of Presidential Libraries." The 1974 statute
also led to the passage of the Presidential Records Act of 1978,
which now governs ownership of presidential papers.

THE VOCATION OF POLITICS

My other major responsibility as a Member of Congress was to serve, by appointment of Speaker of the House of Representatives, Thomas ("Tip") P. O'Neill Jr., as House Majority Whip, third-ranking member of the House Leadership. I found the experience as Whip immensely interesting, for the position gave me an opportunity to work with an organization of nearly fifty other Representatives, each an Assistant Whip, with responsibility for communicating with the Democratic Members in his or her geographical zone and keeping in touch with the Speaker, Majority Leader and with me, as Majority Whip.

In 1980, I was defeated in Ronald Reagan's landslide victory over President Carter. Here I note that I was a candidate for election to Congress fourteen times, five in presidential election years, but that only once did the people of the Third District of Indiana cast a majority of their votes for the Democratic nominee for President. Accordingly, to survive, I had always to run ahead of my party's presidential nominee. In 1980, my district suffered from unemployment, high interest rates and, like the rest of the country, especially the Iran hostage crisis.

Ironically, had I been reelected, to a twelfth term, given that not long thereafter, Speaker O'Neill retired from Congress and Majority Leader Jim Wright resigned, I was in line to become Speaker of the House of Representatives. My loss that year, however, opened an opportunity for another exciting career. I was invited to become President of New York University, a position I assumed in 1981. What followed was, in some respects, a practical extension of commitments I had been pressing for 22 years as a Member of Congress. They resonated with objectives Adlai Stevenson had urged on colleges and universities in our country, especially understanding the cultures and peoples of other countries.

In 2004, I was elected, by the New York State Legislature, to the New York State Board of Regents, the body with supervisory authority over all educational activities, public and private, in the state. In my statement for the Regents, I noted that my wife, Mary Ellen Brademas, a practicing physician, a dermatologist, and I had been residents of the Empire State for twenty-three years.

And in 2004 I echoed Stevensonian concerns for multilateral cooperation with an address in Greece, at The Academy of Athens, on the theme of "Universal Values and World Peace."

In respect of all these activities, as student, legislator, university leader, and participant in pro bono organizations, I hope, without pretense, that I have been making modest contributions that are in harmony with the spirit and legacy of Adlai Stevenson.

-◦-≡⊙⊂≡-◦-

Adlai Stevenson was in 1957 awarded the honorary degree of Doctor of Civil Law by Oxford University, the same honor I was accorded, in 2003, also in the Sheldonian Theatre, during a reunion of Rhodes Scholars.

Having spoken of the Governor's commitment to education, to understanding the world, to encouraging multilateral approaches in the conduct of the foreign policy of the United States, to responding to the impact of the politics of Richard Nixon, I turn to a final dimension of the contribution of Adlai Stevenson to American life.

In an oral history interview nearly forty years ago,[6] I said that Adlai Stevenson gave to politics the sense of its being a high calling, a vocation that was worthy, that should command the best talent; that the life of a politician was not demeaning but, on the contrary, elevating—or could be! Adlai Stevenson's concern with the quality of the processes of politics in a democratic society is, I believe, the heart of the matter. He insisted that political leaders should talk about the issues and that even when it hurt, speak candidly. Indeed, Adlai Stevenson discussed questions of national policy in a way that deeply affected the Administration of John F. Kennedy and the program of President Lyndon B. Johnson. Beautification, pollution control, civil rights, education, the need to cooperate with other countries—Adlai Stevenson addressed an entire range of issues that have to do with the quality of life, both in our country and abroad.

Nearly fifty years ago, I was one of several participants—among others were Senator Eugene McCarthy, British historian Denis Brogan, and one of my former Harvard professors, Merle Fainsod—in a conference at the University of Texas on "The Intellectual in Politics." In my remarks, I spoke of my work with Stevenson's Brain Trust in 1955 and 1956 and said:

> Of Stevenson, in particular, I think it important to note that he elevated the politics of the Republic in two significant ways. He insisted that a candidate had the obligation to discuss the most serious issues facing the country, no matter how controversial they were or what effect they had on his candidacy. Stevenson suffered at the polls from

his 1956 call for a nuclear test ban treaty, but his courageous initiative bore fruit for Kennedy in 1963.

Whereas Senator Dirksen says that a politician's responsibility is to recognize an idea whose time has come, as with civil rights, Stevenson insisted that the highest mission of a politician is to recognize the significance of the idea whose time has not yet come and to try to hasten the day. Second, Stevenson had a profound concern for the quality of American politics and politicians. "He gave us all a little class," I once heard Hubert Humphrey say. Adlai Stevenson made Kennedy possible, and, in my judgment, more than most people realize he prepared the way for Lyndon Johnson's Great Society.[7]

Although Adlai Stevenson did not win the presidency, he shaped the dialogue of American democracy in an enduring way. I reiterate that both Presidents Kennedy and Johnson profited greatly from Stevenson's links with the intellectual and university communities in the country. If, in his tradition, I, both as legislator and university leader, have been engaged—and still am—in activities involving education and foreign affairs, there is another Stevensonian bequest to Americans to which I have enthusiastically resonated. It is his deep respect for the nobility of the vocation of politics, electoral politics, which Stevenson used to describe as "combat politics"!

Indeed, I had reason to pay tribute to Governor Stevenson in another book, *A Time for Heroes* (Phoenix Press, Beverly Hills, CA, 2005, by Robert L. Dilenschneider), when, with several other Americans, I was invited to choose three of my own heroes. I spoke of King Juan Carlos I of Spain for "his brave and enlightened stance that saved Spain's democracy and earned him the genuine love and affection of his people." I praised the late Christian theologian, Reinhold Niebuhr, as "a very compelling figure, intellectually, morally and theologically. Niebuhr's aphorism, 'Man's capacity for justice makes democracy possible, but man's inclination to injustice makes democracy necessary,' was a lodestone for me when I entered the arena of politics." And I cited Adlai Stevenson, whose "importance went beyond what he accomplished in his lifetime. He helped make John Kennedy possible because of the way in which he articulated the nexus among values, ideas and action in the political order."

SOME FINAL THOUGHTS

All these observations bring me to a final one. My own major project now, as President Emeritus of New York University, has to do with the American way of governing, with the politics of the American democracy. The subject was close to the thoughts of Adlai Stevenson and, obviously, is an initiative motivated by *my* twenty-two years of service in the Congress of the United States.

I observe that in our separation-of-powers constitutional system, when it comes to making national policy, Congress, unlike the House of Commons in the British parliamentary system, for example, counts! To illustrate my point, I cite the legislation of which my closest friend in Congress, also son of a Greek immigrant and another Rhodes Scholar, Paul S. Sarbanes, the senior U.S. Senator from Maryland, is chief author of the Sarbanes-Oxley Act, dealing with the reform of corporate governance in the United States. This measure was not developed in the White House or elsewhere in the Executive Branch of the federal government but on Capitol Hill, by a Senator and a Representative elected to Congress.

Yet with 100 Senators and 435 Representatives and customarily, no strict party discipline, Congress is not an easy institution to understand, even for well-informed persons. What we have, therefore, now done is to create, in the Robert F. Wagner Graduate School of Public Service, at New York University, the John Brademas Center for the Study of Congress, of Congress as a policy-making institution. We shall bring to Washington Square Presidents, Senators and Representatives, current and former, Democrats and Republicans; cabinet officers; executive and congressional branch officials; judges; journalists; parliamentarians from other countries; students and scholars, to discuss the processes, the ways by which our national legislature influences and shapes policy, as well as to address significant issues of public policy.

These processes are complicated and not easy to fathom, even for well-informed people, including, I have observed, some Presidents of the United States! This initiative is wholly bipartisan. I have talked about it with both Democratic and Republican leaders in and outside Congress, and I have been heartened by their enthusiastic response. My fundamental purpose in establishing such a Center is to contribute to both public and scholarly understanding of what, after all, in the Constitution of the United States, is the First Branch of Government.

I like to think that Adlai Stevenson would have approved.

NOTES

1. John Bartlow Martin, *Adlai Stevenson and the World: The Life of Adlai E. Stevenson* (New York: Doubleday, 1988), 234.
2. Ibid., 341.
3. Ibid., 224.
4. I discuss Kennedy's education program in my book (with Lynne P. Brown), *The Politics of Education: Conflict and Consensus on Capitol Hill*, based on lectures I delivered in 1986 at the Carl Albert Congressional Research Center at the University of Oklahoma (Norman: University of Oklahoma Press, 1987), and in my Foreword to a study, *John F. Kennedy on Education*, a book edited by William T. O'Hara (New York: Teachers College Press, Columbia University, 1966).
5. Ibid., 30.
6. *Oral History*, Columbia University, July 25, 1966.
7. *The Intellectual in Politics*, edited by H. Malcolm MacDonald (Austin: University of Texas Press, 1966), 113.

CHAPTER 12

REMEMBERING ADLAI STEVENSON*

Arthur Schlesinger Jr.

Dr. Arthur Schlesinger Jr., late renowned historian and author, was assistant to Governor Adlai Stevenson during his 1952 and 1956 Democratic presidential campaigns. In the 1960s he served as special assistant to President John F. Kennedy and, on behalf of the White House, was on numerous occasions in contact with Stevenson while the latter was U.S. Permanent Representative to the United Nations.

I first met Adlai Stevenson in 1946. Edward Weeks, the editor of the *Atlantic Monthly*, suggested that I write a piece about the impending mid-term congressional election. It was the first postwar national election, the first since FDR's death, the first since the dropping of the atomic bomb. It was also the first national test for the Truman administration—and people were already complaining and making condescending cracks, like "To err is Truman." I thought it would be a good idea to take the political temperature in a few key states.

*   This chapter, with the permission of Dr. Schlesinger, was taken from remarks he delivered in a lecture on February 17, 2000, in Springfield, Illinois, sponsored by the Illinois Historical Library in celebration of Adlai E. Stevenson II's centennial birthday.

Illinois, a pivotal state, was high on my itinerary. The day I was to leave Washington on the overnight train to Chicago (people still traveled on sleepers in those faraway days), I happened to lunch with a wartime friend and a one-time Chicago lawyer, George Ball (who later served as Undersecretary of State in the Kennedy and Johnson administrations where he distinguished himself by his opposition to the war in Vietnam). When I told George Ball about my assignment, he said, "You must talk with my old friend Adlai Stevenson—he's been staying with us, and he's going back to Chicago tonight, on the same train. Give me your seat number, and I will pass it along to him."

Soon after I settled in my seat and the train was chugging away from Union Station, an agreeable man of medium height, balding head and beguiling smile introduced himself. He suggested a drink. We had more than one, then went to the dining car (no plastic pre-cooked meals then), then adjourned to the club car and talked till late in the night.

I was utterly delighted by Adlai Stevenson, his intelligence, his wit, his wide range of reference, his shrewd, slightly cynical, insight into people and motives, his belief in high standards of public service, his hopes for the republic. We talked from the start with the easy candor of old friends, and I felt that I had never in my life got to know anyone so well so quickly. Oddly, in the subsequent years of close association, I never felt that I had got to know him much better than that first night. His engaging openness masked a mysterious privacy.

One thing, however, that struck me then and later was his deep love for Illinois. Lincoln was his hero, and he well understood Lincoln's unmatched understanding of the moral dimension of politics, so exquisitely expressed in his speeches and letters, the quality that, joined with a capacity to act, made him the greatest of our presidents. Lincoln too was a man for whom humor concealed mystery.

I was struck also by Adlai's pride in his Illinois ancestors. It is odd, if you think about it, that dynasties play such a role in the politics of a democracy. [In February 2000] we face[d] a likely contest between two famous names—one the son of a president and another son of a distinguished senator. And John McCain after all is the descendant of a well-known naval dynasty.

Adlai found much gratification in recalling that his own great grandfather Jesse Fell, the founder of the Bloomington *Pantograph*, was a close friend and stalwart backer of Lincoln's—and that his grandfather, the first Adlai Stevenson, served as Grover Cleveland's vice president and, if William Jennings Bryan had won in 1900, would have been the first and only vice president to serve under two different presidents. As Governor Stevenson often said, "I have a bad case of hereditary politics." And he would have been even more gratified had he lived to see his son Adlai III serve as a fine United States Senator from Illinois.

--➤〓◉〓✦--

After war broke out in Europe in 1939, debate between isolationists and internationalists assumed an increasingly bitter tone. Adlai became chairman of the Chicago branch of William Allen White's Committee to Defend America by Aiding the Allies. His cool nerve in defying isolationist thunderbolts hurled from the *Tribune* tower impressed Frank Knox, the publisher of the *Chicago Daily News*; and, when FDR called Knox to Washington to serve as Secretary of the Navy, Knox made Stevenson his special assistant. From there he went to the State Department to assist at the founding conference of the United Nations in San Francisco in the spring of 1945 and from there to London to help get the UN organized.

Adlai's interest in world affairs coexisted happily with his solicitude for the State of Illinois. Elected governor in 1948 by the largest margin in the history of the state, he fulfilled a cherished ambition. I visited him two or three times . . . in the gubernatorial mansion, and his delight and pride in his job were unmistakable. Resisting the proposal that he seek the presidential nomination in 1952, he said that his hope and intention were to serve a second term as Governor of Illinois. This was not, I think, a politician's tease. It was what he really felt.

In later years Adlai Stevenson acquired a reputation for indecisiveness. It was claimed that he had chronic difficulty in making up his mind. This reputation was partly due to his habit of thinking aloud before the press and mulling over the pros and cons of one or another choice. And his self-deprecatory manner conveyed an appearance of indecision that did not really exist.

I think that one must distinguish between career decisions and executive decisions. When it came to career changes Stevenson sometimes wavered and dithered. But if he was occasionally indecisive about himself, he was rarely indecisive about his policies.

No one complained about any inability as Governor of Illinois to make executive decisions. As Carl McGowan, his counsel, said, "He could drive you crazy on whether he would accept an invitation or not—but on the really big things he wouldn't do it. . . . I don't remember once that he was indecisive about something on his desk as Governor."

I vividly recall the riot at the Menard Penitentiary in the last days before the 1952 election. Interrupting his national campaign to go back to Menard seemed a no-win situation for the Governor. If he went to the prison and tried to settle the riot by making concessions to the prisoners, he would be accused of softness. If he ordered the police to storm the prison, he would be blamed for any loss of life. I remember when Governor Rockefeller of New York faced a prison riot and, without the excuse of a presidential campaign, declined to go in person to Attica. But Stevenson had no doubt where his responsibility lay. He went in person to Menard, supervised the negotiation and ended the riot.

As I noted, he had not wanted to run for president in 1952. President Truman offered to back him, but Stevenson, as so often when confronted by career choices, wavered and dithered. It was partly his commitment to unfinished business in Illinois. It was partly too his concern about Democratic prospects. Maybe it would be a good idea, he sometimes mused, for the Republicans to take over; after all, the Democrats had held the White House for twenty years.

-*≈◎⟵≈*-

Stevenson never declared a candidacy for the nomination in 1952. The Democratic convention took place in Chicago, and, as the state's governor, he gave the speech welcoming the delegates. His eloquence and wit brought the convention to sudden life and provided stimulus to the Stevenson boom; a boom he had vaguely tried to discourage.

Given Stevenson's non-candidacy I was working in Chicago for Averell Harriman of New York, a declared candidate, a thoughtful and experienced man and a good liberal. But Harriman had insufficient delegate strength, and I found myself playing the role of intermediary between Harriman and Stevenson, resulting in Harriman's withdrawal after the third ballot and his endorsement of Stevenson.

The candidate who did have sufficient delegate strength was Senator Estes Kefauver of Tennessee. Kefauver was a courageous and outspoken liberal. But the party bosses hated him because his investigations of organized crime threatened to expose relations between crime and politics. His victory in the New Hampshire primary in February had confirmed Truman's decision not to run, and Kefauver had thereafter taken the primary road to the convention, winning all but two primaries and arriving with half again as many delegates as his closest rival. Enthusiasm for Stevenson and fear of Kefauver rapidly enlarged a draft movement to which Stevenson finally capitulated. He was nominated on the fourth ballot.

The 1952 convention was the last in which the presidential nomination has required more that a single ballot. In the half century since, all presidential candidates have been nominated on the first ballot—which has meant the transformation of the national convention from its historic role as a forum for decision into a new role as a ceremony of ratification—ratification, that is, of choices already made in primaries and caucuses.

⟞⟞⟞◯⟝⟝⟝

It was a brilliant campaign. He proposed to win the election, Stevenson said in his acceptance speech. But even more important than winning the election, he continued, was governing the nation. "This is the test of a political party—the acid, final test. When the tumult and the shouting die, when the bands are gone and the lights are dimmed, there is the stark reality of responsibility in an hour of history haunted with those gaunt, grim specters of strife, dissension and materialism at home, ruthless, inscrutable and hostile power abroad."

"Let's talk sense to the American people," he concluded. "Let's tell them the truth, that there are no gains without pains, that we are now on the eve of great decisions, not easy decisions, like resistance when you're attacked, but a long, patient, costly struggle which alone can assure triumph over the great enemies of man—war, poverty and tyranny—and the assaults upon human dignity which are the most grievous consequences of each."

Stevenson was striking a new note in Democratic politics; or rather he was renewing the idealism of Woodrow Wilson and Franklin Roosevelt. In the last days of Truman the motto of the Democratic Party seemed to be "You never had it so good." The essence of the party's appeal was not to demand exertions but to promise benefits. Stevenson changed all that. His lofty conception of politics and citizenship, his conviction that affluence was not enough for the good life, his impatience with liberal clichés, his demand for new ideas, his regard for people who had them, his contempt for conservative complacency, his summons to the young, his call for strong public leadership, his belief in the nobility of public service, his sense that history had no easy answers—all this set the tone for a new era in Democratic politics. He redeemed politics from its sordid and selfish side and made political life significant and exciting for a new generation. What would we give today if candidates addressed so effectively what Lincoln had called the better angels of our nature!

This was still an age of whistlestops on the countryside and mass rallies in the cities. Though he complained at times, Stevenson was a joyous campaigner. He loved giving political speeches before highly partisan audiences—or at least he loved them when he was giving them but hated them before-hand and hated them afterward when his Lake Forest friends reproached him for being so unkind to the Republicans.

It was indeed a brilliant campaign. It lifted the hearts of millions and instructed a new generation in the possibilities of politics. But it was hard to run against a national hero. Moreover, the political cycle was due to turn. The grim years of depression and war had left [in 1952] a weary electorate in search of rest and recuperation. Stevenson's soaring oratory and his challenge to the best side of the national character were greatly admired by a passionate minority— but it was a minority that the complacent majority derided as "eggheads."

◄───○◄═══◄►─

The approach of 1956 brought him back to elective politics. This time he was an active contender for the nomination, especially after Estes Kefauver beat him in the Minnesota primary. Stevenson fought back and was nominated on the first ballot. He threw the vice presidential choice to the convention, and Kefauver emerged as his running mate.

Stevenson's campaign in 1956 was less rhetorical and more liberal, substantive and programmatic than in 1952. His advocacy of a nuclear test ban treaty and of the abolition of the draft was ahead of its time, but it availed little against the General in the White House.

Stevenson polled a million fewer votes than four years before. When
some expressed disappointment over the impact of the campaign as
compared to 1952, Stevenson gave a wry explanation: "You can only
be a virgin once."

Four years later, Adlai insisted that he was not a candidate and
that we should back the man of our choice. A group of Stevensonian
liberals—John Kenneth Galbraith, Arthur Goldberg, Joseph Rauh,
the historians Allan Nevins, Henry Steele Commager, James MacGregor
Burns and me—decided to come out for Kennedy. My then wife told
the *Boston Globe* that she was still for Stevenson. A few days later I
received a letter from Robert Kennedy on another matter but with a
scrawled postscript: "Can't you control your own wife—or are you
like me?"

The Stevenson-Kennedy relationship, while nominally still friendly,
had become uneasy. Kennedy had backed Stevenson with enthusiasm in 1952 and 1956, and Stevenson had rather hoped that
Kennedy would be his running-mate in 1956. In spite of differences
in temperament and disparities in age, they had affinities in background and taste. A relaxed afternoon at Libertyville or Hyannis
Port had much the same mood and tempo—the same sort of spacious, comfortable country house; the same patrician ease of man-
ners; the same sounds of children and dogs in the background; the
same kind of irrelevant European visitors; the same style of humor
and of gossip; the same free and wide-ranging conversation about a
variety of subjects; the same quick transition from the serious to the
frivolous and back again.

Moreover, they were in substantial agreement on the great issues
of public policy. And in a sense Stevenson had made Kennedy's
rise possible. Stevenson had redefined the Democratic Party and
brought a new generation of idealists and activists into politics. By
1960 the candidates for the Democratic nomination, and Kennedy
most of all, were talking in the Stevensonian idiom and stressing
peril, uncertainty, responsibility, purpose. More than either of them
recognized or admitted, Kennedy was the heir and executor of the
Stevenson revolution.

But by 1960 it was too late for them ever really to know one
another. The age gap of seventeen years marked them as of different
generations. Each felt that the other did not understand his problems. Each doubted whether the other appreciated what had been
done for him—Stevenson by giving Kennedy his opportunities in the
1956 convention, Kennedy by campaigning for Stevenson in 26

states in the 1956 election. Rivalry now made differences in age and temperament emotionally more important than their many affinities. The contrast between Stevenson's diffidence and Kennedy's determination in the spring of 1960 heightened for each his misgivings about the other. And Stevenson, like all the political leaders of his generation, thought that Kennedy was a young man pushing too hard; he ought to wait his turn.

Kennedy of course was nominated on the first ballot, Stevenson coming in fourth. Moved by his contempt for the Republican candidate, Richard Nixon, and by his hope of becoming Secretary of State, Adlai gave nearly a hundred speeches in the fall campaign. Introducing the nominee to a California audience, he drew the contrast between himself and Kennedy with typical grace and insight: "In classical times when Cicero had finished speaking, the people said, 'How well he spoke'—but when Demosthenes had finished speaking, the people said, 'Let us march.'"

The victorious Kennedy did not want a senior man of independent mind and constituency heading the State Department. Instead he offered Stevenson the Ambassadorship to the United Nations— an offer that Stevenson rather glumly accepted. As one of Kennedy's special assistants, I was assigned the sometimes uncomfortable job of serving as middleman between the President and the UN Ambassador—two men whom I admired but whose own rapport was perhaps less than perfect.

Kennedy, who had an essential respect and liking for Stevenson, tried, when he thought of it, to make their relationship effective. He understood Stevenson's standing in the world, admired his public presence and wit, valued his skills as diplomat and orator and respected his taste in people. Nearly everyone close to Stevenson received jobs in the Kennedy Administration. But certain of Stevenson's idiosyncrasies did try him; and his own effect on Stevenson in their fact-to-face encounters was unfortunately to heighten those that tried him most.

The relationship was of course harder on Stevenson. He was the older man, and in one way or another Kennedy had denied him his highest hopes. Though Stevenson respected the President's intelligence and judgment, he never seemed wholly at ease on visits to the White House. He tended to freeze a little, much as he used to do in the 1950s on television shows like Meet the Press, and instead of the pungent, astute and beguiling man he characteristically was, he would come over as stiff, even at times as prim and pedantic. Kennedy consequently never saw Stevenson at his best.

Adlai was at his best in the UN where he exerted considerable influence through his stature, intelligence and charm. His high point was his performance during that most dangerous moment in human history—the Cuba missile crisis. It was the most dangerous moment in the history of the world because never before had war threatened between two powers that had between them the technical capacity to blow up the planet and all the people on it. Kennedy wired him: I WATCHED YOUR SPEECH THIS AFTERNOON WITH GREAT SATISFACTION. IT HAS GIVEN OUR CAUSE A GREAT START. . . . THE UNITED STATES IS FORTUNATE TO HAVE YOUR ADVOCACY. YOU HAVE MY WARM AND PERSONAL THANKS.

After Kennedy's assassination and the return of Stevenson's generation to power with Lyndon Johnson, Adlai hoped for a larger role in shaping foreign policy. But he was to have less influence with LBJ than with JFK. Meanwhile his frenetic life of work, speeches, parties and travel was wearing him down. He was overweight, smoked too much, suffered from arteriosclerosis and hypertension and disdained the advice of doctors. Walking down a London street in July 1965 with his dear friend Marietta Tree, he suffered a fatal heart attack.

Nineteen sixty-five was more than a third of a century ago. Kids entering college [in 2000] were not even born till about 1982, seventeen years after Stevenson's death. To the young today Adlai Stevenson is a dimly remembered textbook name, a historical relic. Yet historians will look on him, I believe, as a noble example of the power of positive losing. He articulated the values of democracy with a force and eloquence that kept those values alive in a time of materialism and complacency. He lived the passage from John Buchan that John Kennedy liked so much to quote: "Public life is regarded as the crown of a career, and to young men it is the worthiest ambition. Politics is still the greatest and the most honourable adventure."

CHAPTER 13

ADLAI'S INTEGRITY AND CREDIBILITY
WERE IMPRESSIVE NATIONAL
RESOURCES

Carl McGowan

The following, with the permission of Judge McGowan's surviving spouse, Jodie, was taken from his remarks on March 11, 1966, before the Law and Legal Clubs in Chicago, a few months after the untimely death of Governor Stevenson in London. From 1963, for several years, the judge sat on the United States Court of Appeals for the District of Columbia Circuit and served briefly, in 1981, as Chief Judge before assuming senior status. His tenure there followed years of friendship and professional association with Stevenson dating back to 1939, when he moved to Chicago from New York to teach law at Northwestern University. The judge accompanied Stevenson to Springfield as his legal counsel on the latter's becoming Governor in 1949. In 1952, he was an integral member of the Governor's first campaign for President. Judge McGowan took part in a number of landmark cases while on the Court of Appeals, including those involving the Pentagon Papers and Watergate tapes and authored significant opinions on use of prior convictions to impeach criminal defendants, the right of members of Congress to sue in federal court concerning legislative matters, the scope of judicial review of federal administrative actions, and the ownership and disposition of presidential papers. His death occurred in December 1987.

PROLOGUE

Hope P. McGowan*

Among the items contained in the folder labeled "Adlai" from my father's old file cabinet is a brittle, yellowed clipping of a Doonesbury cartoon. Drawn soon after the 1984 election in which the popularity of the incumbent president helped sweep a new Republican majority—including a new congressman from Georgia—into office, the first panel shows journalist Rick Redfern waking up after a night of heavy drinking. After apologizing to his wife for his behavior, Rick goes on to bemoan the election results: "What if it wasn't just a triumph of personality, Joanie? What if it's a real revolution? What if one day my kid wakes up in a country run by Newt Gingrich?" In his anguish, he begs her, "Joanie . . . if something happens to me . . . you must tell our son about Adlai Stevenson!"

Carl McGowan loved that cartoon and would have enthusiastically endorsed this book's mission of telling new generations and reminding others about Adlai Stevenson. His long, productive, and mutually beneficial association with Stevenson began in 1939 when one of his first social engagements upon moving to Chicago from New York was a luncheon invitation from Adlai, a law school classmate of his former boss. The two men immediately forged a friendship, and after Pearl Harbor Adlai helped my father obtain a position with the Navy Department where Adlai was then serving as an assistant to the Secretary. Happily for me and my siblings, I might add—for it was during his war years in Washington that my father met and married my mother.

In 1949, the future Judge McGowan became legal counsel to the recently elected Illinois Governor, little dreaming that his duties would expand less than four years later to include the design and assembly of a nationwide presidential campaign. When asked in subsequent years what it had been like to work for and with Governor Stevenson, he replied simply that "it was the greatest fun imaginable" and described Adlai himself as "the best company in the world," a phrase, he noted, that was "quite precisely understood in the small Illinois town (Paris) where I grew up." During those years, despite the stress of ever-present crises and the bitterness of the later loss of

---

* Carl McGowan's daughter and Justice Department attorney.

the presidency, Adlai never "lost his cool," my father reported, "nor did he ever fail to bring to bear upon these strenuous encounters the saving grace of humor."

The 1952 campaign served as the climax of their professional relationship, and a stunning climax it was, remarkable for the eloquence of the Democratic candidate's language and his refusal either to "talk down" to his listeners or compromise his position on substantive issues in order to win more votes. The tone and quality of the campaign reflected the personal characteristics shared by Adlai and his closest advisor: modesty, civility, common sense, and a reverence for clarity and precision in writing and thought, as well as an approach to public life that valued adherence to principle over a desire to be elected at any cost.

Both men could also lay claim to a lack of arrogance, an open-mindedness, and a deep and abiding faith in human reason as the solvent of society's ills, assets that served them well in their later incursions into public service, Adlai as our Ambassador to the United Nations, my father as a federal appellate court judge.

For many of us, the virtues embodied by Adlai Stevenson and Carl McGowan are sadly absent in twenty-first-century life, and the high standards they set during the 1952 campaign and afterward appear doomed to be forgotten by future generations. But, as the following set of remarks indicates, my father never doubted that the world would long remember the legacy of Adlai Stevenson and be influenced—and inspired—by it. He expressed this belief most powerfully in the eulogy he delivered for Adlai at Washington's National Cathedral, in words that cannot help but be of comfort to anyone who remembers Adlai Stevenson today: "Adlai's voice is still now. But its echoes are likely to be sounding down the corridors of history for a long time. For it is the essence of faith to believe that the world in its advancing age will set no less store than have we upon reason, upon intelligence, upon gaiety, upon charity and compassion and grace—all those things and more of and with which this voice has spoken to us so often and so clearly in the past."

THE JUDGE'S REMARKS

For the fact is, of course, that no one has a monopoly on Adlai Stevenson. One of the striking things about his life is that he lived it at so many levels. Journalism, law, politics, private practice, public office, business and finance, social and civic causes, private organizations, charitable foundations, education, literature, the worlds of the university and the arts, the sporting field—he was at home in all and known in all. This catalogue is, indeed, far from complete. And there is the further circumstance that these many lives of his were led not only in this country but abroad. His foreign friendships alone were astonishing in their number and variety.

The whole story about Adlai Stevenson is, thus, one that will only be told, if ever, by many voices. Those . . . [who] speak from the associations of private life and work have pieces to add to this intricate and many-colored mosaic, which are as essential as those from the public sphere. The flash-bulb, the headline, the motor-cycle escort, all do their best to foster the illusion that the public man is always and inescapably a more interesting human being than one whose work and life are carried on without these raucous accompaniments.

One of the marks of maturity of a society is for at least a respectable number of its members to know that, at bottom, this is not so. It is hard to assert with any confidence the maturity of our own time by this standard, but Adlai Stevenson was a vital and interesting man wholly apart from his public fame. The calcium lights in his case did not create a personality. They rather focused a wider span of attention upon one that existed in its own right and by its own force.

⊷⇒◯⇐⊶

[President Kennedy is quoted in Arthur Schlesinger's book on the Kennedy Administration as saying:]

"The integrity and credibility of Adlai Stevenson constitute one of our great national assets. I don't want anything to be done which might jeopardize that."

⊷⇒◯⇐⊶

How was it that the "integrity and credibility" of our friend and fellow-lawyer became "one of our great national assets"? The accuracy of President Kennedy's characterization is beyond challenge. It was a fact perhaps most acutely apprehended by chiefs of state and others whose business it is to sense the popular temper and to weigh their actions accordingly. But it was also felt by the unlearned as well as the egghead, by the opponent as well as the partisan. It exists as one of the most extraordinary phenomena of the political life of our time. Reams remain to be written about it by future historians and political scientists. It is undoubtedly too early to articulate the final and definitive explanation of why it was so.

⋅⊷⟹◉⟸⊷⋅

Perhaps it would be well first to try to spell out what abstractions like "integrity" and "credibility" mean in this context. For me they merge into something best defined by an answer to the question of whether a particular public figure is as honest with others as he is with himself. There are some people, of course, who are congenitally unable to be honest with themselves and, accordingly, are incapacitated for meaningful communication with their fellows. There are others who are quite capable of doing the one, but deliberately project a different point of view to the world about them.

The world of politics has many examples of both kinds—and the public knows it. Thus it is always refreshed by, and gives its respect to, the man whom it believes to be doing both. It finds that person to have a rational aspect—a sort of bed-rock believability, if you please—which commands attention, if not agreement. Since we are all so conscious of the extent to which we are constantly fooling ourselves as well as those around us even in the concerns of private life, we are greatly complimented when the public man, who must depend on our uncertain favor, appears to be telling us exactly what he is telling himself.

Throughout Adlai's lengthy career in the public eye, he persisted in doing just this. He would be the last to claim that he was endowed with all the copy-book virtues, or that he never fell from the path of grace. But, in the conduct of the public's business, he simply found it more natural to operate without guile. It was the easier way for him, although it seemed on occasion recklessly to invite pressure and attack. He appeared to find these consequences less painful than the personal discomfort of blurring an issue by sweeping an inconvenient fact under the rug, or by tailoring his view of it to that which his hearers might be expected to hold. The cynic might suspect that this habit resulted form either fantastic naiveté or shrewd political calculation. But to try to categorize Adlai as either a Boy Scout or a Machiavelli is a vain inquiry. The fact remains that, whatever the springs of action within the depths of his being, this was his way of life, his way of coming to grips with the public business.

It was a way which may be traced throughout his public career—in office and out. It was certainly the star he steered by as Governor of this state. I continue to think of Adlai as one of the last of the practicing federalists, with a small "f." He did not accept the view that everything can be done better in Washington; he had seen that operation from the inside. He knew, of course, that in this increasingly interdependent world, as in our vastly changing country, there are some areas in which precept and action must come through the single medium of the national state. As an informed realist about international relations, he thought these areas were likely to increase rather than to decline.

But this he conceived to be all the more reason why we should strive valiantly to keep the federal decks clear for action in those fields where only a federal response could be effective, and not to clutter them with responsibilities which could be met at the state level. He did not believe that a President preoccupied with a problem like Vietnam should have to worry also about mental hospitals, or local law enforcement, or the deficiencies of garbage collection in New York City. He was painfully conscious of the fact that our genius for devising governmental solutions for emerging problems has not been balanced by any apparent capacity whatsoever for dismantling the machinery once the problem has either been solved or has disappeared under the impact of time and change.

Adlai was not a "big government" man as such, as any study of the budgetary policies he pursued as Governor will show. He hated to spend the public's money as much as he did his own. After the Democratic Convention in 1952, some of the members of the government in Washington came to Springfield to discuss their plans with the man who might become their boss. A couple of them departed in dazed anguish after those interviews, more than ready to jettison their hopes of a couple of billions for new programs in return for some assurance that under the new regime they would not have to drive themselves to the office or type their own letters. Those who said they were for Eisenhower solely for reasons of fiscal responsibility knew not whereof they spoke. They voted against the man who was, if they could but [have] known, their dream candidate.

Economy in government was simply one aspect of Adlai's goal of efficiency in government. A small-staff man himself, he preferred fewer—but better—public servants. And he genuinely subscribed to the belief of Brandeis in the continuing vitality of the federal scheme of our governmental structure, including the Justice's view of the values that reside in variety. Anyone who observed the intensity and eagerness with which Adlai, at the annual conferences of all the state governors, took part in the discussion of common problems realized that for him there was real meaning in the Brandeisian concept that many separate laboratories for social and political experiment have great advantages over one.

At those meetings, he was invariably one of the two or three who stood out markedly from the rest. His performances there, founded upon the deep and absorbing interest he had in his job, had a lot to do with the swift growth of his national reputation. It was Adlai's cruel dilemma to be placed under intolerable pressures to seek, against long odds which were visible to everyone in the country except those in Washington, another public office because of the skill and assurance with which he was functioning in the one he was in—and which he loved.

He succeeded as Governor of this state because he went about that work with the same integrity and credibility [about] which President Kennedy later remarked.

⋆⟿⊜⟾⋆

The Springfield story is still a familiar reality . . . , and it need not be pursued here. Out of it all—the ups and the downs, the disappointments as well as the achievements—there began to filter out through the country the impression that perhaps here was a politician with a difference. When, at the beginning of the 1952 presidential campaign, he said his purpose would be "to talk sense to the American people," there was already a glimmering of hope that maybe he meant just what he said. And, of course, he proceeded to do just that. By "sense" he did not mean that his listeners must uniformly agree with what he told them. As it turned out, too many of them apparently did not. What was clear was that he intended to convey the sense of any subject as it appeared to him, that his purpose was to talk out loud on issues in the presence of millions as he would if he were turning the matter around in his own mind in the privacy of his office.

His appearance before the American Legion Convention in New York City early in September of 1952 remains for many of us one of life's authentically thrilling experiences. Whatever may have been its impact upon the Legionnaires—and it was surprisingly favorable—it set that cynical and sophisticated town by the heels. Its long and lasting love affair with Adlai really began that day.

He did the same kind of thing, however, in other places quite as unlikely. He talked turkey about labor rough-stuff to forbiddingly silent audiences outside factory gates on a cold gray afternoon in the Detroit suburbs. He told employer groups throughout the nation to stop pining for a vanished world. He ignored the carnival character of a New Orleans rally to suggest that it was time to grow up in the area of race relations. In Texas, he cautioned that maybe the tidelands really did belong to the federal government, and that perhaps it was not shocking for the latter to claim its own in view of all it had done for the Lone Star State.

His finest moment in this respect came later. In 1952 he was, after all, riding high as a presidential nominee who was still Governor of Illinois and who was obviously making a lot of friends in the other 47 states. During the next four years, he was only a private citizen who had been crushingly defeated. If the fates of those to whom the same thing had happened were any guide, his prospects were dim and his influence slight. It is also true, as we all know, that defeat inevitably saps self-confidence and tends to cause one to play everything safe.

Not so with Adlai. This is the period in which he was the first truly national political figure to look at Joe McCarthy and to observe out loud that the Emperor appeared to have no clothes on. This later became visible to most people, but those times proved that Hans Christian Andersen was a shrewd popular psychologist. It was Adlai, the losing candidate, who helped greatly to set in train the ultimate deliverance of the Eisenhower Administration from the biggest albatross it had, in the process of winning, hung around its own neck.

It is by no means certain that Adlai was conscious of any personal heroism in all this. A civilized man himself, Senator McCarthy struck him as an absurd individual who surely must appear so to all civilized people, a public figure who was simply not credible in the sense of entitlement to be taken seriously. Thus, Adlai spoke out with essentially the same innocence of precocity as did the child in the fairy tale.

⟶⟫◎⟪⟵

Adlai had a deep sense of obligation to his immediate audience. He always felt that, if as many as two people inconvenienced themselves by gathering together to hear him speak, they were entitled to his best effort-and that included a subject matter falling squarely within their range of interest. His allegiance to the values of the craft of public speaking was such that he would rather risk an audience's irritation than its boredom.

But whether he fancied himself as cast in the heroic mold or not, he came to be so regarded in the eyes of many millions of his fellow-citizens. You probably did not see an advertisement that appeared in a Washington paper on [the] birthday . . . that would have been his sixty-sixth. It was paid for by a commercial establishment, but what it said, below a good photograph of Adlai and his birth date, was that it was in memory of "the gentlest hero of the 20th Century." He would have regarded this as more than a little hyperbolic, and turned it off with some typically wry jest. But he who aspires to a similar sobriquet for the century to follow ours would do well to study the public career of Adlai Stevenson.

And there will be those who will aspire, largely because of him. Dick Goodwin, himself old enough to have served well both Presidents Kennedy and Johnson but a mere schoolboy when Stevenson first ran for President, has, in one of the best pieces yet written about Adlai, said that "he changed the face of American politics; enriching the democracy, providing a base on which talent could aspire to power, opening a gateway to public life through which many who never heard his voice will some day enter." Adlai's political disappointments were deep and devastating, but there are many Presidents of the United States of whom that could not even begin to be said.

He was an ornament of our generation, but his greatest and most lasting gifts have been bestowed upon our children and those who come after them. He proved that one can, although denied power, make of integrity and credibility a great national asset. That is the kind of accomplishment which speaks to the young in accents their elders cannot always hear.

It was, at all events, an asset which served us well in a time of great peril—the Cuba missile crisis of 1962. After all the partisan political rancor which often surrounded Adlai in the years before that, it is gratifying to his friends that, in his last major appearance on the public scene, he spoke for a united people. Because, in those terrifying

October days, only the proceedings at the United Nations could be in the public view, Adlai's was the only voice through which our government could speak in public; and it was, in a sense, our only point of contact with what was going on behind the scenes.

He never rose more completely to the occasion. He cast confusion upon the heads of our foes. He gave comfort, determination, and pride to ourselves. That whole incident seems, in retrospect, to have demonstrated that moral power remains a vital force in the ordering of world politics. It was the good fortune of all mankind that its instrument on that fateful occasion was [our] friend and fellow member [of the bar of many of us] . . . .

It had been a long—and often hard—journey to that focal point in the consciousness of the whole world. It was a journey which had stretched from Bloomington, and the law school at Northwestern, and 11 South LaSalle Street, and the noon committee meetings at the Bar Association, and the treks over to the County Building to file a brief or get a certified copy, and the staying down in the Loop on a winter night to attend a dinner . . . .

It was a journey which we all watched with fascinated interest. The sweep and verve of Adlai's life gave an added dimension to our own. We had always an exciting sense of participation in it because, after all, he was one of us—a Chicago lawyer who had trod our daily rounds and who had sat in our midst as personal friend and professional brother. When the news came last summer that it had ended, there was a feeling in each of us that, as in George Santayana's lament for a friend:

> Chapel and fireside, country road and bay,
> Have something of their friendliness resigned;
> Another, if I would, I could not find,
> And I am grown much older in a day.

Our memories of him abide. And they are not all, or even in the larger part, solemn or sad, because that was not his way. We have known at first hand the gayety, the sparkle, the idealism, which did not stray into self-righteousness.

We are met . . . to recall our delight in a friend, and not to assign him his place in history. He will, in any event, be much in the minds of his generation as long as any survive. His contributions to the quality of American life seem likely to command attention and respect for a long time after that.

Stephen Spender has written a moving modern poem, the first line of which is: "I think continually of those who were truly great." Greatness is, at best, a complex concept. The mists which shroud it seldom clear away, if ever, except in the lengthening perspective of time. Adlai himself did not believe that high-flown abstractions of this kind were very useful ways of thinking about people. Although he would characteristically deny the relevance to himself of Spender's opening line, surely we may join his name, in the closing lines, with:

> The names of those who in their lives fought for life,
> Who wore at their hearts the fire's center.
> Born of the sun they traveled a short while towards the sun,
> And left the vivid air signed with their honor.

EDITOR'S NOTE

All of which brings to mind the thoughts of those expressed above and of others: my former law school professor, Willard Wirtz, of his compatriot Judge McGowan on the life and times of the Governor; William McCormick Blair Jr., a friend and law partner of Stevenson who accompanied him throughout the United States and sixty-four nations in the 1950s, afterward becoming Ambassador to Denmark and the Philippine Republic; and Newton Minow, who also practiced law with Stevenson, remembering that the Governor had been "ridiculed by his opponents on . . . [the nuclear] issue, as on others which subsequently became sound national policies . . . [but lived] to see a treaty outlawing . . . testing" and that "millions of children, born and unborn, can thank him for being so right, so brave, and so faithful to his own convictions" *As We Knew Adlai*. Harper & Row, Publishers, New York, 1966, p. 185. Now asking, whether one could "imagine" a national politician today taking that sort of electoral risk, telling the American public the truth notwithstanding. Also, the thoughts of Mrs. Edison (Jane) Dick, a friend of the Stevensons for four decades and supporter throughout, an Ambassador to the UN during the Governor's tenure. Many have wondered why Stevenson held back on his presidential leanings in

1960. Her view was that the "reason he did not make a Sherman-like statement . . . was his reluctance to dash the hopes of all those who had been so . . . loyal [as Mrs. Roosevelt] and who mounted the most amazing demonstration of support for a noncandidate in our political history. This loyalty, I know, touched Adlai deeply; it was one of his major resources in coping with disappointments, frustrations and personal loneliness" (ibid., p. 274). In like manner to Judge McGowan's reference, she noted the recent passing of a friend who Stevenson had said "'was lucky—he died with his boots on'" and opines that the Governor "went as he would have wanted to go," quoting the English press that it was symbolic, as a world citizen, it had occurred there "in a country where he was as greatly beloved as in his own.'" Mrs. Dick then remarked (ibid., p. 288):

> Let me be honest. I pretend to no objectivity in trying to find an answer to the question: 'Who can name what he was?' My views are colored by heartwarming recollections of forty years. . . . But I believe they may provide an insight into his hold on the imagination and affection of a world that will miss him for many tomorrows.

My memory also recalls what former Senator Eugene McCarthy had said only a few years ago, that if Adlai Stevenson had been elected President in 1960 the Vietnam War undoubtedly would have been avoided, a statement that Ambassador Harlan Cleveland's chapter helps materially to explain. Further, I remember a cousin asking what, after all, was so important about Stevenson since "he had failed to reach the presidency," and my frank response to him, that "Moses hadn't reached the Promised Land either." Finally, for America in the years to come, I am reminded of the wisdom of Stevenson's earlier words in *Look Magazine*, 1957:

> . . . I believe that the United States must take the initiative that the great struggle for men's minds, which is the essence of the Cold War, will be won not with bigger bombs but with better ideas. The battle for the uncommitted peoples of the world, for their friendship and respect, will go to the nation that is wise, compassionate and considerate, as well as strong.

He had the touch of greatness. It was his humanity, integrity, and intellect; and his tireless mission for understanding and peace in this troubled world.

Epilogue

Adlai Stevenson:
The Past and a Look at the Future

Adlai Stevenson, a warm and intelligent man with a great sense of humor
Source: Abraham Lincoln Memorial Library

HIS PAST IS PROLOGUE

Alvin Liebling *

. . . one of the most enduring political figures of our time, he continues to light the path to peace in our nuclear age.

Former Governor and U.S. Ambassador to the UN Adlai E. Stevenson II's one-hundredth birthday celebration a few years ago and contemporary international and political concerns have sparked a renewed awareness of the societal impact of this extraordinary Illinoisan. That is what this book is about. From the 1930s into the 1960s, Stevenson steadily and selflessly served his state and the nation, yet at all times he was a man of the world and so admired.

He did not reach the presidency though he was twice nominated as the Democratic candidate, and many in his party supported him for a third try. Yet, as Drs. John Brademas and Arthur Schlesinger, Ken Hechler, and Judge Carl McGowan indicate, more than most who achieved the office, Stevenson is acknowledged to have influenced the policies of his party and the nation. And as Secretaries Cleveland and Urquhart and Ambassadors Yost and vanden Heuvel note, as a founder and later our Permanent Representative to the UN, he identified the patient effort the U.S. must exert, sometimes courageously, to achieve a multilateral consensus to sustain the conditions of peace in a nuclear age.

---

* Judge Alvin Liebling, editor of this volume

Alarmed by the vastly increased radioactive fallout and destructive effect associated with recent U.S. hydrogen bomb testing, Stevenson made pursuit of an international ban on further aboveground testing a major issue of his 1956 presidential campaign. Although the proposal was ridiculed by his opposition before the election, only two years later it was adopted and comprehensively expanded upon by President Eisenhower.

It became a driving force for a limited test ban treaty in 1963 and a more comprehensive treaty, which we signed in 1996 but have not yet ratified. According to Dr. Sidney D. Drell and Ambassadors James E. Goodby and George Bunn, those treaties and anticipation of nuclear disarmament have been the stimulus for the multinational sign-on and adherence so far of the nonnuclear states to the Non-Proliferation Treaty of 1970. With the unfinished business of Stevenson's initiative, respecting a comprehensive test ban treaty, nonproliferation has been put into question. And Iran and North Korea have been dangerously challenging this part of the regimen for the world's survival.

Adlai Stevenson's collaborative legacy has thus impacted the past through several U.S. administrations until recent date, with the acts of unilateralism of the present Bush Administration in Iraq and elsewhere seen as an effort to set it aside, with heavy penalty. Now, the Administration calls for furtherance of the Third World's freedom. Given this as a long-desired national goal, the issue is how we, the eminent power in the world, are best advised to regain our tarnished global leadership and foster achievement of this objective—by patient Stevensonian consensus-building, where our example and assistance are our might, or by continuing a too often go-it-alone assertion of our will.

As the Introduction notes, this book differs from prior literary efforts that have dwelt upon interesting personal reminiscences about the Governor. The concern here is rather with the specifics of his lengthy public career and their significance—the lessons they hold for those who follow. First mentioned is the need to return to the better politics of his time. Then, the importance of his pattern of international problem solving, done in the crucible of the means calculated and still available for that use, the United Nations. It was a different approach for the United States, which before World War II had proceeded without a participation in the League of Nations.

That world body was to have ended all wars after World War I, but the United States turned away and war came again. After it was over, in the spirit of Wilson, Adlai Stevenson of Bloomington, Illinois, as spokesman for the U.S. State Department, was a key member of America's team that established the UN at San Francisco. This time the Senate approved. He was a leader of the preparatory sessions in London and moved it along on its path in the 1940s. In the 1960s, he returned to the UN as U.S. Ambassador and showed how it could work in the Congo, Cuba and elsewhere. Based on the initiative he introduced in the 1956 presidential election, the limited nuclear test ban treaty of 1963 was followed before long by the Non-Proliferation Treaty. The latter treaty is still in effect.

Former Secretary of State Colin Powell has said the Non-Proliferation Treaty is the centerpiece of the nonproliferation "global regime"; making it—with nuclear disarmament—the hope of mankind. The world now watches for our action on the Comprehensive Nuclear Test Ban Treaty, progress on disarmament and Iran and North Korea's adherence to nonproliferation. The Stevenson-built pattern of nuclear control thus continues, along with the need for the patient pursuit of multilateral consensus, which he espoused as the tool of the civilized world to keep the peace. Which, with his other credentials, is why Adlai Stevenson remains one of the most enduring political figures of our time.

What can we expect will be the international and political impact of Stevenson's legacy in the future? The above chapters deal with various aspects of his effect in the period in and since his time, but the issues requiring an application of his legacy will predictably continue. Therefore, a further analysis of where the country is now and can move toward, in his view, is obviously pertinent. There are two persons especially positioned to shed light on this. First, Adlai Stevenson's close, daily friend and Washington backup during his last four-and-a-half years at the UN, former Assistant Secretary of State for International Organization Affairs and then, Ambassador to NATO, Harlan Cleveland, and the second, his eldest son, former U.S. Senator from Illinois, Adlai E. Stevenson III. Their incisive remarks immediately follow.

✦⇒◉⇐✦

A Final Editor's Note: Reflective of the words of Adlai Stevenson on our joining in the creation of the United Nations, our response to the problems remaining in Iraq, as elsewhere, must this time be more resourceful, patient, and truly international to help ensure the peace and re-enshrine our lost world leadership. The recent bipartisan plan of the Baker-Hamilton Iraq Study Group is fundamentally an acknowledgment of this. Choosing an effective way of assuring and enforcing, as required, the necessary benchmarks under that plan without broadening conflict or creating instability in the region is seen as the crux of the matter.

A MORE SENSITIVE FOREIGN POLICY

*Harlan Cleveland**

> *... shouting is not a substitute for thinking*
> *and reason is not the subversion but the*
> *salvation of freedom.*

> —*Adlai E. Stevenson, Godkin Lecture,*
> *Harvard University, March 1954*

I.

The international legacy of Adlai Stevenson has long survived him. In the second half of the twentieth century, the United States emerged as powerful but prudent, drawing nations together to build a workable world order. We Americans and our government, our business, and our cultural outreach, became players in every world region—and this was much more the consequence of thinking and reason than of shouting or subversion.

"International relations" came to be, more and more, deep involvements in each other's "internal affairs." Some of this mutual interpenetration was widely applauded; the Marshall Plan for European recovery, 1948–52, was popular (for different reasons) on both sides of the Atlantic. Some involvements raised eyebrows even in the countries that sponsored them: peacetime espionage and clandestine operations were chronically suspect and often controversial.

* Former Assistant Secretary of State and Ambassador to NATO.

Issues about human rights, such as treatment of political prison-ers, the status of women, race discrimination, and a whole catalogue of economic/social rights reaching deep into what had earlier been regarded as the "domestic policy" of nations, naturally proved sensi-tive to those who governed, or tried to influence governance. Whether they were also resisted as political interference depended of course on whose oxen seemed gored.

Much of this mutual interpenetration wasn't even thought of as foreign policy: trade and investment, cross-border aid for public health, cultural and educational exchange, and especially the mostly uninhibited cross-border flows of information. In practice all of these were handled increasingly by "nongovernments"—by civil society's many operating agencies.

When Adlai Stevenson was the ranking U.S. Ambassador at the United Nations from 1961 to 1965, one of his favorite themes was the idea that the UN should, with U.S. help, develop "the capacity to act." During its "thousand days," the Kennedy Administration, for example, consistently supported the effective UN peacekeeping force in the Congo. That was the first substantial UN force, consist-ing mostly of troops from India, Malaysia, Canada, and Scandinavia, supervised by Ralph Bunche, the African-American Undersecretary-General of the UN.

In the half century after World War II, more and more interna-tional *operations* were delegated by nation-states to international organizations. This was done not only to soften (by spreading the responsibility for) the political impact of "intervening in internal affairs." It was also intended to spread the costs as widely as possible among donor countries, helping the largest contributing govern-ments reassure their taxpayers that "we are not in this by ourselves." International operations were not limited to economic and financial aid. They were equally necessary each time a peace-and-security cri-sis created a need for neutral mediators, large-scale refugee relief, armed peacekeeping forces, or resources for post-hostilities peace building.

Moreover, many functions were turning out to be so inherently international that governments had to pool their sovereignties to regulate the dangers of uninhibited enterprise in the "global commons." The largest, wettest, and emptiest parts of our global surround—Antarctica, the world's oceans, the global atmosphere, and outer space—were early and obvious candidates for treatment as

parts of a Global Commons. So were some widespread environmental impacts. And so, during the last quarter of the twentieth century,
were issues of access and barriers to the global information-flow that
kept multiplying as more and more of the world's people made use
of far-reaching information technologies and communicated via
wireless, the Internet, and its World Wide Web.

II.

Not long before he died in 1965, the interrupted foreign policy
ambitions of Adlai Stevenson were well expressed in a talk he gave to
students at Princeton, his own alma mater, gathered for a lecture in
honor of Dag Hammarskjöld:

> [A]t this time the only sane policy for America—in its own interests
> and in the wider interests of humanity—lies in the patient, unspectac-
> ular, and if need be lonely search for the interests which unite nations,
> for the policies which draw them together, for institutions which tran-
> scend rival national interests, for the international instruments of law
> and security, for the strengthening of what we have already built
> inside and outside the United Nations, for the elaboration of a chang-
> ing world, for a stable, workable society.

At the dawn of the twenty-first century, American foreign policy still
bore the imprint of Adlai Stevenson's thinking—and his patented
rhetoric, too. Early in 2000, I tried to summarize what "we, the people" thought was our foreign policy—not necessarily the government's, but "our" foreign policy. Some of the items in my list were
strikingly Stevensonesque—not surprising, perhaps, since he and I
had worked together in the 1960s on so many of them:

We are for the rights of human beings, a fair chance of life, liberty,
and the pursuit of happiness for all, just as it says in our Declaration
of Independence, the Preamble to the U.S. Constitution, and the
United Nations founding documents we helped write. We can't
seem to accomplish this for everyone just yet, even in our own country, but we'll keep working at it because it's our nation's very reason
for being.

We understand that the first fifty-five years since the end of World
War II were replete with reasons why we need a United Nations with

the capacity to act—to act in our interest, or to bless a coalition of the willing that is ready to act. But we need to keep remembering that the United Nations is not "the other guys." The UN is us, complicated to be sure by the fact that we have to act in the collective interest of many others as well.

We know now that nuclear weapons are unusable except for deterrence. After all, we were willing to let one war drift into stalemate (Korea) and lose another (Vietnam) without using the Big Bang ourselves. But we must prevent nuclear spread. That will become more possible worldwide when, as we should, we agree with others to ban nuclear tests—as Adlai presciently advocated during his 1956 presidential campaign—and slice our own bulging nuclear stockpiles to the minimum levels needed for deterrence in a world no longer threatened by an arms race between two superpowers.

We think we have the world's best allies—and want to stay close to them. Some of them handle some economic or social issues better than we do, so maybe we have something to learn from them. When it comes to the collective use of NATO, in Europe or farther afield, we'll be a loyal and supportive member of the club, but the Europeans are going to have to assume more of the joint responsibility.

We now realize that turbulence and uncertainty in the developing world—the product of rising expectations, rising resentments, and rising frustrations—have become the main change-agent, and the root of much terrorism, in world affairs. Local wars, humanitarian disasters, and global epidemics will keep requiring new ways to cooperate and new kinds of international institutions.

We really want to see a fair shake for the world's poor. Poverty is "the seedbed of world disorder," as Adlai said; he saw the "line of demarcation between social problems and political problems" as already disappearing in his time. Now we know that modern science and technology actually provide the wherewithal to eradicate poverty. But to do that will take both political will (in the United States first of all) and new dimensions of international cooperation. What's physically and economically possible shouldn't be held back by what's politically unprecedented.

We're proud of the science and technology that has learned to use outer space, not only to get humans to the moon and robots beyond that, but for worldwide human benefits—satellite communications, arms control inspection, weather forecasting, resource sensing from space, monitoring environmental risks. Global systems will have to be invented to secure the human benefits which space technologies will make both possible and necessary. Plenty of international cooperation is going to be required, and U.S. leadership is going to be indispensable. (It's hard to understand why, since President John F. Kennedy's initiatives on satellite communication and the World Weather Watch—which Adlai Stevenson helped get through the UN General Assembly with a unanimous vote—no American political leader has grabbed this quintessentially American torch.)

III.

That was a snapshot of the American people's foreign policy at the start of the new millennium. But in the first years of the twenty-first century, our long record of American leadership for constructive international cooperation was seriously derailed—by American leaders.

Shocked by the scale and suddenness of the September 11, 2001, attacks in New York and Washington, the U.S. government first acted with wide popular and international approval—invading Afghanistan, brushing aside the Taliban, and chasing after al-Qaeda, the loose-knit terrorist group blamed for the unprecedented attack on the U.S. mainland.

But then a series of secret decisions in Washington and unilateral moves elsewhere, the product of ideological mind-sets and deeply flawed intelligence, embroiled U.S. armed forces in invading Iraq. For the invasion itself, they were, if anything, overprepared; Iraq's defenders soon melted into the countryside and the inner cities. For what happened next, our forces and our political leaders were woefully unprepared.

The top Pentagon planners evidently assumed that their role would be as liberators: a cheering, friendly Iraqi population, freed at last from thirty years of dictatorship, would self-organize to put their own country back together.

But even in the most favorable historical case—the reoccupation of Italy in World War II, which Adlai Stevenson had seen up close and personal—the lesson was crystal clear. As the Allies pushed the Germans north out of an already "co-belligerent" Italy, an ambitious occupation authority—the Allied Control Commission—had to be put in place with security forces at the ready and a civil affairs staff moving north with the troops to organize local government, fix power plants, rebuild ports and roads, and provide huge inputs of food and fuel for many months before a traumatized people could start organizing their own democratic future.

In Iraq, contrary to all the experience of successful post-hostilities planning, the "civil affairs" (G-5) elements were initially held back in offices in Kuwait, instead of accompanying the fighting forces as they advanced—until looting and disorder in Baghdad belatedly awakened the Americans to the need for an occupation authority.

Even then, our occupiers' first big move was to disband Iraq's forces that would sooner or later be needed to take over internal security from the occupation. The disbanded soldiers, their pay cut off, went home with their weapons, disgruntled and jobless. Some of them soon became part of a scattered insurgency against the occupation led and reinforced by Saddam loyalists, resentful young Shiite clerics, and a growing number of terrorists—al-Qaeda and copycats—from abroad.

The resulting mess radiated far beyond the borders of Iraq. The doctrine of preemptive war was used to reinforce the U.S. Administration's evident reluctance to consult NATO allies or work with the United Nations. But many Americans, misled by what they had heard from Washington, started changing their minds; popular support for the war in Iraq slipped to a minority in public opinion polls. Congress was inert and compliant, voting large grants of authority and huge sums of money in a rush that precluded a serious national debate about either the decision to go to war or an exit strategy from the mess to which the U.S became deeply and unilaterally committed.

IV.

Meanwhile, the impact on public attitudes in Europe and "the Muslim world"—crucial segments just then of what our Founders called "the general opinion of Mankind"—was sudden and profound. Daniel Yankelovich, our most thoughtful interpreter of public opinion, assembled some numbers that told an appalling story. The data cited here are drawn from Gallup, Zogby, and Pew polls. They showed, for example, that:

In the Middle East, the ratio of people holding favorable opinions of America ranged from a high of 13 percent in Egypt to 3 percent in Saudi Arabia. It was only 6 percent in Morocco and Jordan, which most Americans would have considered the most friendly Arab countries. (Only 18 percent of citizens in the Muslim countries polled believed the 9/11 attacks were carried out by Arabs.)

In France, Germany, and Russia the percentages of "unfavorable opinion of the U.S." doubled from 2002 to 2003. Italy's unfavorable opinion went from 23 percent to 59 percent. It more than tripled in Britain, and quadrupled in Poland. In NATO ally Turkey, where the U.S. already had a 55 percent unfavorable rating, it soared to 84 percent.

The Pew Global Attitudes Project published a summary conclusion in 2004: "The war [in Iraq] has widened the rift between Americans and Western Europeans, further inflamed the Muslim world, softened support for the war on terror, and significantly weakened global public support for the pillars of the post-World War II era—the UN and the North Atlantic Alliance."

This sudden turn in "the general opinion of Mankind" was even more serious than the reluctance of so many governments to cooperate with the United States in so many ways. Governments can and do change their policies and their international behavior much more rapidly than bodies politic typically change their minds.

The international fallout of the mostly unilateral decisions that produced "the mess we are in" contrasted dramatically and sadly with the instant, almost universal "rally 'round the United States" reaction in world opinion (including the opinions of governments) just after the 9/11 attacks. For the U.S. government to have blown that golden opportunity to keep building international institutions with "the capacity to act" ran directly counter to what eleven U.S. Presidents, of both political parties and with mostly bipartisan support in Congress, had been aiming to accomplish ever since before World War II was even won.

V.

Acting alone does not serve the U.S. interest, does not serve our global presence, does not win friends or partners or allies. It can win a small war but risks making a mess of the peace that should follow.

The American people and the political leaders they elect are having to climb a steep learning curve about the new game of post–Cold War politics. It's evidently no longer good enough to lead by strutting our military stuff without thinking hard about where that will lead. It is no longer feasible even to lead with our imagination backed by the power of the purse, Marshall Plan style.

Our imagination now has to be matched, as Adlai Stevenson foresaw, by the willingness to listen, the capacity to consult, and the power to persuade. It's a difficult style to master. Much will depend on the quality of its mastery.

When Adlai was active in U.S. international leadership, he was often motivated by the thought that if the U.S. government was dead in the water, the international system was likely to be becalmed as well.

The remarkably fundamental and far-sighted ideas on which our nation was founded are bound to provide worldwide stimulation for those seeking freedom and equality. But for the time being, in this new century, the rest-of-the-world may no longer be able to count on the U.S. government making so many of the constructive bugle calls—as long as its bugle remains rusty and its leaders can't remember the score.

A BETTER POLITICS

Adlai E. Stevenson III*

> ... democracy was not a means to an end. It was an end in itself
> and propagated in the world by our example and assistance.

The Guv's politics may no longer be possible. The presidential
selection process has become a multiyear physical and financial
endurance contest. Candidates compete in fifty state primary and
caucus systems, pandering to local interests, raising money, and stag-
ing events for commercial television that trivializes "news" and tai-
lors it to audience preferences. The federal election-year cycle is a
multibillion-dollar money-raising and marketing exercise that the
fittest have difficulty surviving.

In the Guv's time political leaders with some knowledge of the
candidates and issues selected candidates in national conventions.
Now the conventions are media events that the media begins to
shun. The principal function of party organization is to raise money
for marketing. The Democratic Party's "titular" leader and advisory
committees, which formulated public policy during the Eisenhower
interregnum, are of the past.

Electoral politics is uninterrupted by election. One former confi-
dant of President Clinton estimates he spent one third of his time
while in the country raising political funds. President George W.
Bush does likewise. Absent is the parade of ideas of Democratic

* Former United States Senator, Illinois.

presidential candidates of the past under the banner of a New Freedom, New Deal, Fair Deal, New Frontier, Great Society or New America of Adlai II, or even a New Foundation of President Carter. Politics became tactics. For neoconservatives, it became tactics spawned by ideology, religiosity, and oil, convenient substitutes for wisdom and reason. Tactics thus inspired are well financed, messianic, and uncompromising.

The Guv's schooling was in the world and on the ground. His politics was empirical and rational. He revered our democracy and, contrary to the image, loved people and retail politics—"pressing the flesh." "Trust the people with the truth," he said, "all the truth."

What won was more important than who won. Patriotism was not worn on the lapel. It was the tranquil, steady dedication of a lifetime. He did not need polls and consultants to tell him what was right. He labored over the message—the ideas, policies, and their articulation.

For the Guv, democracy was not a means to an end. It was an end in itself and propagated in the world by our example and assistance. He spoke to the decency and good sense of people. Lacking guile, he could trust his instincts and his cause. He was eloquent, spontaneous, and humorous. The humor and wisdom evoked a warmth that my brothers and I encountered in markets, ministries, and mansions the world over. Humor, as Adlai I reminds us in the *Black Book*, is a universal language. It "scans the brother man." Adlai II lost two presidential elections to the returning war hero but won the hearts and minds of people everywhere. America was a superpower and secure then. Today, conditions have changed.

The Guv was a candidate of the politicians like all great presidents in modern American history. His was a more representative form of democracy. It was possible for the fittest to survive.

Al Liebling and the contributors to this book, all friends, supporters, or colleagues, have described another time and politics, another kind of politician. In doing so, they remind us of what our politics was and might again be. Nothing gave the Guv greater satisfaction than the good citizens he involved in their politics. Nothing would give him more satisfaction today than the possibility that some, being reminded, might still be moved to follow after him. The American people might still respond and restore to their politics the values that created the American republic and the Guv exemplified.

Adlai Stevenson's chair is empty but his legacy endures

Source: Abraham Lincoln Memorial Library, by Bill Mauldin. *Chicago Sun-Times*, 1965

INDEX